THE DEFENDERS

KINGPINS OF NEW YORK

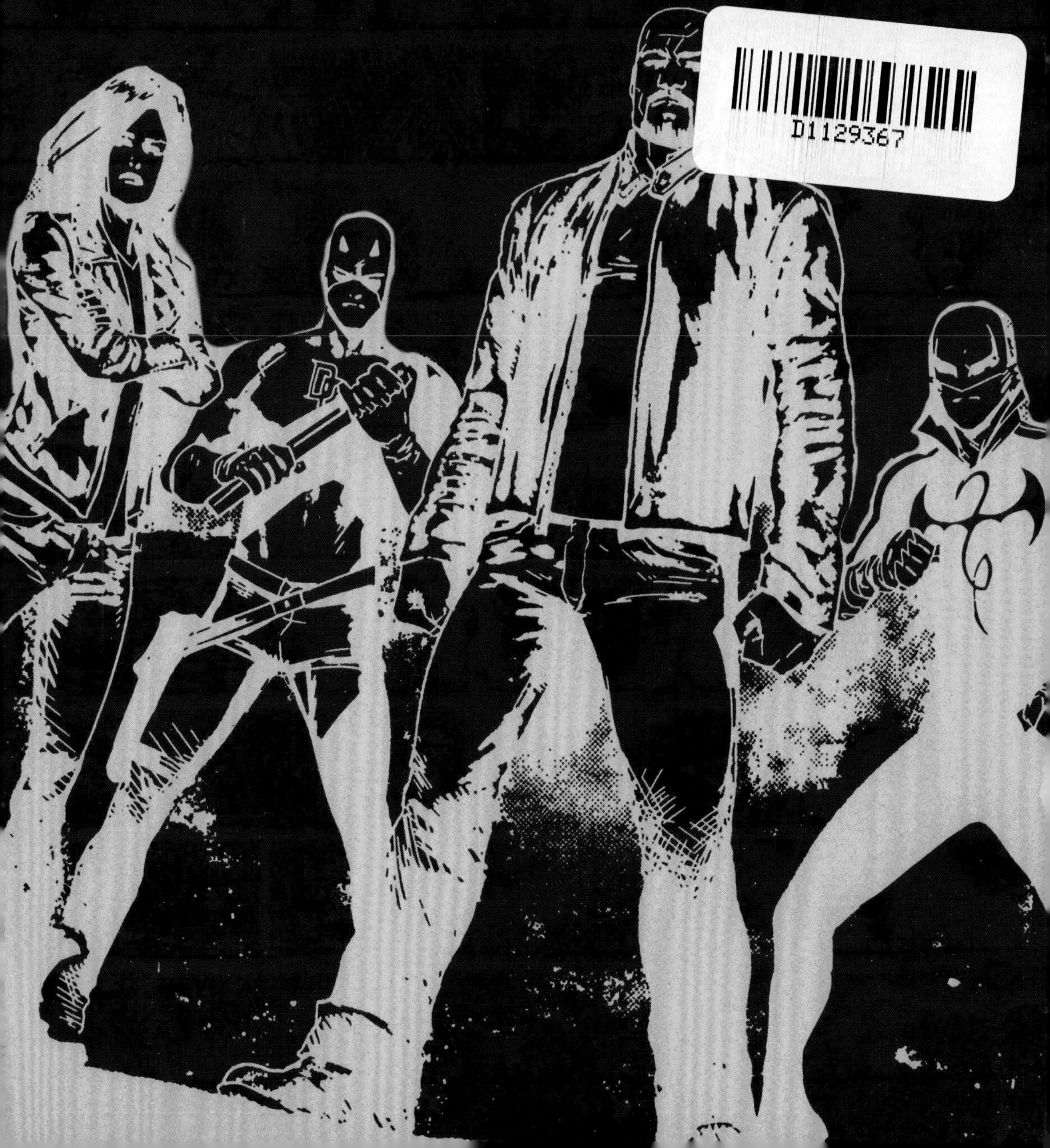

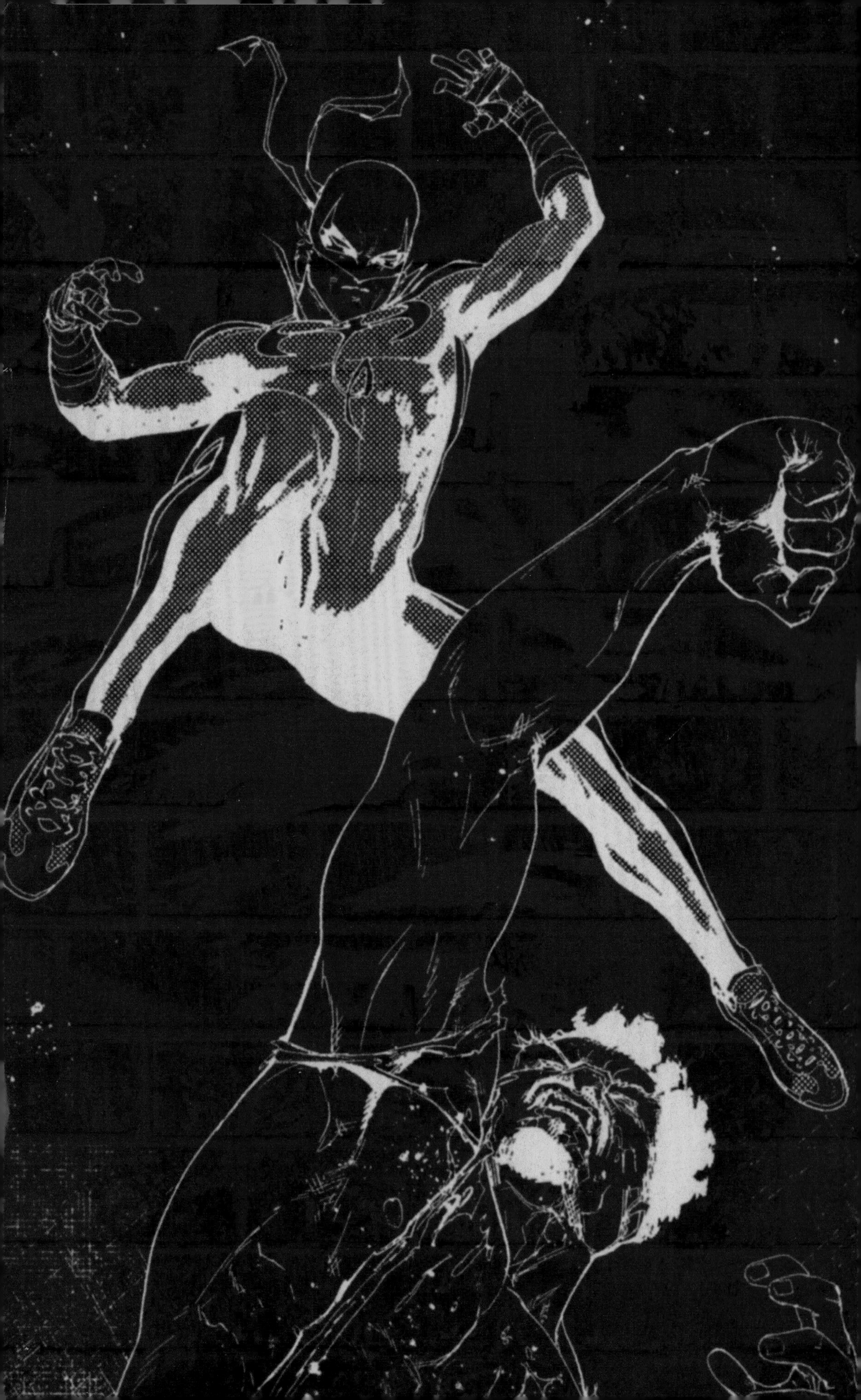

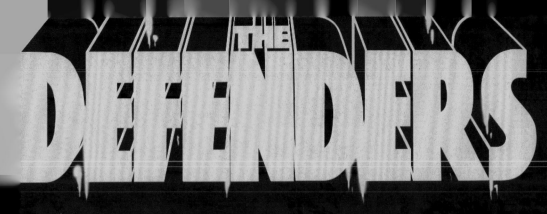

THE DEFENDERS

KINGPINS OF NEW YORK

BRIAN MICHAEL BENDIS
WRITER

DAVID MARQUEZ
WITH **MICHAEL AVON OEMING** (NO. 8)
ARTISTS

JUSTIN PONSOR WITH **PAUL MOUNTS** (NO. 7)
COLOR ARTISTS

VC's CORY PETIT
LETTERER

DAVID MARQUEZ & JUSTIN PONSOR
COVER ART

ALANNA SMITH
ASSISTANT EDITOR

TOM BREVOORT
EDITOR

COLLECTION EDITOR: **JENNIFER GRÜNWALD**
ASSISTANT EDITOR: **CAITLIN O'CONNELL**
SSOCIATE MANAGING EDITOR: **KATERI WOODY**
DITOR, SPECIAL PROJECTS: **MARK D. BEAZLEY**

VP PRODUCTION & SPECIAL PROJECTS: **JEFF YOUNGQUIST**
SVP PRINT, SALES & MARKETING: **DAVID GABRIEL**
BOOK DESIGNER: **ADAM DEL RE**

EDITOR IN CHIEF: **C.B. CEBULSKI**
CHIEF CREATIVE OFFICER: **JOE QUESADA**
PRESIDENT: **DAN BUCKLEY**
EXECUTIVE PRODUCER: **ALAN FINE**

ERS VOL. 2: KINGPINS OF NEW YORK. Contains material originally published in magazine form as DEFENDERS #6-10. First printing 2018. ISBN 978-1-302-90747-1. Published by MARVEL WORLDWIDE, subsidiary of MARVEL ENTERTAINMENT, LLC. OFFICE OF PUBLICATION: 135 West 50th Street, New York, NY 10020. Copyright © 2018 MARVEL No similarity between any of the names, characters, and/or institutions in this magazine with those of any living or dead person or institution is intended, and any such similarity which may exist is purely coincidental. **Printed in Canada.** DAN BUCKLEY, t, Marvel Entertainment; JOHN NEE, Publisher; JOE QUESADA, Chief Creative Officer; TOM BREVOORT, SVP of Publishing; DAVID BOGART, SVP of Business Affairs & Operations, Publishing & Partnership; ABRIEL, SVP of Sales & Marketing, Publishing; JEFF YOUNGQUIST, VP of Production & Special Projects; DAN CARR, Executive Director of Publishing Technology; ALEX MORALES, Director of Publishing ns; DAN EDINGTON, Managing Editor; SUSAN CRESPI, Production Manager; STAN LEE, Chairman Emeritus. For information regarding advertising in Marvel Comics or on Marvel.com, please contact Vit Custom Solutions & Integrated Advertising Manager, at vdebellis@marvel.com. For Marvel subscription inquiries, please call 888-511-5480. **Manufactured between 4/20/2018 and 5/22/2018 by**

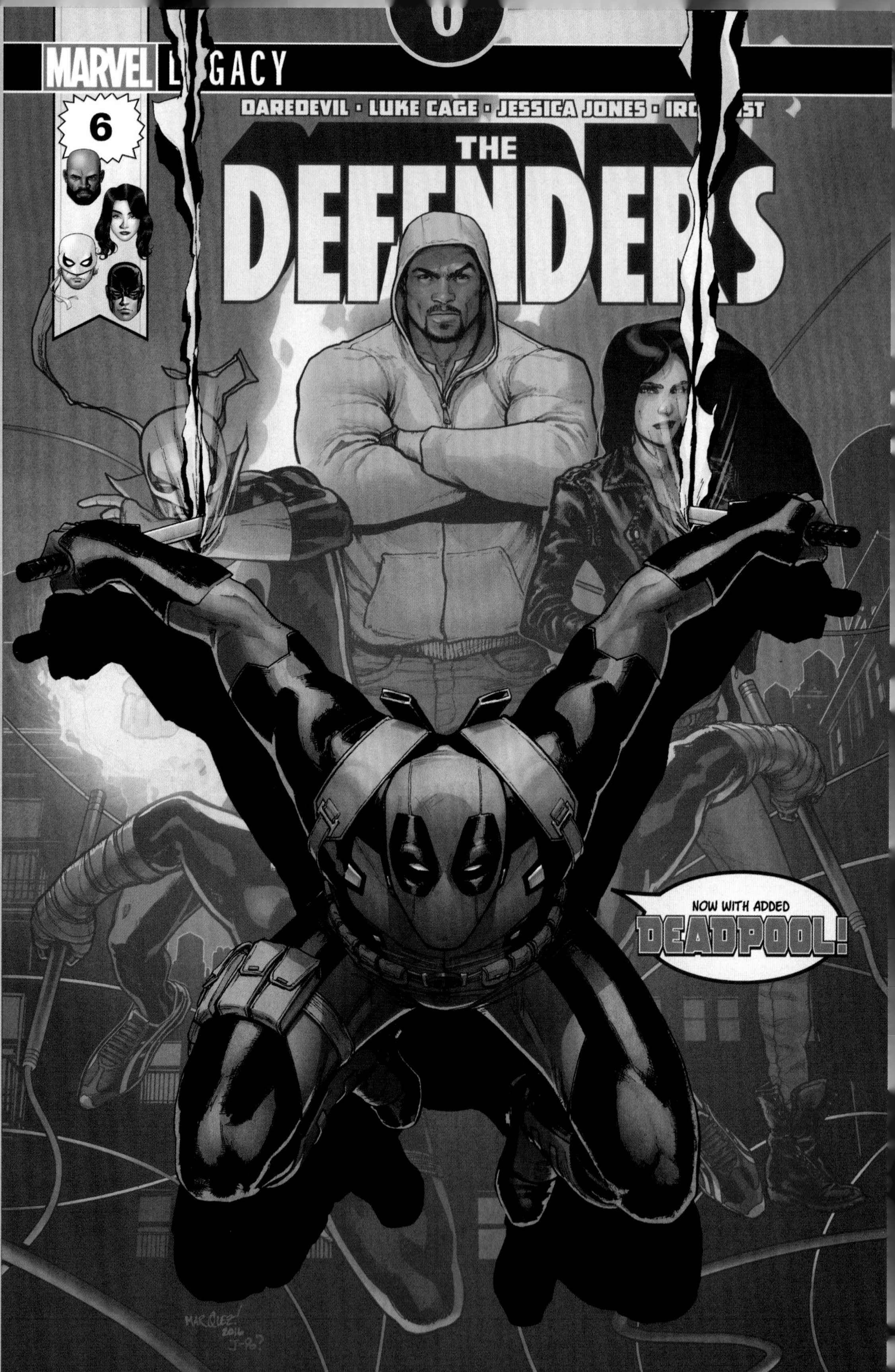
MARVEL LEGACY
6
DAREDEVIL · LUKE CAGE · JESSICA JONES ·
THE DEFENDERS
NOW WITH ADDED
DEADPOOL!

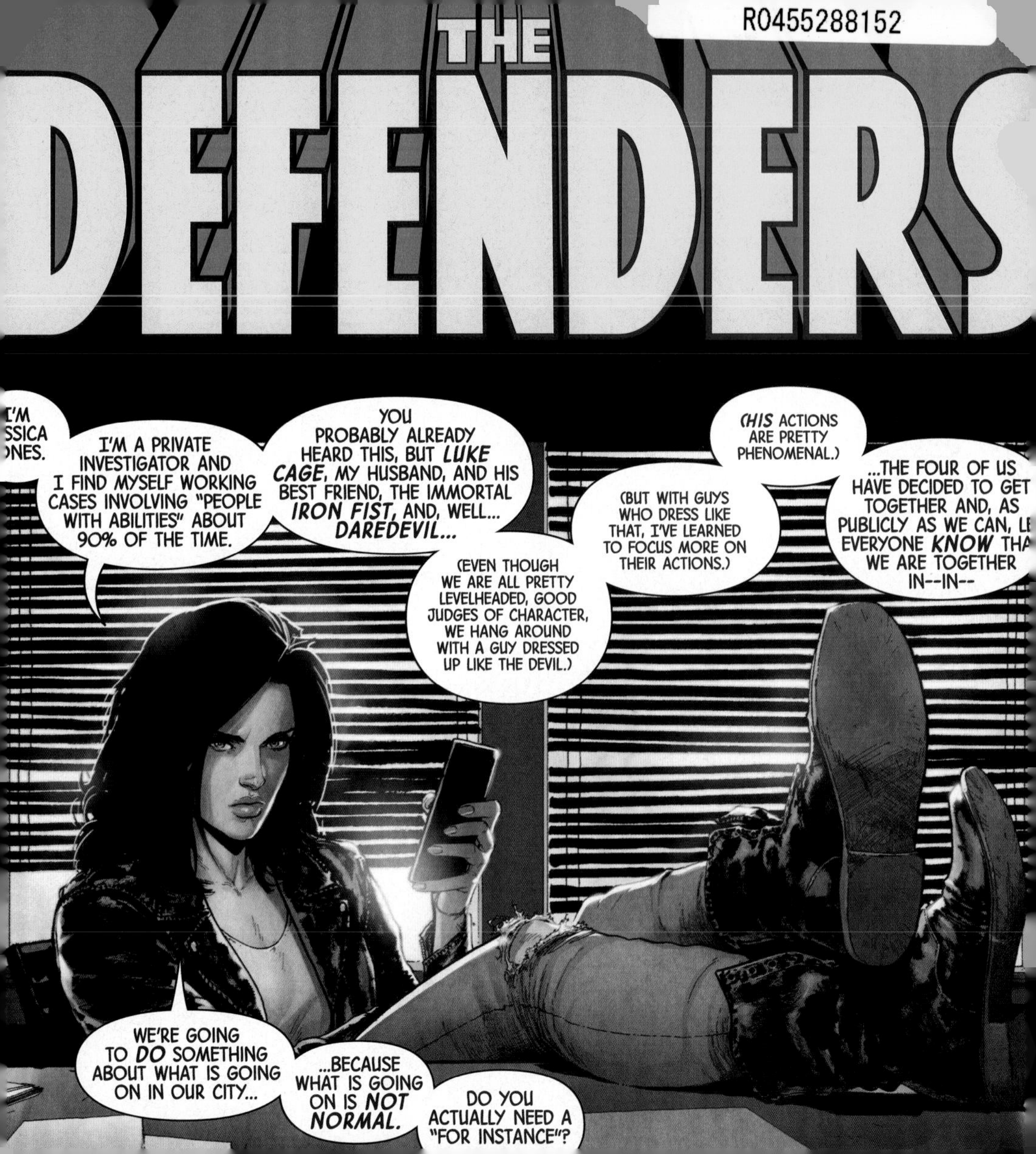
THE DEFENDERS
I'M SSICA NES.
I'M A PRIVATE INVESTIGATOR AND I FIND MYSELF WORKING CASES INVOLVING "PEOPLE WITH ABILITIES" ABOUT 90% OF THE TIME.
YOU PROBABLY ALREADY HEARD THIS, BUT LUKE CAGE, MY HUSBAND, AND HIS BEST FRIEND, THE IMMORTAL IRON FIST, AND, WELL... DAREDEVIL...
(EVEN THOUGH WE ARE ALL PRETTY LEVELHEADED, GOOD JUDGES OF CHARACTER, WE HANG AROUND WITH A GUY DRESSED UP LIKE THE DEVIL.)
(BUT WITH GUYS WHO DRESS LIKE THAT, I'VE LEARNED TO FOCUS MORE ON THEIR ACTIONS.)
(HIS ACTIONS ARE PRETTY PHENOMENAL.)
...THE FOUR OF US HAVE DECIDED TO GET TOGETHER AND, AS PUBLICLY AS WE CAN, LE EVERYONE KNOW THA WE ARE TOGETHER IN--IN--
WE'RE GOING TO DO SOMETHING ABOUT WHAT IS GOING ON IN OUR CITY...
...BECAUSE WHAT IS GOING ON IS NOT NORMAL.
DO YOU ACTUALLY NEED A "FOR INSTANCE"?

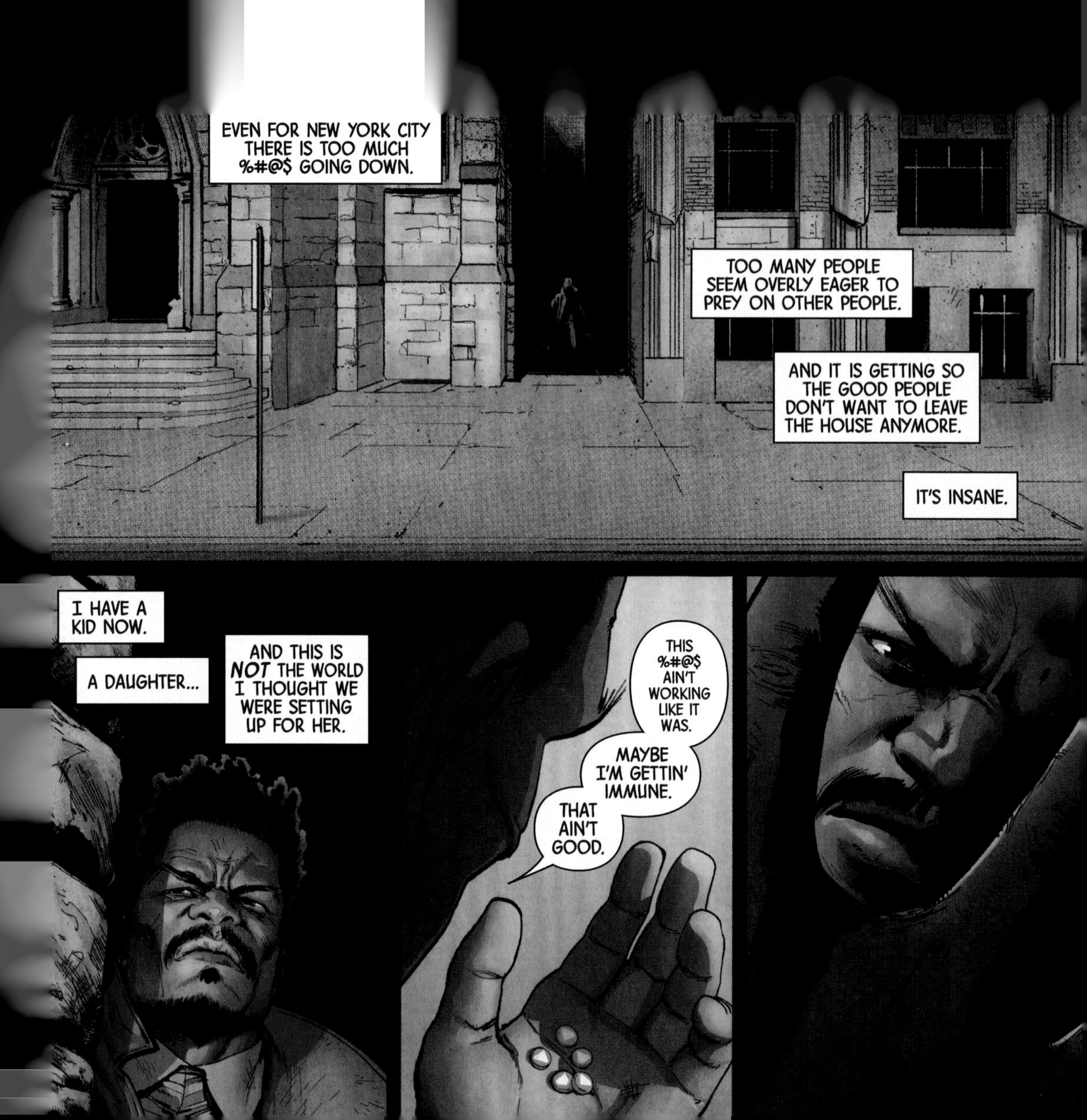
EVEN FOR NEW YORK CITY THERE IS TOO MUCH %#@$ GOING DOWN.
TOO MANY PEOPLE SEEM OVERLY EAGER TO PREY ON OTHER PEOPLE.
AND IT IS GETTING SO THE GOOD PEOPLE DON'T WANT TO LEAVE THE HOUSE ANYMORE.
IT'S INSANE.
I HAVE A KID NOW.
A DAUGHTER...
AND THIS IS *NOT* THE WORLD I THOUGHT WE WERE SETTING UP FOR HER.
THIS %#@$ AIN'T WORKING LIKE IT WAS.
MAYBE I'M GETTIN' IMMUNE.
THAT AIN'T GOOD.

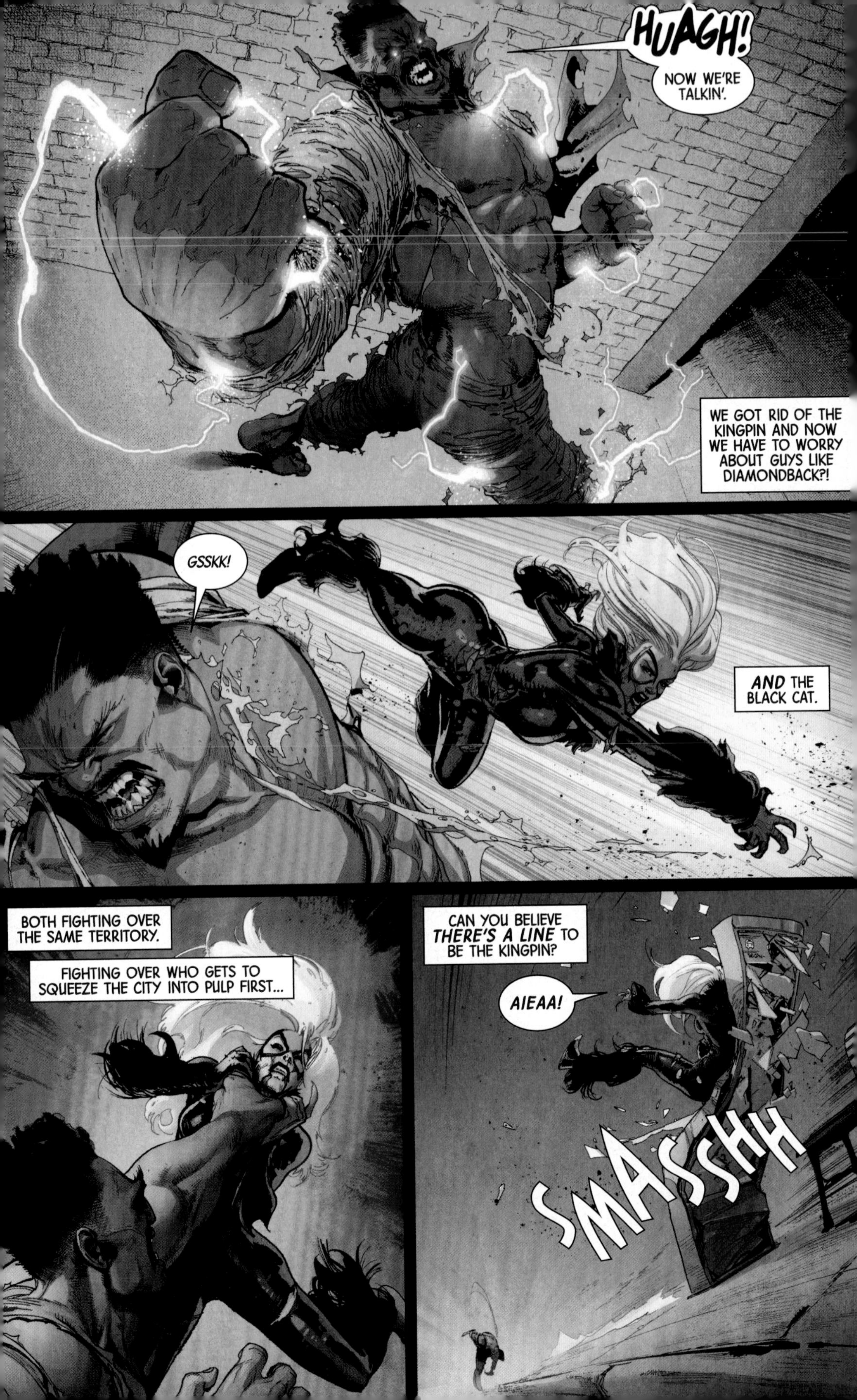
HUAGH!
NOW WE'RE TALKIN'.
WE GOT RID OF THE KINGPIN AND NOW WE HAVE TO WORRY ABOUT GUYS LIKE DIAMONDBACK?!
GSSKK!
AND THE BLACK CAT.
BOTH FIGHTING OVER THE SAME TERRITORY.
FIGHTING OVER WHO GETS TO SQUEEZE THE CITY INTO PULP FIRST...
CAN YOU BELIEVE THERE'S A LINE TO BE THE KINGPIN?
AIEAA!
SMASSHH

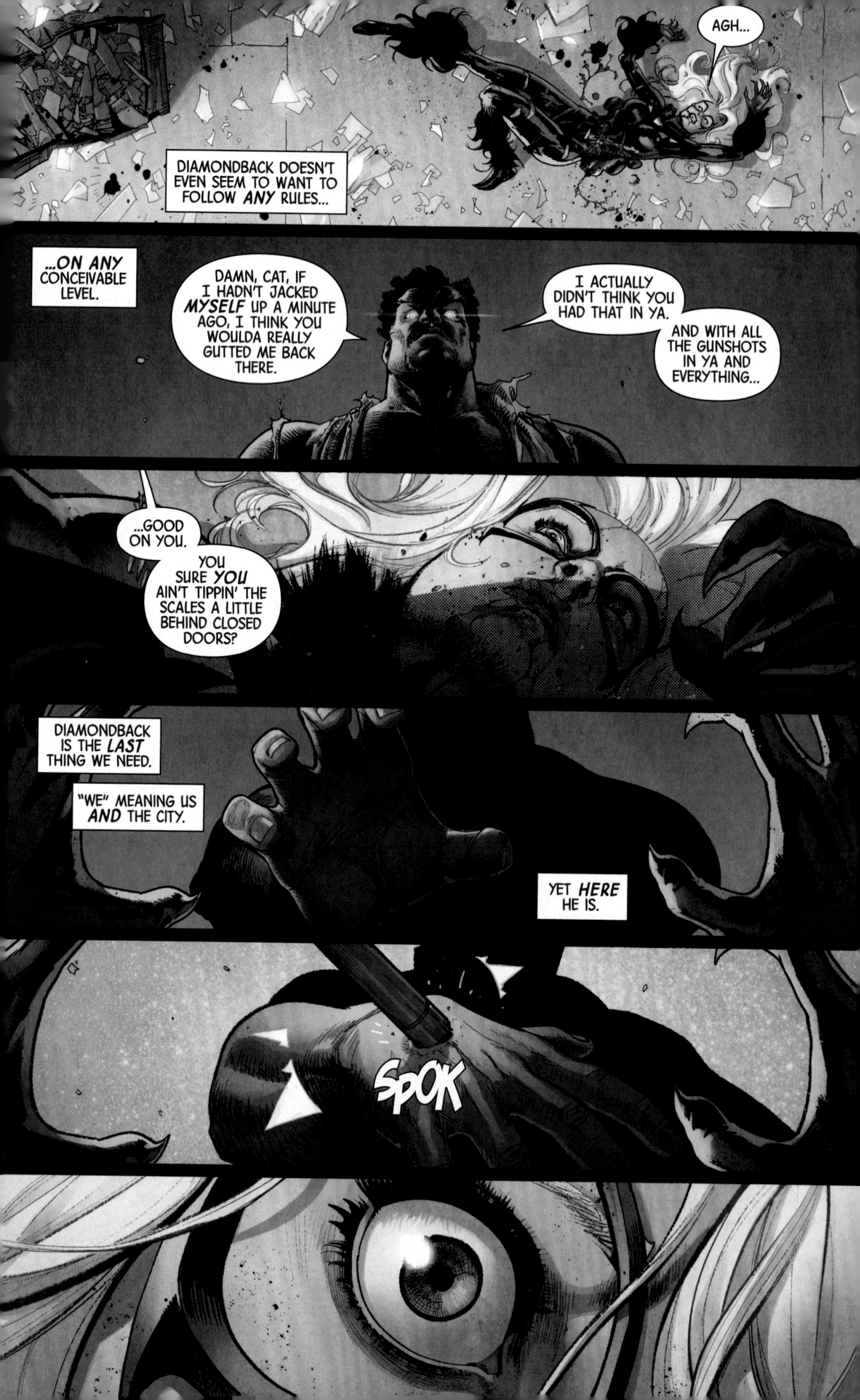
AGH...
DIAMONDBACK DOESN'T EVEN SEEM TO WANT TO FOLLOW ANY RULES...
...ON ANY CONCEIVABLE LEVEL.
DAMN, CAT, IF I HADN'T JACKED MYSELF UP A MINUTE AGO, I THINK YOU WOULDA REALLY GUTTED ME BACK THERE.
I ACTUALLY DIDN'T THINK YOU HAD THAT IN YA.
AND WITH ALL THE GUNSHOTS IN YA AND EVERYTHING...
...GOOD ON YOU.
YOU SURE YOU AIN'T TIPPIN' THE SCALES A LITTLE BEHIND CLOSED DOORS?
DIAMONDBACK IS THE LAST THING WE NEED.
"WE" MEANING US AND THE CITY.
YET HERE HE IS.
SPOK

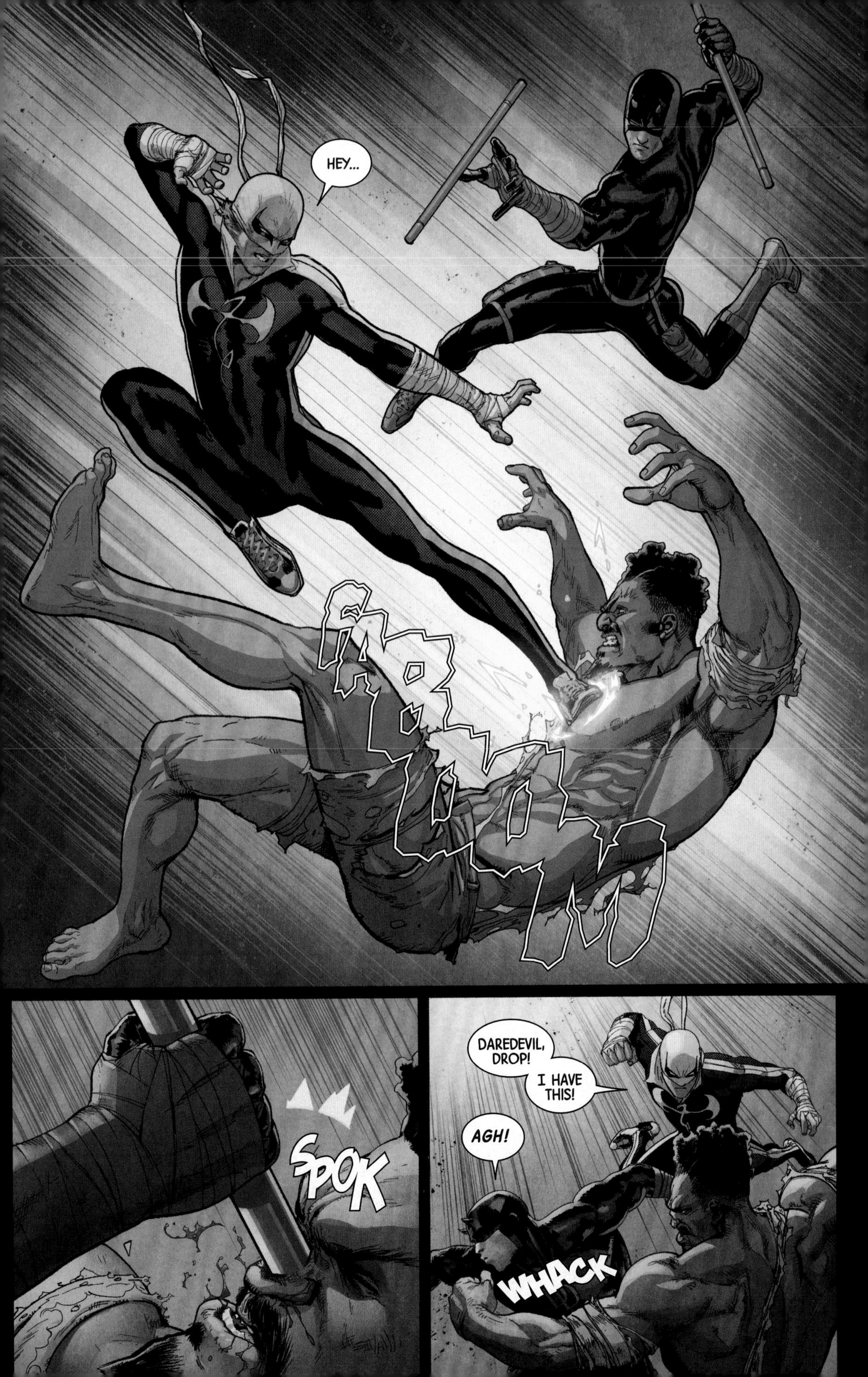
HEY...
SPOK
DAREDEVIL, DROP!
I HAVE THIS!
AGH!
WHACK

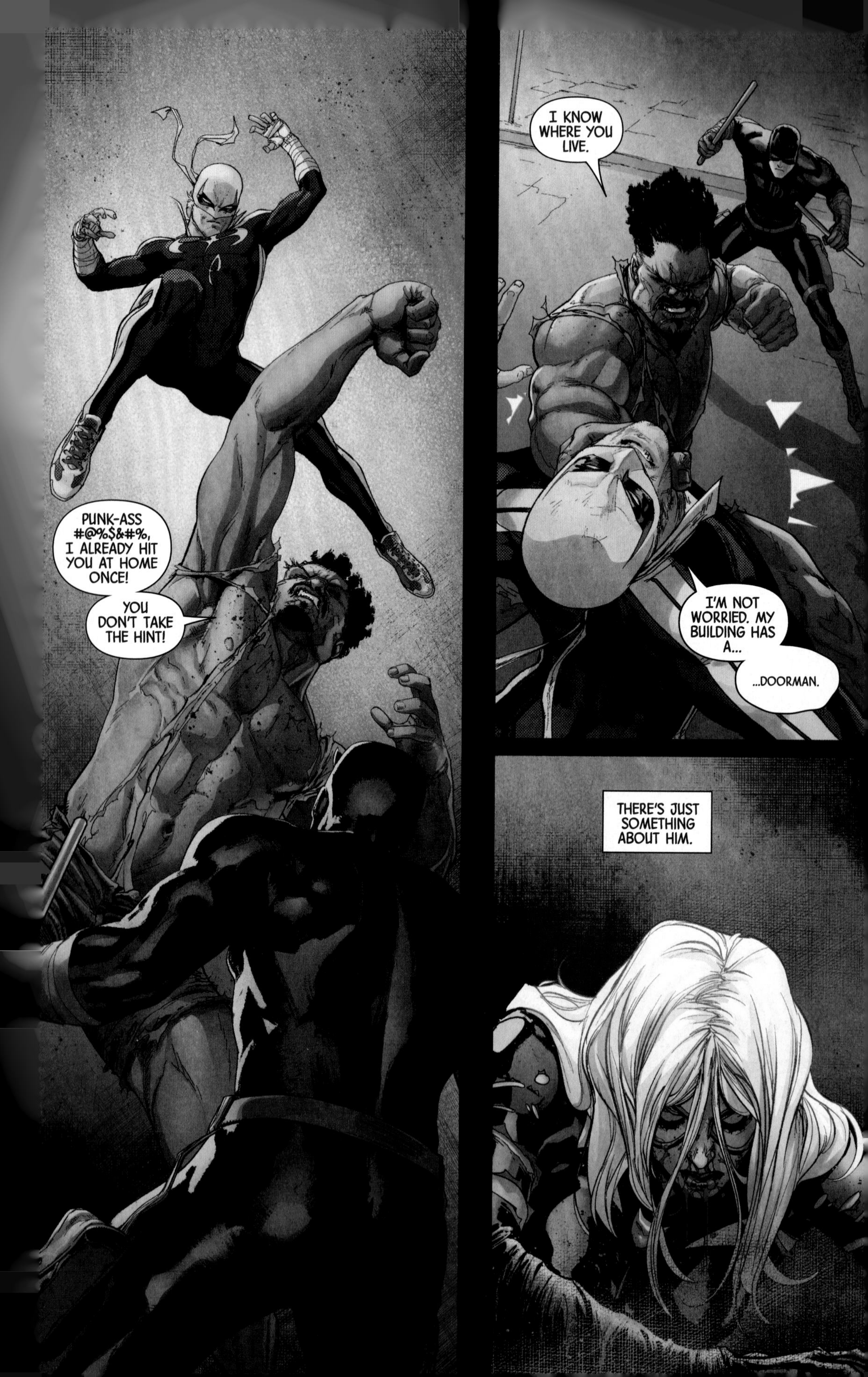
PUNK-ASS #@%$&#%, I ALREADY HIT YOU AT HOME ONCE!
YOU DON'T TAKE THE HINT!
I KNOW WHERE YOU LIVE.
I'M NOT WORRIED. MY BUILDING HAS A...
...DOORMAN.
THERE'S JUST SOMETHING ABOUT HIM.

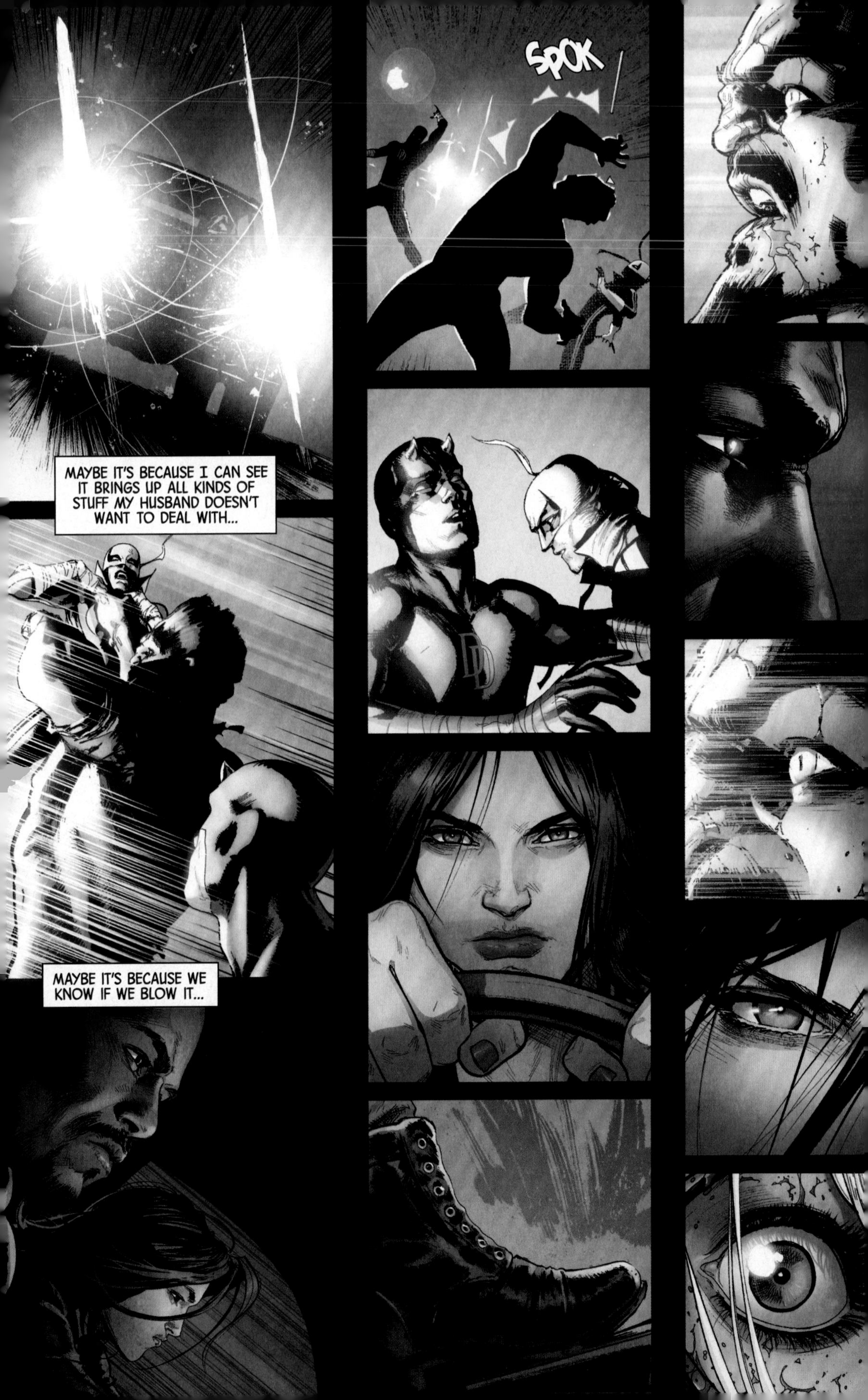

SPOK
MAYBE IT'S BECAUSE I CAN SEE IT BRINGS UP ALL KINDS OF STUFF MY HUSBAND DOESN'T WANT TO DEAL WITH...
MAYBE IT'S BECAUSE WE KNOW IF WE BLOW IT...

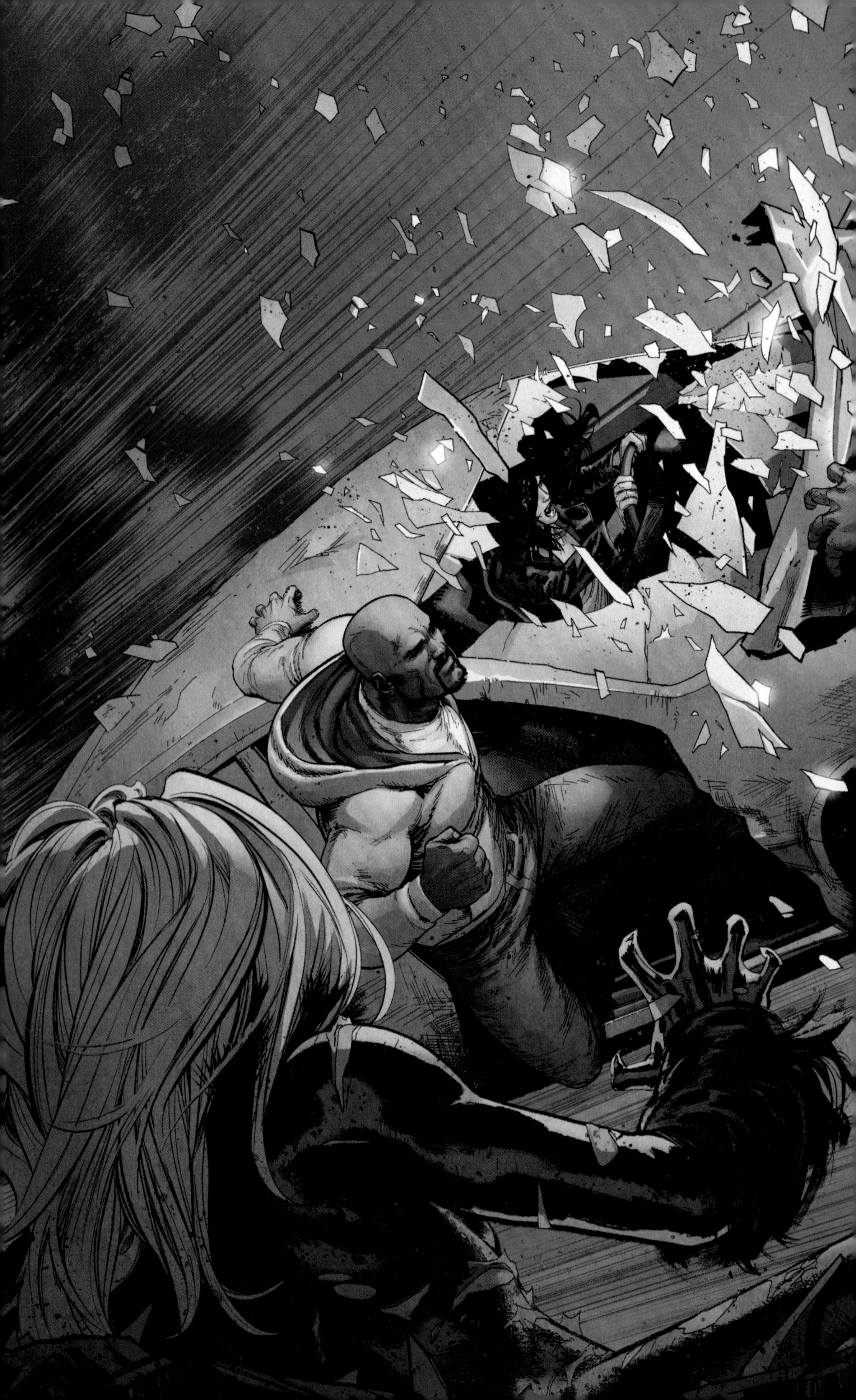

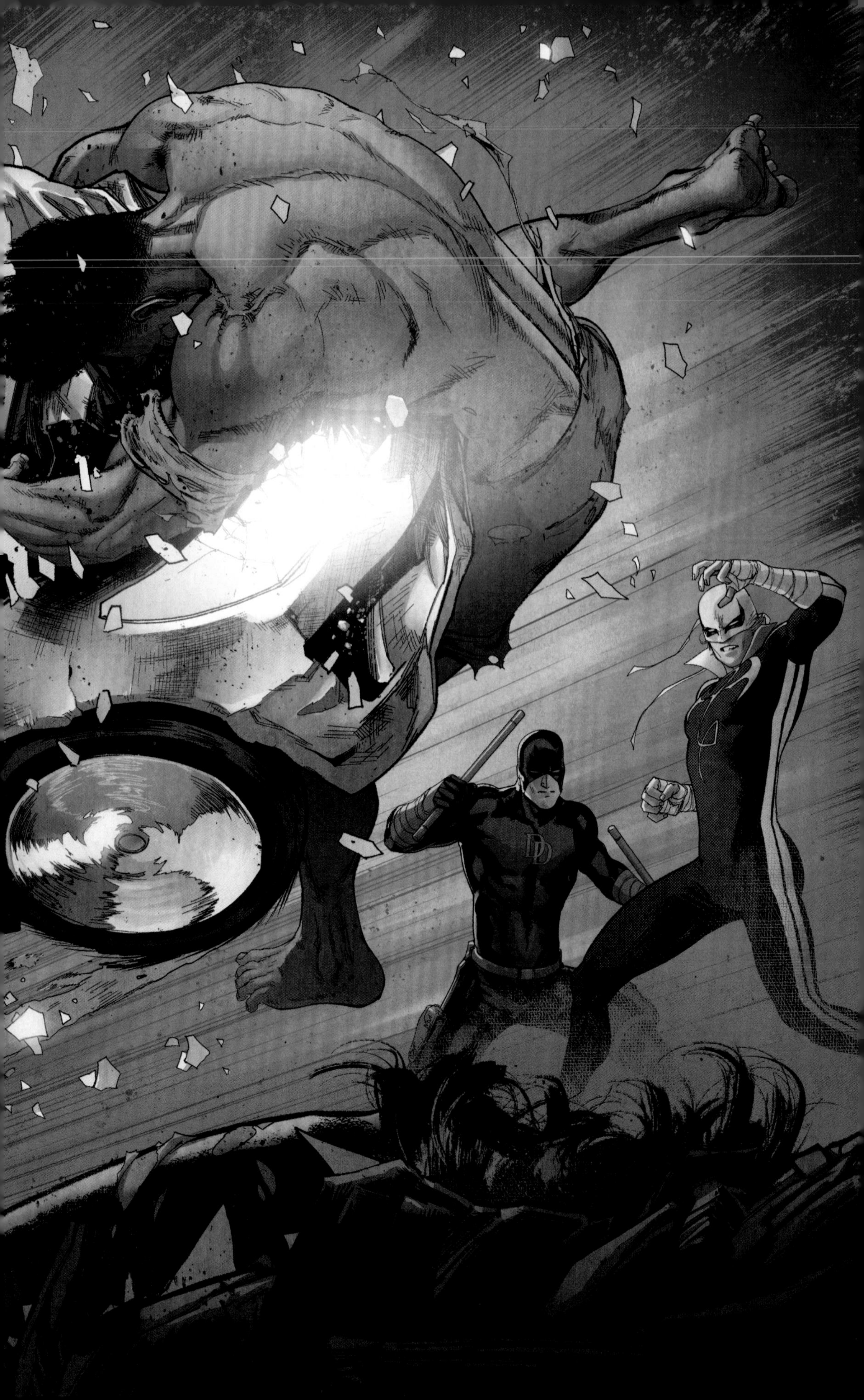

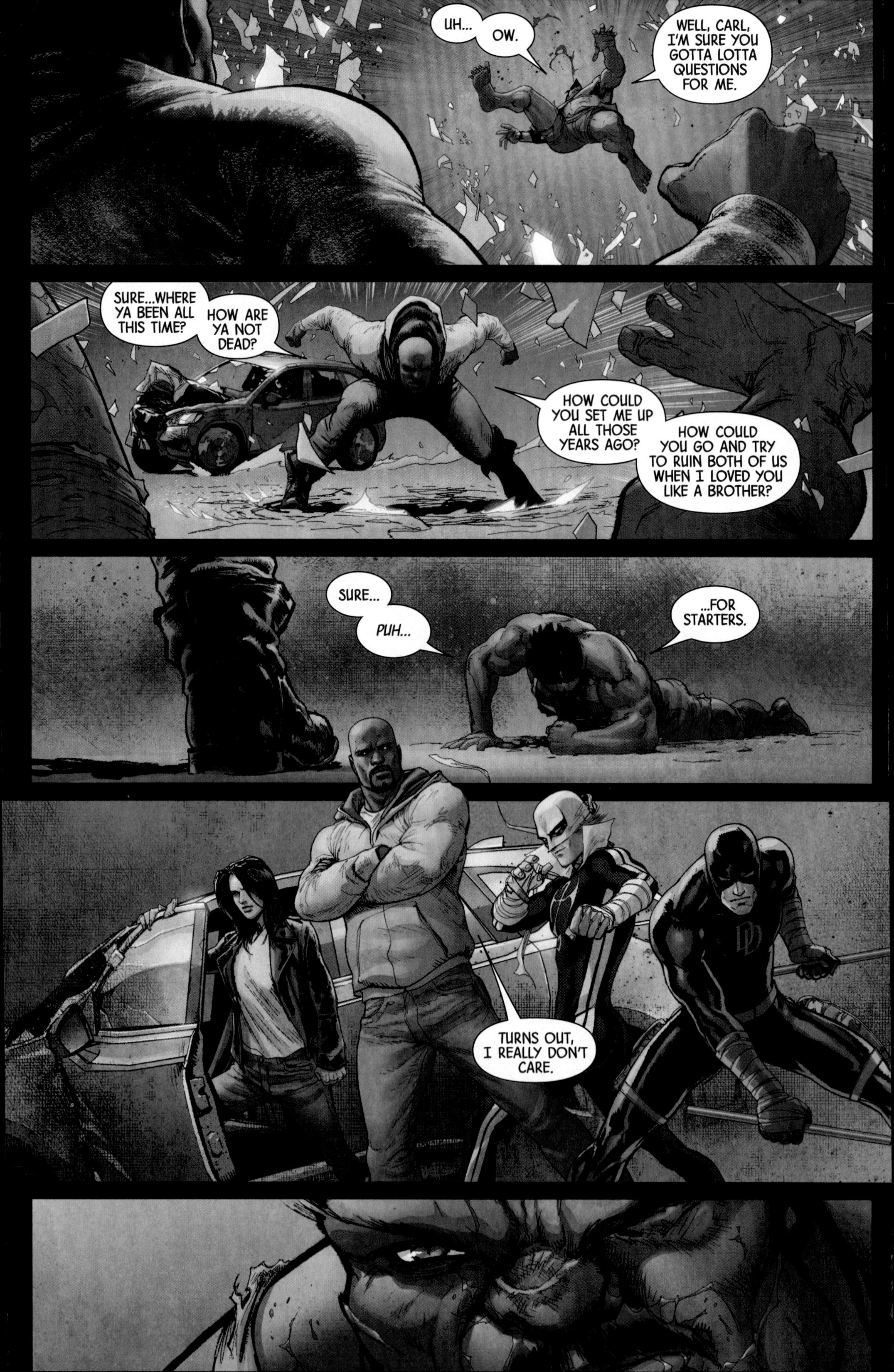

UH...
OW.
WELL, CARL, I'M SURE YOU GOTTA LOTTA QUESTIONS FOR ME.
SURE...WHERE YA BEEN ALL THIS TIME?
HOW ARE YA NOT DEAD?
HOW COULD YOU SET ME UP ALL THOSE YEARS AGO?
HOW COULD YOU GO AND TRY TO RUIN BOTH OF US WHEN I LOVED YOU LIKE A BROTHER?
SURE...
PUH...
...FOR STARTERS.
TURNS OUT, I REALLY DON'T CARE.

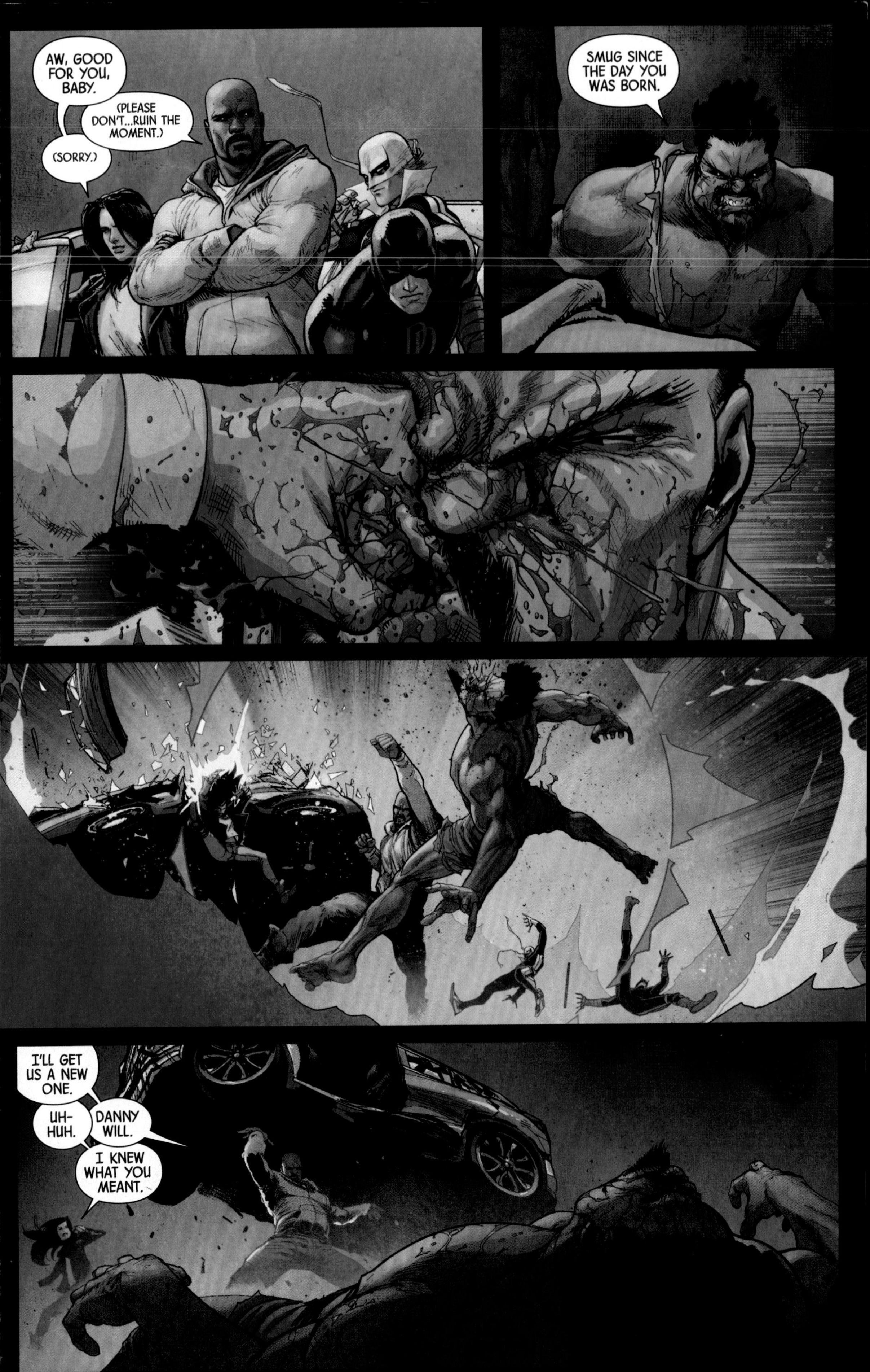
AW, GOOD FOR YOU, BABY.
(PLEASE DON'T...RUIN THE MOMENT.)
(SORRY.)
SMUG SINCE THE DAY YOU WAS BORN.
I'LL GET US A NEW ONE.
UH-HUH.
DANNY WILL.
I KNEW WHAT YOU MEANT.

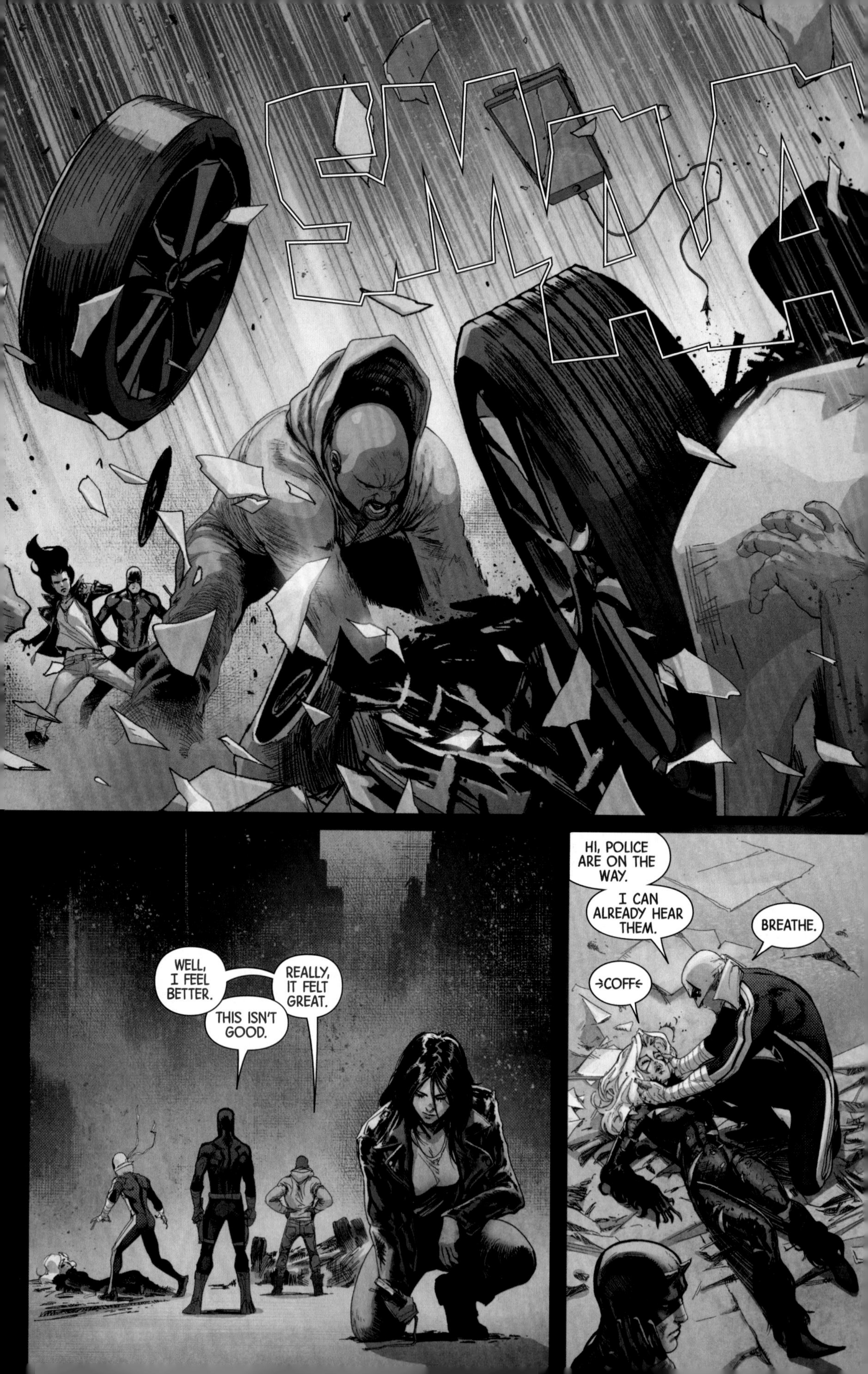
SMASH
WELL, I FEEL BETTER.
REALLY, IT FELT GREAT.
THIS ISN'T GOOD.
HI, POLICE ARE ON THE WAY.
I CAN ALREADY HEAR THEM.
BREATHE.
COFF

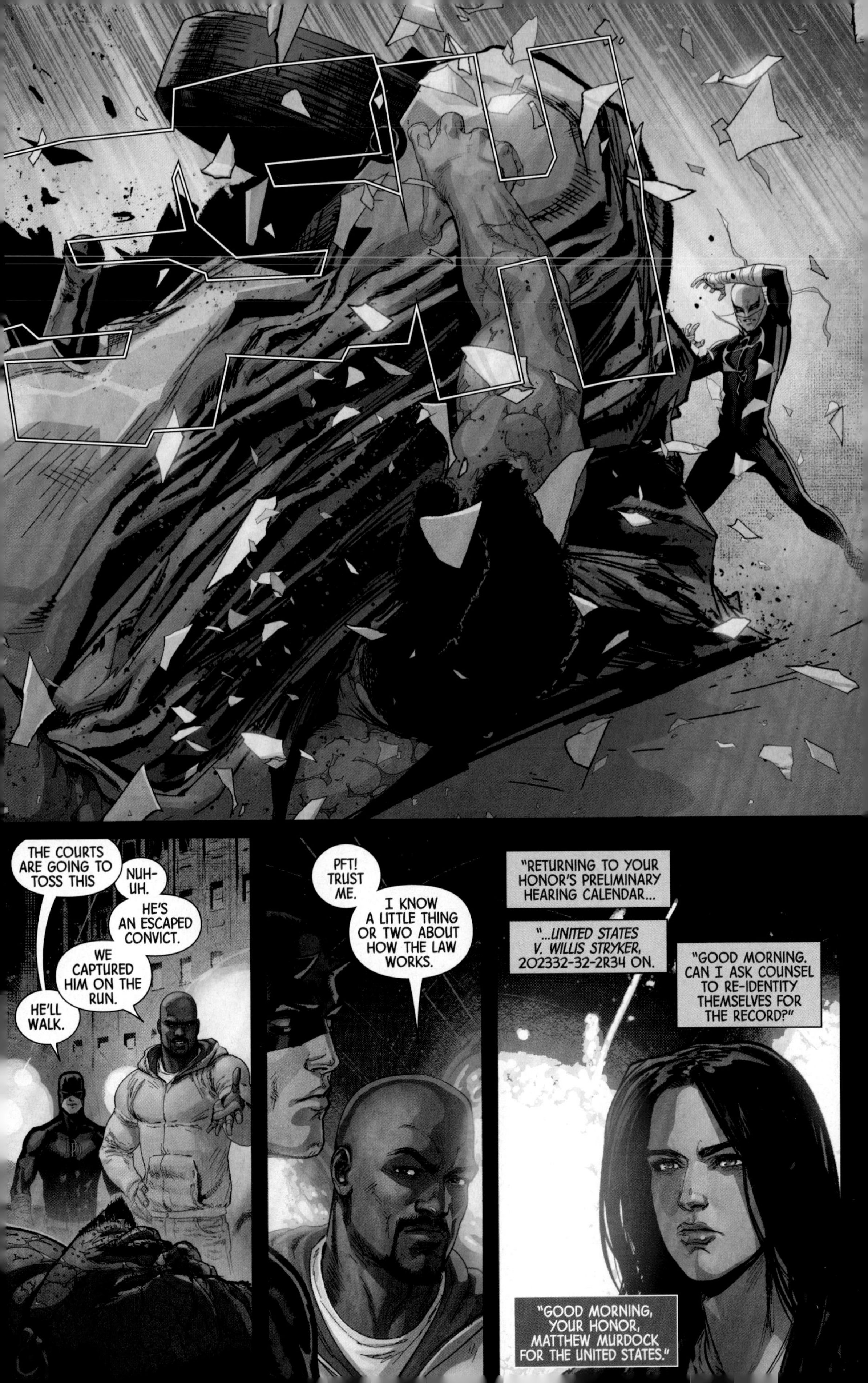
THE COURTS ARE GOING TO TOSS THIS
NUH-UH.
HE'S AN ESCAPED CONVICT.
WE CAPTURED HIM ON THE RUN.
HE'LL WALK.
PFT! TRUST ME.
I KNOW A LITTLE THING OR TWO ABOUT HOW THE LAW WORKS.
"RETURNING TO YOUR HONOR'S PRELIMINARY HEARING CALENDAR...
"...UNITED STATES V. WILLIS STRYKER, 202332-32-2R34 ON.
"GOOD MORNING. CAN I ASK COUNSEL TO RE-IDENTITY THEMSELVES FOR THE RECORD?"
"GOOD MORNING, YOUR HONOR, MATTHEW MURDOCK FOR THE UNITED STATES."

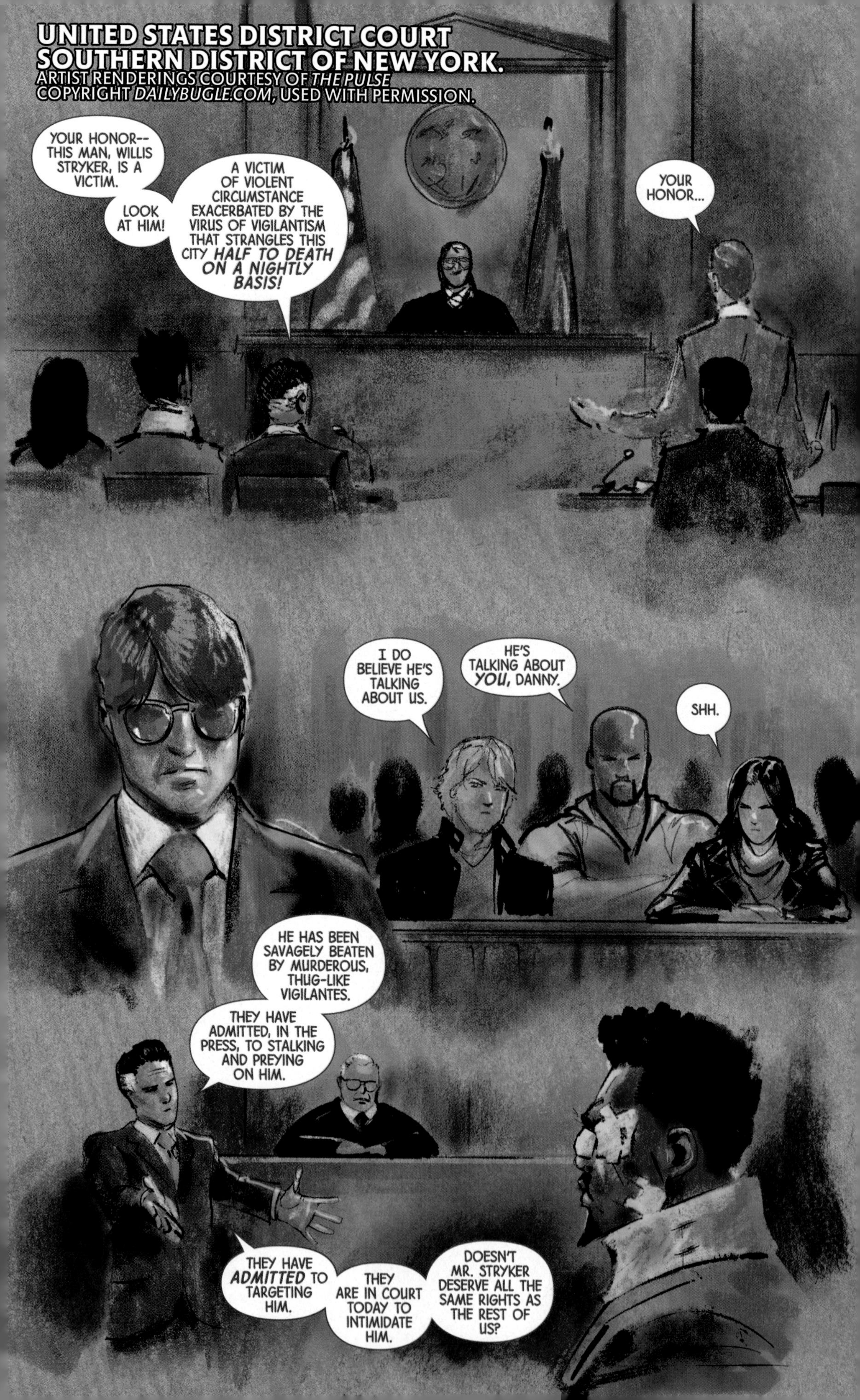
UNITED STATES DISTRICT COURT SOUTHERN DISTRICT OF NEW YORK.
ARTIST RENDERINGS COURTESY OF THE PULSE
COPYRIGHT DAILYBUGLE.COM, USED WITH PERMISSION.
YOUR HONOR-- THIS MAN, WILLIS STRYKER, IS A VICTIM.
LOOK AT HIM!
A VICTIM OF VIOLENT CIRCUMSTANCE EXACERBATED BY THE VIRUS OF VIGILANTISM THAT STRANGLES THIS CITY HALF TO DEATH ON A NIGHTLY BASIS!
YOUR HONOR...
I DO BELIEVE HE'S TALKING ABOUT US.
HE'S TALKING ABOUT YOU, DANNY.
SHH.
HE HAS BEEN SAVAGELY BEATEN BY MURDEROUS, THUG-LIKE VIGILANTES.
THEY HAVE ADMITTED, IN THE PRESS, TO STALKING AND PREYING ON HIM.
THEY HAVE ADMITTED TO TARGETING HIM.
THEY ARE IN COURT TODAY TO INTIMIDATE HIM.
DOESN'T MR. STRYKER DESERVE ALL THE SAME RIGHTS AS THE REST OF US?

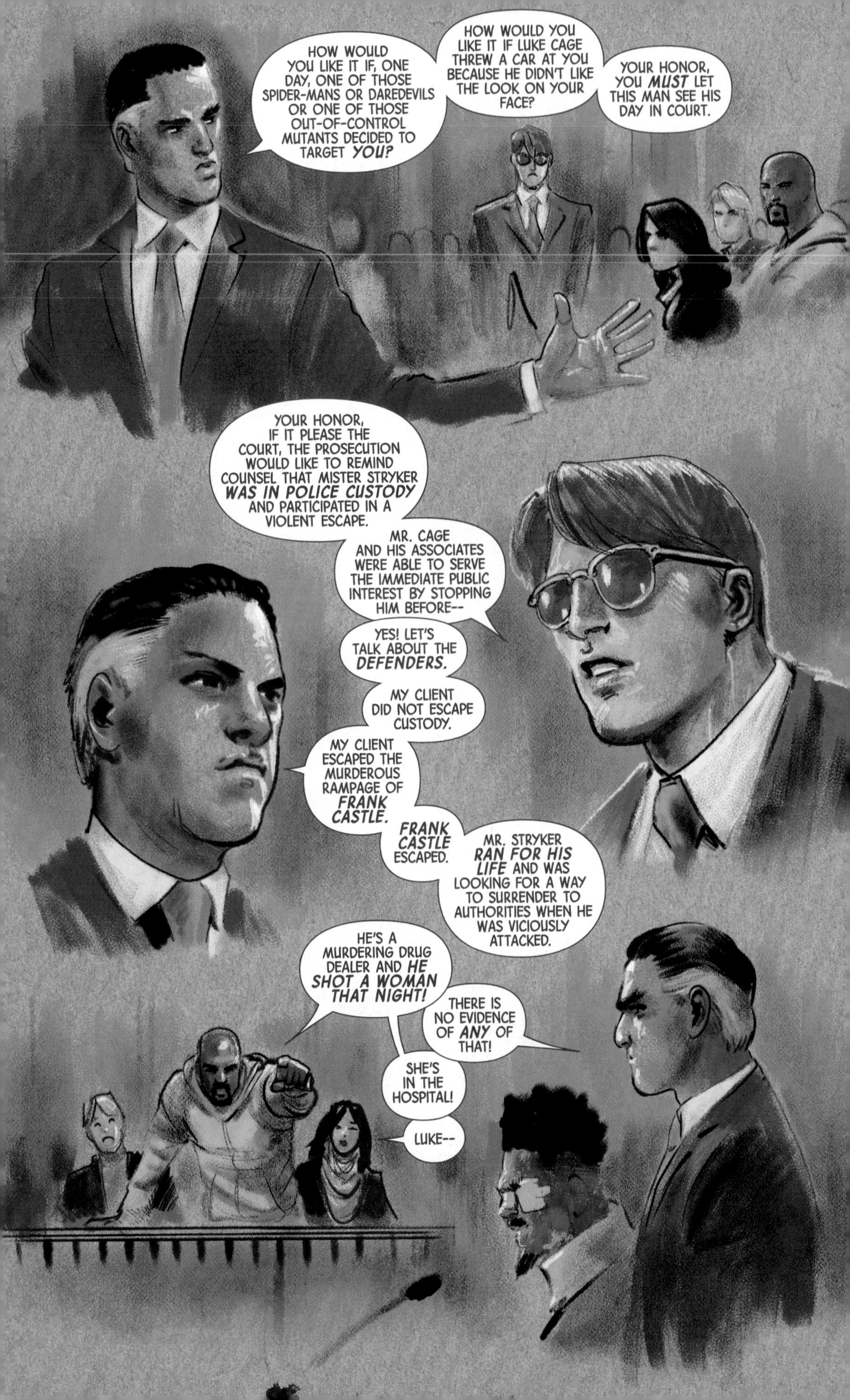
HOW WOULD YOU LIKE IT IF, ONE DAY, ONE OF THOSE SPIDER-MANS OR DAREDEVILS OR ONE OF THOSE OUT-OF-CONTROL MUTANTS DECIDED TO TARGET *YOU?*
HOW WOULD YOU LIKE IT IF LUKE CAGE THREW A CAR AT YOU BECAUSE HE DIDN'T LIKE THE LOOK ON YOUR FACE?
YOUR HONOR, YOU *MUST* LET THIS MAN SEE HIS DAY IN COURT.
YOUR HONOR, IF IT PLEASE THE COURT, THE PROSECUTION WOULD LIKE TO REMIND COUNSEL THAT MISTER STRYKER *WAS IN POLICE CUSTODY* AND PARTICIPATED IN A VIOLENT ESCAPE.
MR. CAGE AND HIS ASSOCIATES WERE ABLE TO SERVE THE IMMEDIATE PUBLIC INTEREST BY STOPPING HIM BEFORE--
YES! LET'S TALK ABOUT THE *DEFENDERS.*
MY CLIENT DID NOT ESCAPE CUSTODY.
MY CLIENT ESCAPED THE MURDEROUS RAMPAGE OF *FRANK CASTLE.*
FRANK CASTLE ESCAPED.
MR. STRYKER *RAN FOR HIS LIFE* AND WAS LOOKING FOR A WAY TO SURRENDER TO AUTHORITIES WHEN HE WAS VICIOUSLY ATTACKED.
HE'S A MURDERING DRUG DEALER AND *HE SHOT A WOMAN THAT NIGHT!*
THERE IS NO EVIDENCE OF *ANY* OF THAT!
SHE'S IN THE HOSPITAL!
LUKE--

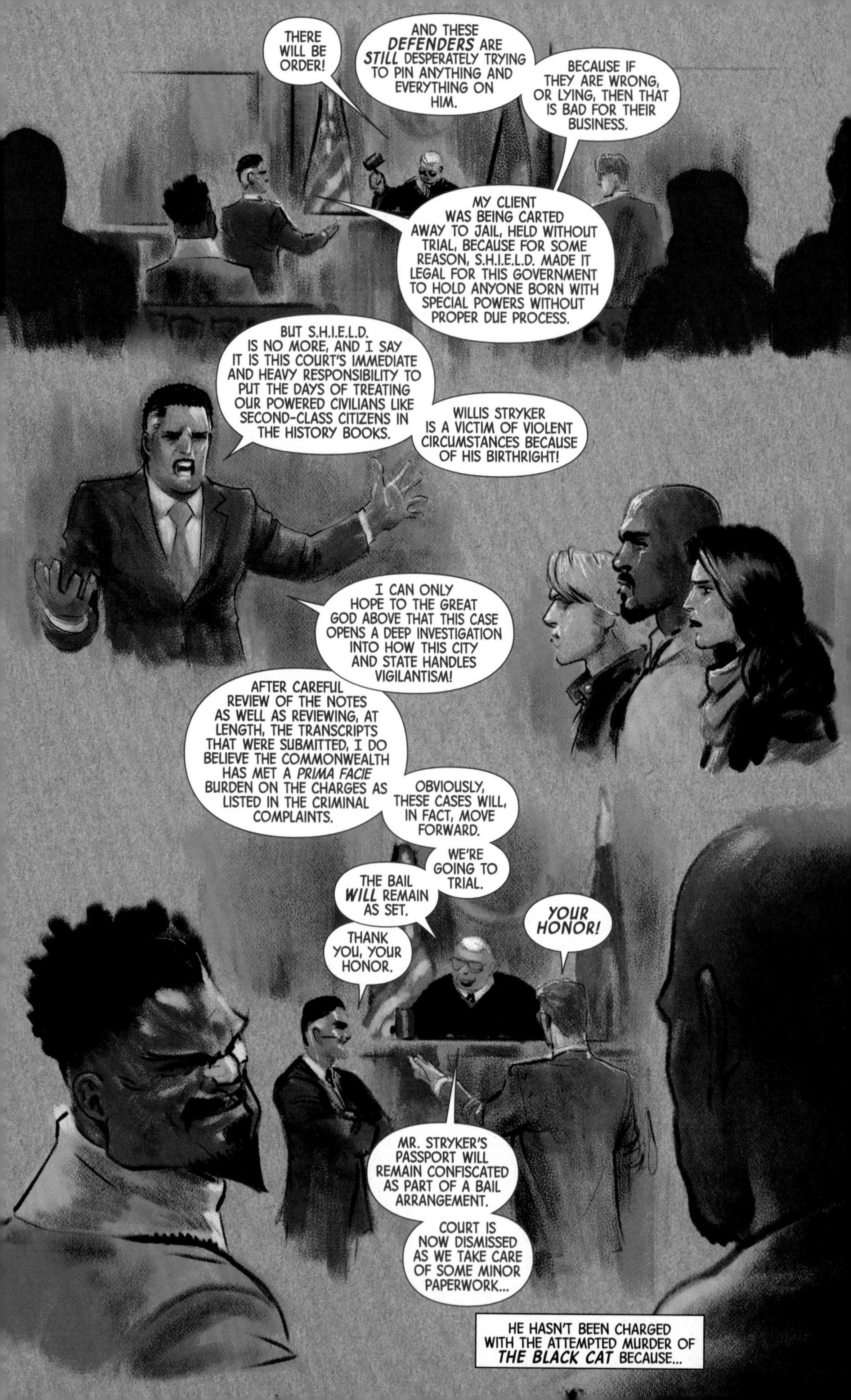
THERE WILL BE ORDER!
AND THESE DEFENDERS ARE STILL DESPERATELY TRYING TO PIN ANYTHING AND EVERYTHING ON HIM.
BECAUSE IF THEY ARE WRONG, OR LYING, THEN THAT IS BAD FOR THEIR BUSINESS.
MY CLIENT WAS BEING CARTED AWAY TO JAIL, HELD WITHOUT TRIAL, BECAUSE FOR SOME REASON, S.H.I.E.L.D. MADE IT LEGAL FOR THIS GOVERNMENT TO HOLD ANYONE BORN WITH SPECIAL POWERS WITHOUT PROPER DUE PROCESS.
BUT S.H.I.E.L.D. IS NO MORE, AND I SAY IT IS THIS COURT'S IMMEDIATE AND HEAVY RESPONSIBILITY TO PUT THE DAYS OF TREATING OUR POWERED CIVILIANS LIKE SECOND-CLASS CITIZENS IN THE HISTORY BOOKS.
WILLIS STRYKER IS A VICTIM OF VIOLENT CIRCUMSTANCES BECAUSE OF HIS BIRTHRIGHT!
I CAN ONLY HOPE TO THE GREAT GOD ABOVE THAT THIS CASE OPENS A DEEP INVESTIGATION INTO HOW THIS CITY AND STATE HANDLES VIGILANTISM!
AFTER CAREFUL REVIEW OF THE NOTES AS WELL AS REVIEWING, AT LENGTH, THE TRANSCRIPTS THAT WERE SUBMITTED, I DO BELIEVE THE COMMONWEALTH HAS MET A PRIMA FACIE BURDEN ON THE CHARGES AS LISTED IN THE CRIMINAL COMPLAINTS.
OBVIOUSLY, THESE CASES WILL, IN FACT, MOVE FORWARD.
WE'RE GOING TO TRIAL.
THE BAIL WILL REMAIN AS SET.
THANK YOU, YOUR HONOR.
YOUR HONOR!
MR. STRYKER'S PASSPORT WILL REMAIN CONFISCATED AS PART OF A BAIL ARRANGEMENT.
COURT IS NOW DISMISSED AS WE TAKE CARE OF SOME MINOR PAPERWORK...
HE HASN'T BEEN CHARGED WITH THE ATTEMPTED MURDER OF THE BLACK CAT BECAUSE...

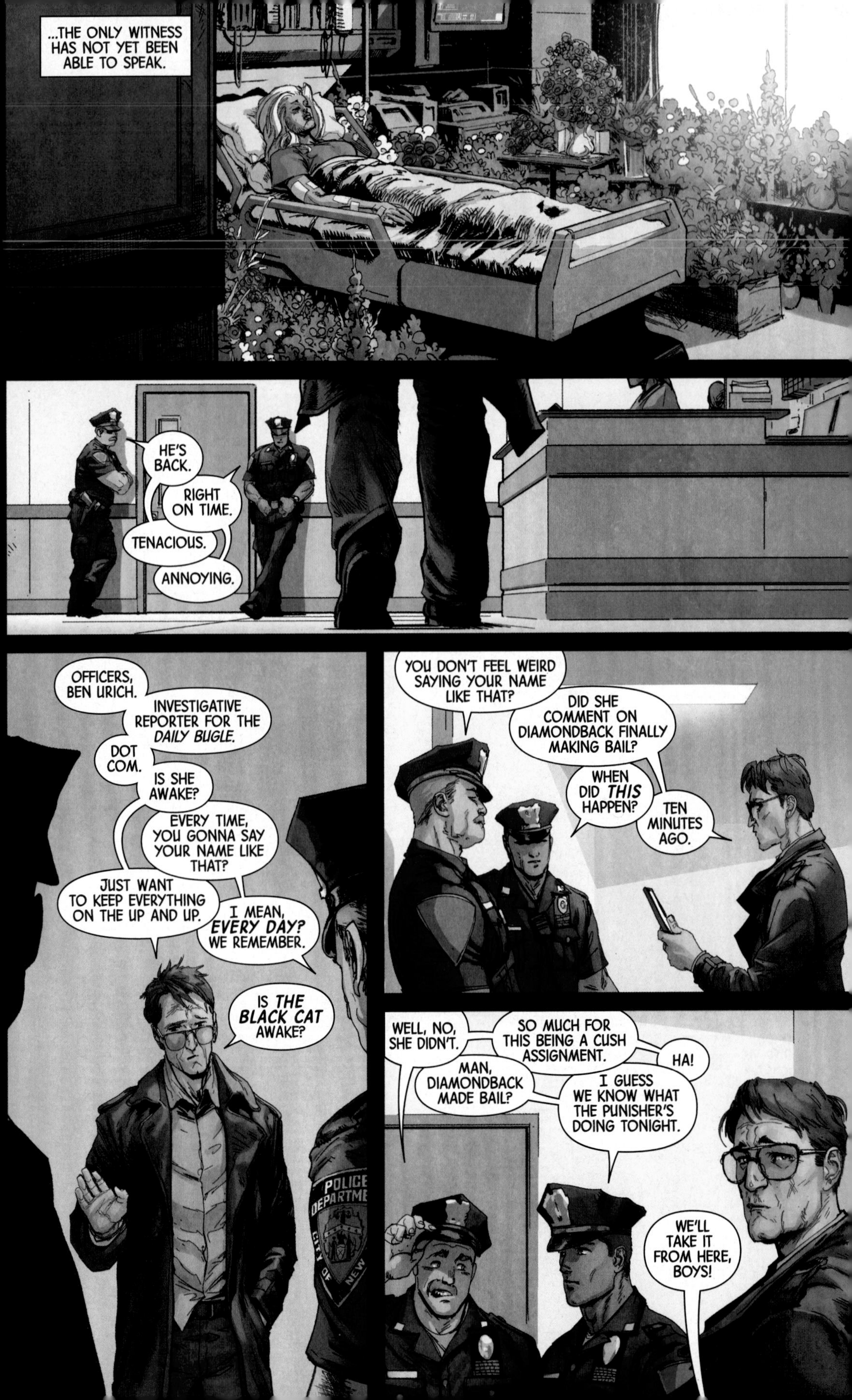

...THE ONLY WITNESS HAS NOT YET BEEN ABLE TO SPEAK.
HE'S BACK.
RIGHT ON TIME.
TENACIOUS.
ANNOYING.
OFFICERS, BEN URICH.
INVESTIGATIVE REPORTER FOR THE DAILY BUGLE.
DOT COM.
IS SHE AWAKE?
EVERY TIME, YOU GONNA SAY YOUR NAME LIKE THAT?
JUST WANT TO KEEP EVERYTHING ON THE UP AND UP.
I MEAN, EVERY DAY? WE REMEMBER.
IS THE BLACK CAT AWAKE?
YOU DON'T FEEL WEIRD SAYING YOUR NAME LIKE THAT?
DID SHE COMMENT ON DIAMONDBACK FINALLY MAKING BAIL?
WHEN DID THIS HAPPEN?
TEN MINUTES AGO.
WELL, NO, SHE DIDN'T.
SO MUCH FOR THIS BEING A CUSH ASSIGNMENT.
HA!
MAN, DIAMONDBACK MADE BAIL?
I GUESS WE KNOW WHAT THE PUNISHER'S DOING TONIGHT.
WE'LL TAKE IT FROM HERE, BOYS!

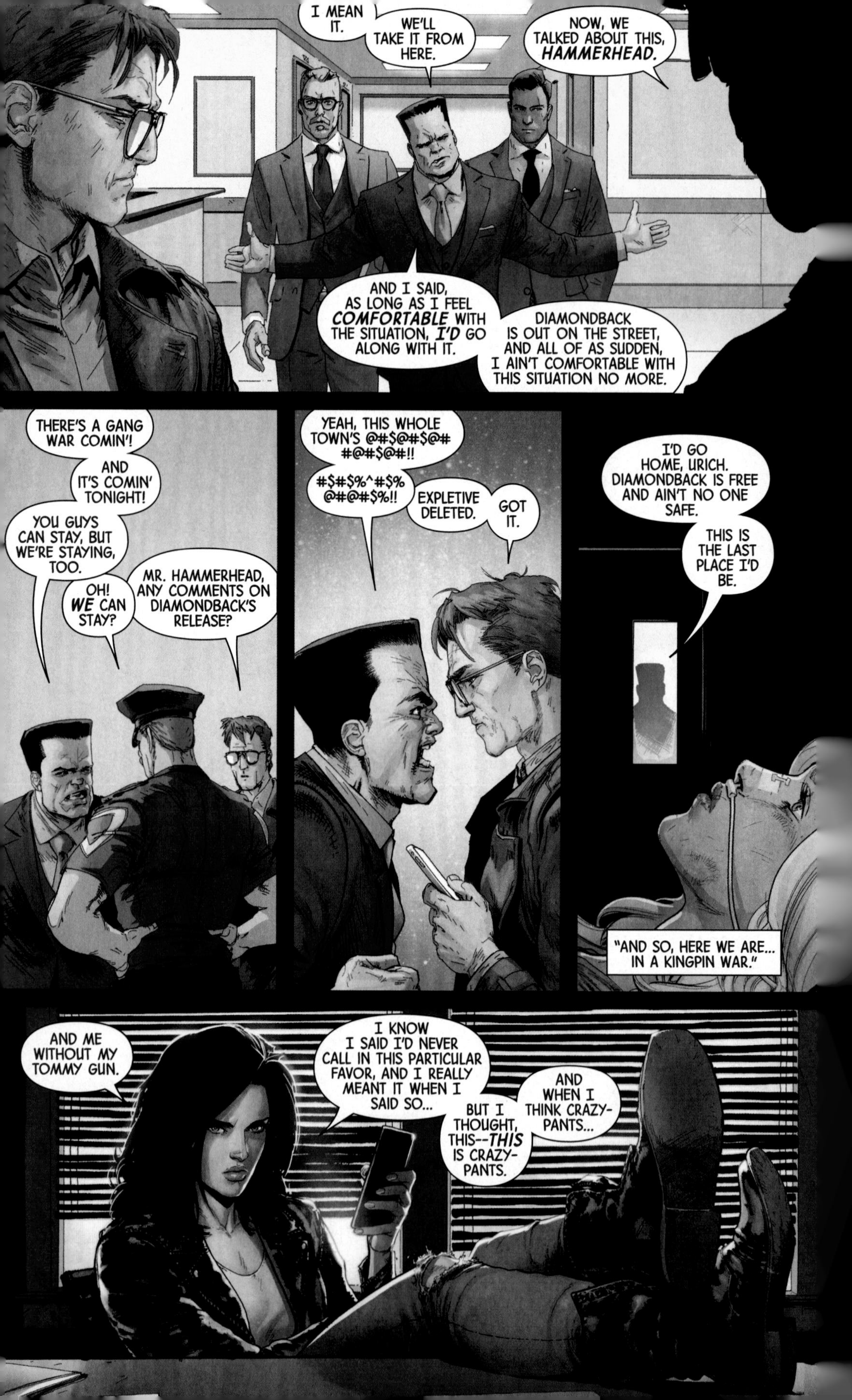
I MEAN IT.
WE'LL TAKE IT FROM HERE.
NOW, WE TALKED ABOUT THIS, HAMMERHEAD.
AND I SAID, AS LONG AS I FEEL COMFORTABLE WITH THE SITUATION, I'D GO ALONG WITH IT.
DIAMONDBACK IS OUT ON THE STREET, AND ALL OF AS SUDDEN, I AIN'T COMFORTABLE WITH THIS SITUATION NO MORE.
THERE'S A GANG WAR COMIN'!
AND IT'S COMIN' TONIGHT!
YOU GUYS CAN STAY, BUT WE'RE STAYING, TOO.
OH! WE CAN STAY?
MR. HAMMERHEAD, ANY COMMENTS ON DIAMONDBACK'S RELEASE?
YEAH, THIS WHOLE TOWN'S @#$@#$@# #@#$@#!!
#$#$%^#$% @#@#$%!!
EXPLETIVE DELETED.
GOT IT.
I'D GO HOME, URICH. DIAMONDBACK IS FREE AND AIN'T NO ONE SAFE.
THIS IS THE LAST PLACE I'D BE.
"AND SO, HERE WE ARE... IN A KINGPIN WAR."
AND ME WITHOUT MY TOMMY GUN.
I KNOW I SAID I'D NEVER CALL IN THIS PARTICULAR FAVOR, AND I REALLY MEANT IT WHEN I SAID SO...
BUT I THOUGHT, THIS--THIS IS CRAZY-PANTS.
AND WHEN I THINK CRAZY-PANTS...

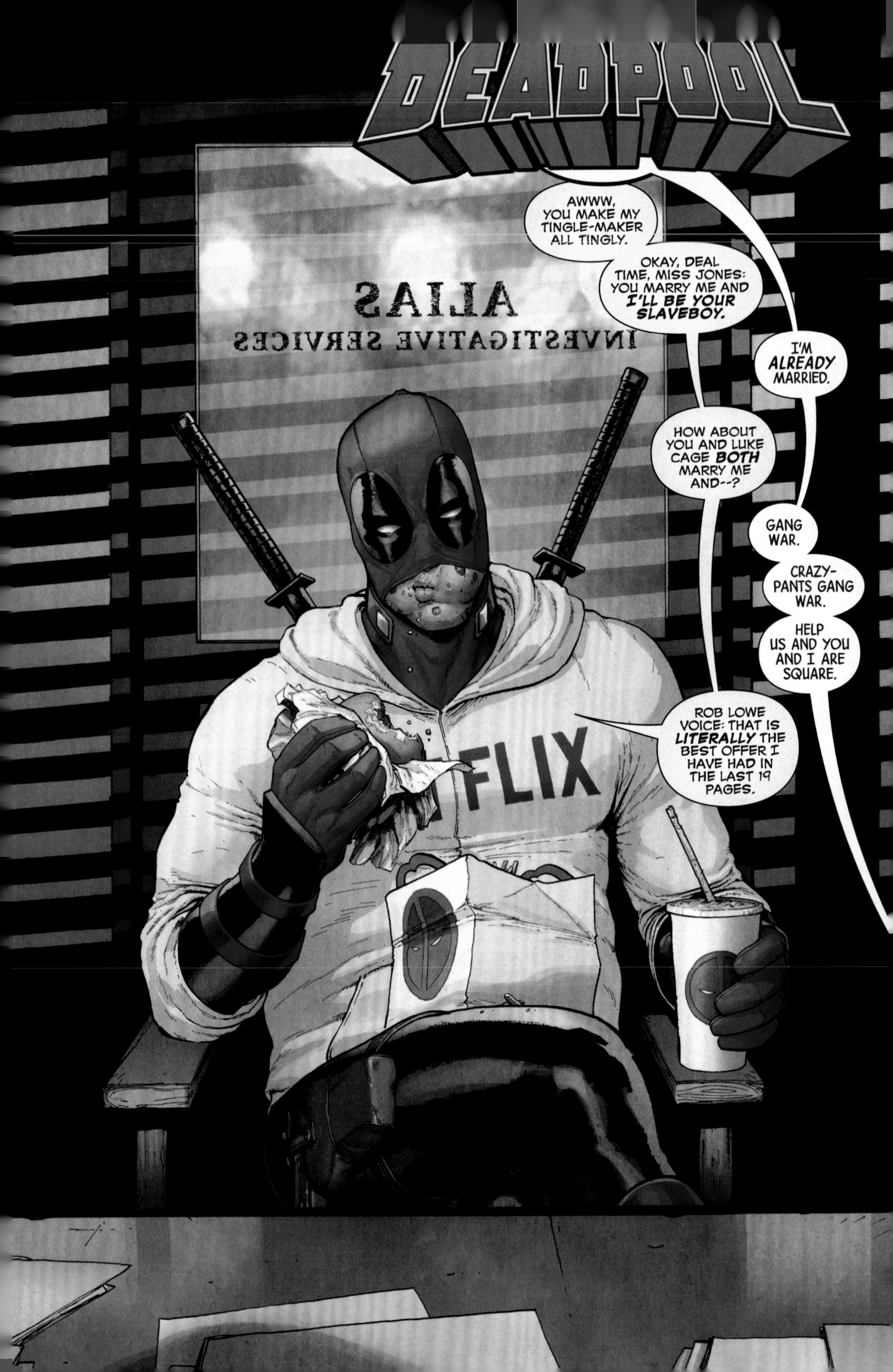
DEADPOOL
AWWW, YOU MAKE MY TINGLE-MAKER ALL TINGLY.
OKAY, DEAL TIME, MISS JONES: YOU MARRY ME AND *I'LL BE YOUR SLAVEBOY.*
I'M *ALREADY* MARRIED.
HOW ABOUT YOU AND LUKE CAGE *BOTH* MARRY ME AND--?
GANG WAR.
CRAZY-PANTS GANG WAR.
HELP US AND YOU AND I ARE SQUARE.
ROB LOWE VOICE: THAT IS *LITERALLY* THE BEST OFFER I HAVE HAD IN THE LAST 19 PAGES.
ALIAS INVESTIGATIVE SERVICES
FLIX

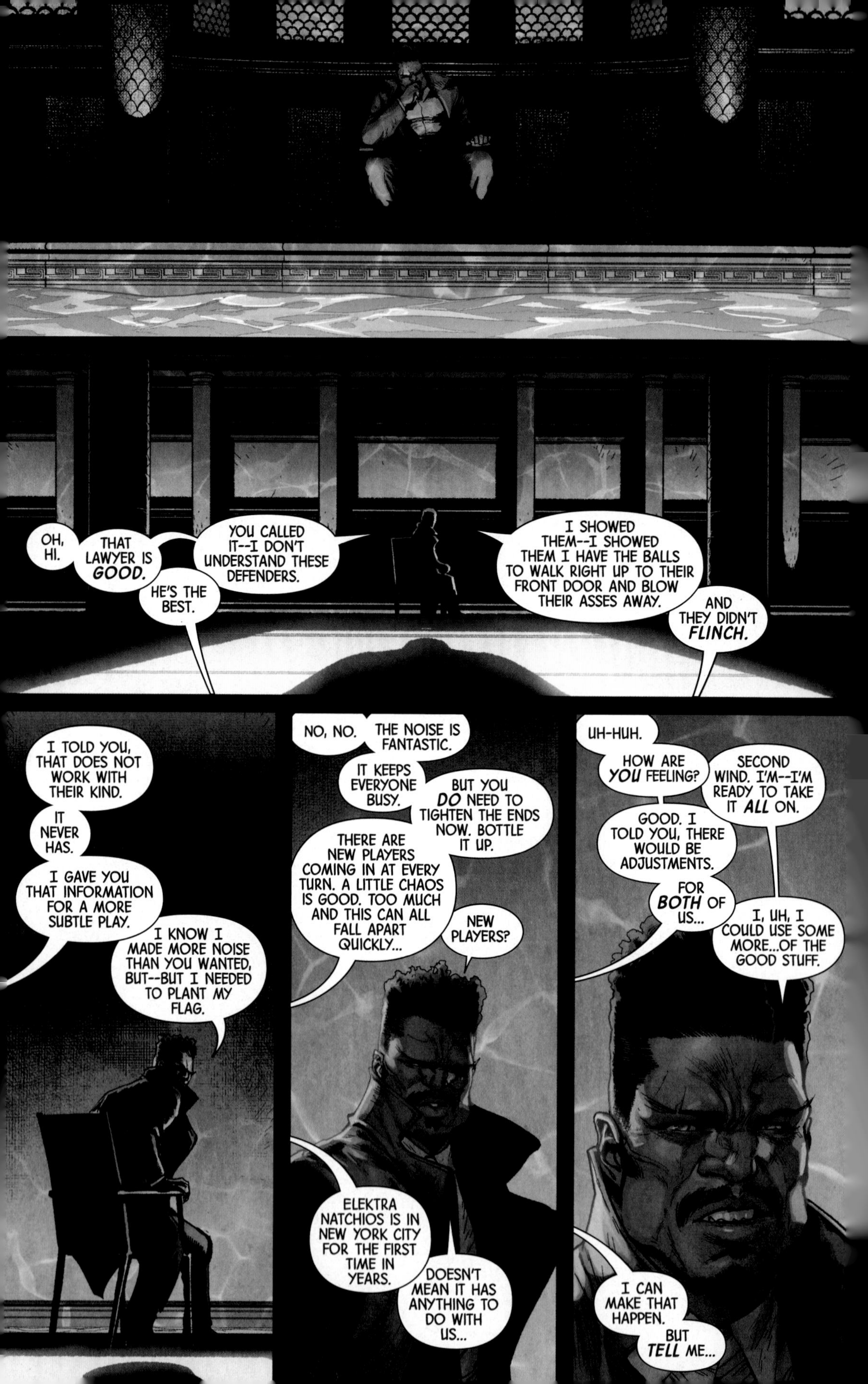
OH, HI.
THAT LAWYER IS GOOD.
HE'S THE BEST.
YOU CALLED IT--I DON'T UNDERSTAND THESE DEFENDERS.
I SHOWED THEM--I SHOWED THEM I HAVE THE BALLS TO WALK RIGHT UP TO THEIR FRONT DOOR AND BLOW THEIR ASSES AWAY.
AND THEY DIDN'T FLINCH.
I TOLD YOU, THAT DOES NOT WORK WITH THEIR KIND.
IT NEVER HAS.
I GAVE YOU THAT INFORMATION FOR A MORE SUBTLE PLAY.
I KNOW I MADE MORE NOISE THAN YOU WANTED, BUT--BUT I NEEDED TO PLANT MY FLAG.
NO, NO.
THE NOISE IS FANTASTIC.
IT KEEPS EVERYONE BUSY.
BUT YOU DO NEED TO TIGHTEN THE ENDS NOW. BOTTLE IT UP.
THERE ARE NEW PLAYERS COMING IN AT EVERY TURN. A LITTLE CHAOS IS GOOD. TOO MUCH AND THIS CAN ALL FALL APART QUICKLY...
NEW PLAYERS?
ELEKTRA NATCHIOS IS IN NEW YORK CITY FOR THE FIRST TIME IN YEARS.
DOESN'T MEAN IT HAS ANYTHING TO DO WITH US...
UH-HUH.
HOW ARE YOU FEELING?
SECOND WIND. I'M--I'M READY TO TAKE IT ALL ON.
GOOD. I TOLD YOU, THERE WOULD BE ADJUSTMENTS.
FOR BOTH OF US...
I, UH, I COULD USE SOME MORE...OF THE GOOD STUFF.
I CAN MAKE THAT HAPPEN.
BUT TELL ME...

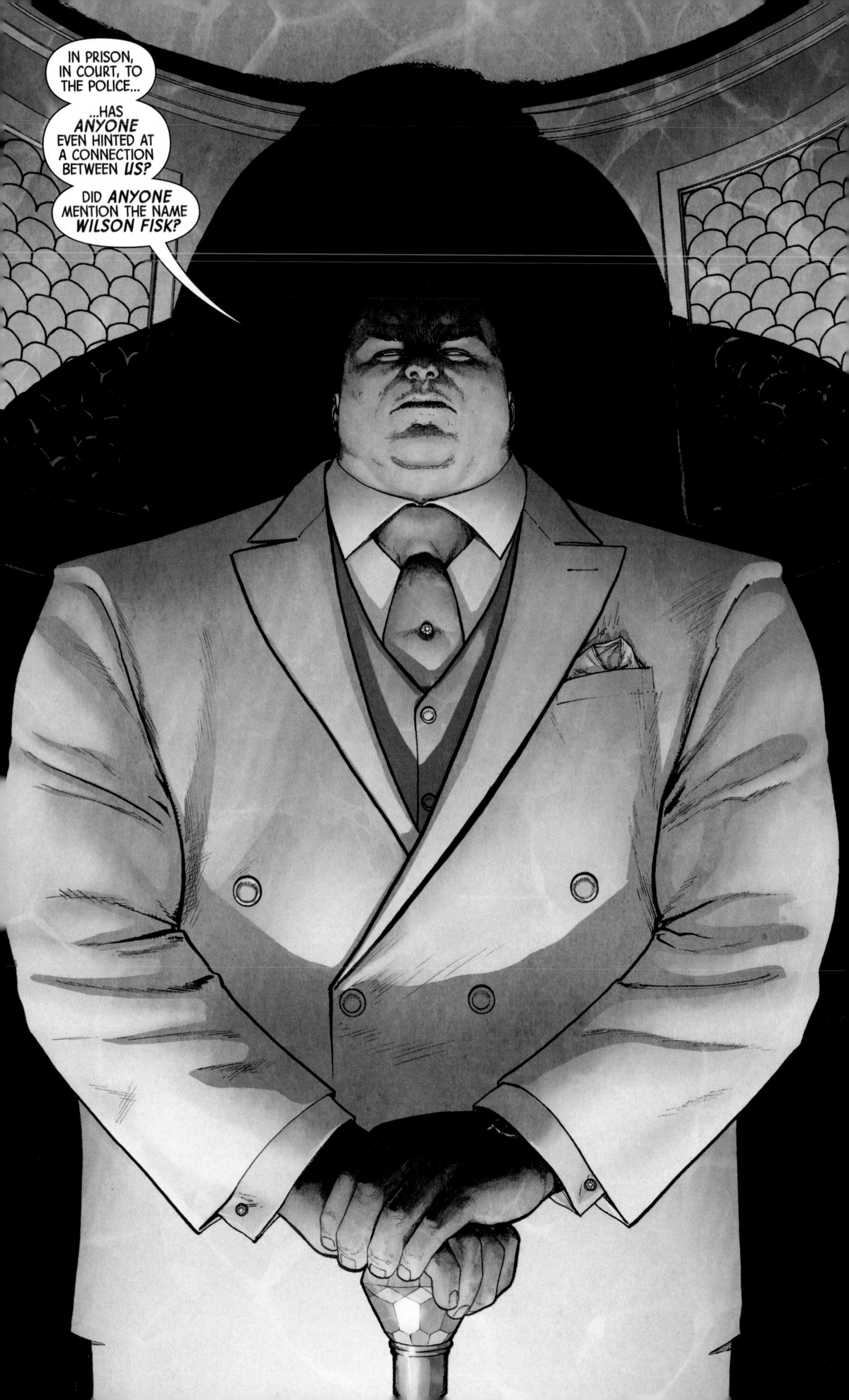
IN PRISON, IN COURT, TO THE POLICE...
...HAS *ANYONE* EVEN HINTED AT A CONNECTION BETWEEN *US?*
DID *ANYONE* MENTION THE NAME *WILSON FISK?*

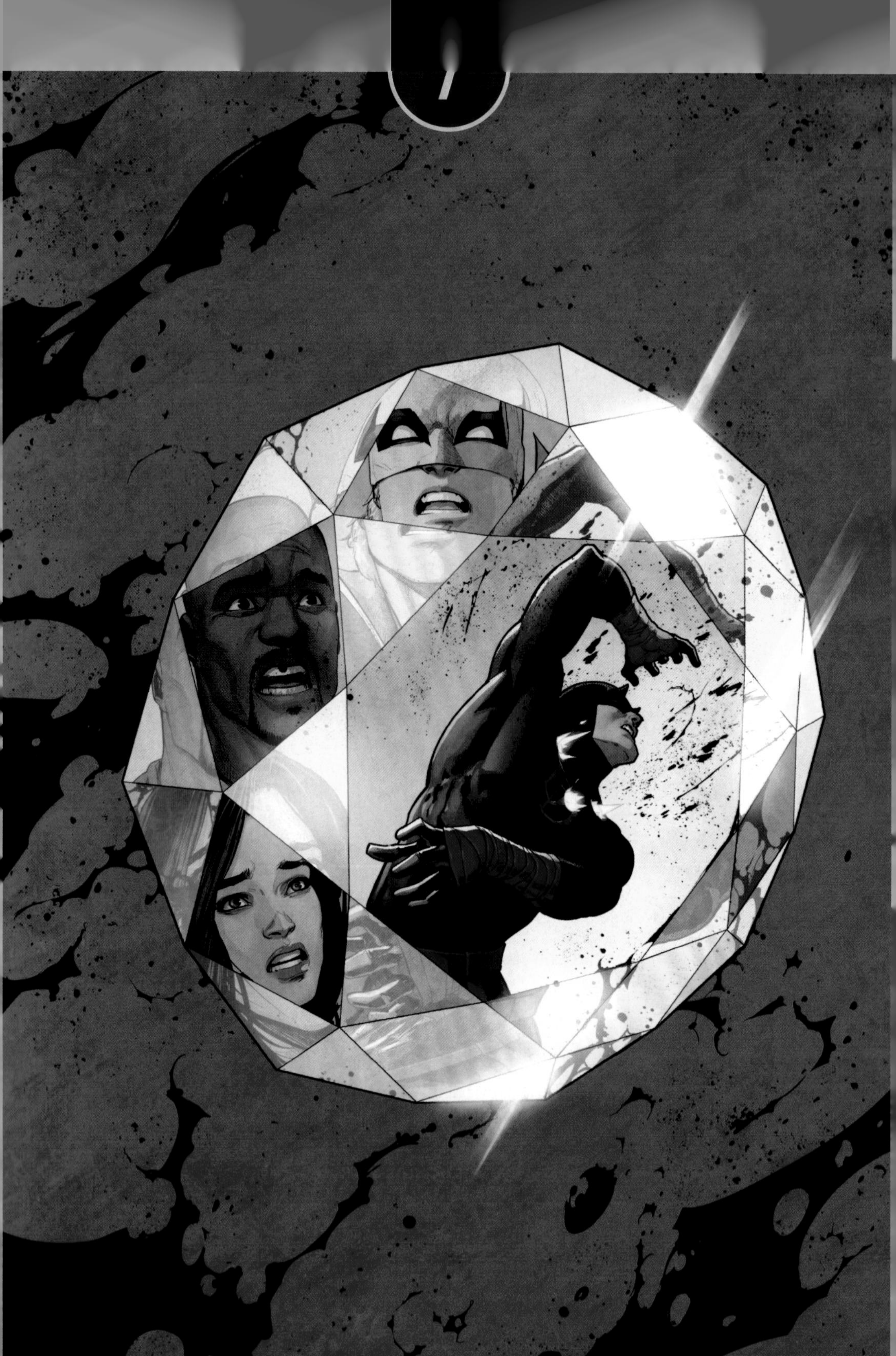

THE DEFENDERS

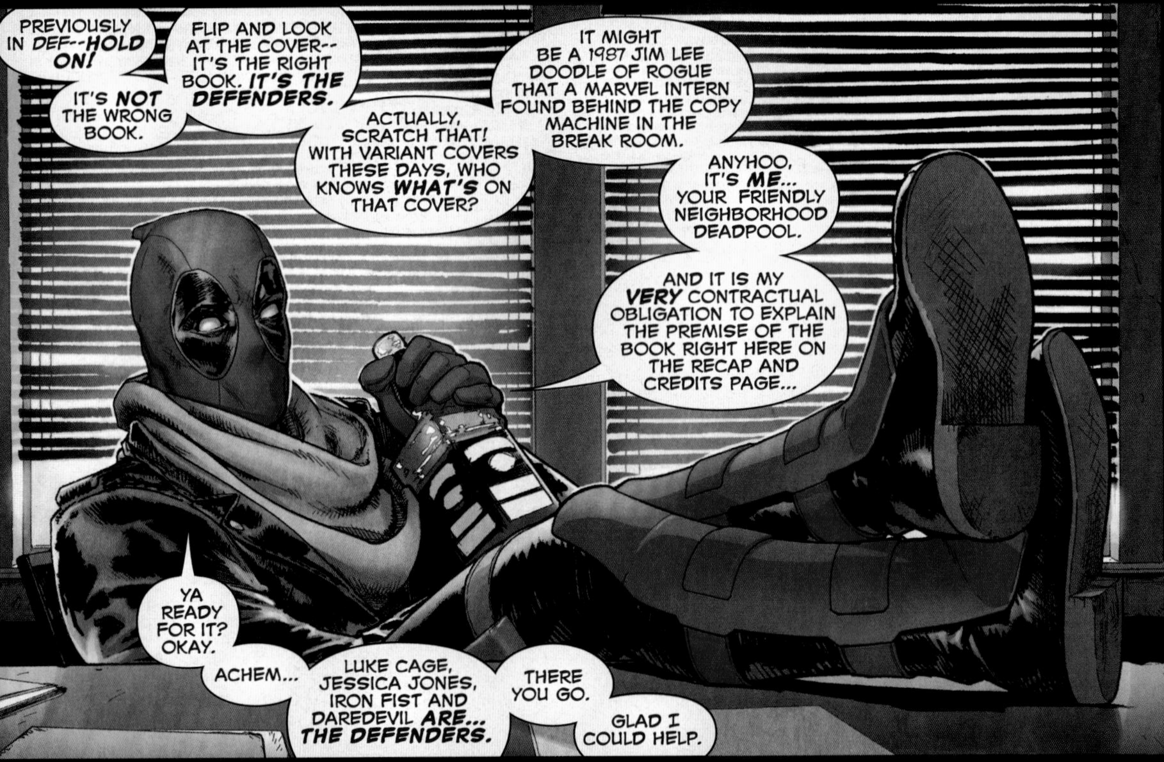
PREVIOUSLY IN DEF--HOLD ON!
IT'S NOT THE WRONG BOOK.
FLIP AND LOOK AT THE COVER-- IT'S THE RIGHT BOOK. IT'S THE DEFENDERS.
ACTUALLY, SCRATCH THAT! WITH VARIANT COVERS THESE DAYS, WHO KNOWS WHAT'S ON THAT COVER?
IT MIGHT BE A 1987 JIM LEE DOODLE OF ROGUE THAT A MARVEL INTERN FOUND BEHIND THE COPY MACHINE IN THE BREAK ROOM.
ANYHOO, IT'S ME... YOUR FRIENDLY NEIGHBORHOOD DEADPOOL.
AND IT IS MY VERY CONTRACTUAL OBLIGATION TO EXPLAIN THE PREMISE OF THE BOOK RIGHT HERE ON THE RECAP AND CREDITS PAGE...
YA READY FOR IT? OKAY.
ACHEM...
LUKE CAGE, JESSICA JONES, IRON FIST AND DAREDEVIL ARE... THE DEFENDERS.
THERE YOU GO.
GLAD I COULD HELP.

WRITER
BRIAN MICHAEL BENDIS

ARTIST
DAVID MARQUEZ

COLOR ARTISTS
JUSTIN PONSOR
with PAUL MOUNTS

LETTERER
VC's CORY PETIT

COVER ARTISTS
DAVID MARQUEZ & JUSTIN PONSOR

ASSISTANT EDITOR
ALANNA SMITH

EDITOR
TOM BREVOORT

EDITOR IN CHIEF
AXEL ALONSO

CHIEF CREATIVE OFFICER
JOE QUESADA

PRESIDENT
DAN BUCKLEY

EXECUTIVE PRODUCER
ALAN FINE

DEFENDERS No. 7, January 2018. Published Monthly except in June by MARVEL WORLDWIDE, INC., a subsidiary of MARVEL ENTERTAINMENT, LLC. OFFICE OF PUBLICATION: 135 West 50th Street, New York, NY 10020. **BULK MAIL POSTAGE PAID AT NEW YORK, NY AND AT ADDITIONAL MAILING OFFICES.** © 2017 MARVEL No similarity between any of the names, characters, persons, and/or institutions in this magazine with those of any living or dead person or institution is intended, and any such similarity which may exist is purely coincidental. $3.99 per copy in the U.S. (GST #R127032852) in the direct market; Canadian Agreement #40668537. **Printed in the USA.** Subscription rate (U.S. dollars) for 12 issues: U.S. $26.99; Canada $42.99; Foreign $42.99. **POSTMASTER: SEND ALL ADDRESS CHANGES TO DEFENDERS, C/O MARVEL SUBSCRIPTIONS P.O. BOX 727 NEW HYDE PARK, NY 11040. TELEPHONE # (888) 511-5480. FAX # (347) 537-2649. subscriptions@marvel.com.** DAN BUCKLEY, President, Marvel Entertainment; JOE QUESADA, Chief Creative Officer; TOM BREVOORT, SVP of Publishing; DAVID BOGART, SVP of Business Affairs & Operations, Publishing & Partnership; C.B. CEBULSKI, VP of Brand Management & Development, Asia; DAVID GABRIEL, SVP of Sales & Marketing, Publishing; JEFF YOUNGQUIST, VP of Production & Special Projects; DAN CARR, Executive Director of Publishing Technology; ALEX MORALES, Director of Publishing Operations; SUSAN CRESPI, Production Manager; STAN LEE, Chairman Emeritus. For information regarding advertising in Marvel Comics or on Marvel.com, please contact Jonathan Parkhideh, VP of Digital Media & Marketing Solutions, at jparkhideh@marvel.com. For Marvel subscription inquiries, please call 888-511-5480. **Manufactured between 10/20/2017 and 10/31/2017 by LSC COMMUNICATIONS INC., GLASGOW, KY, USA.**

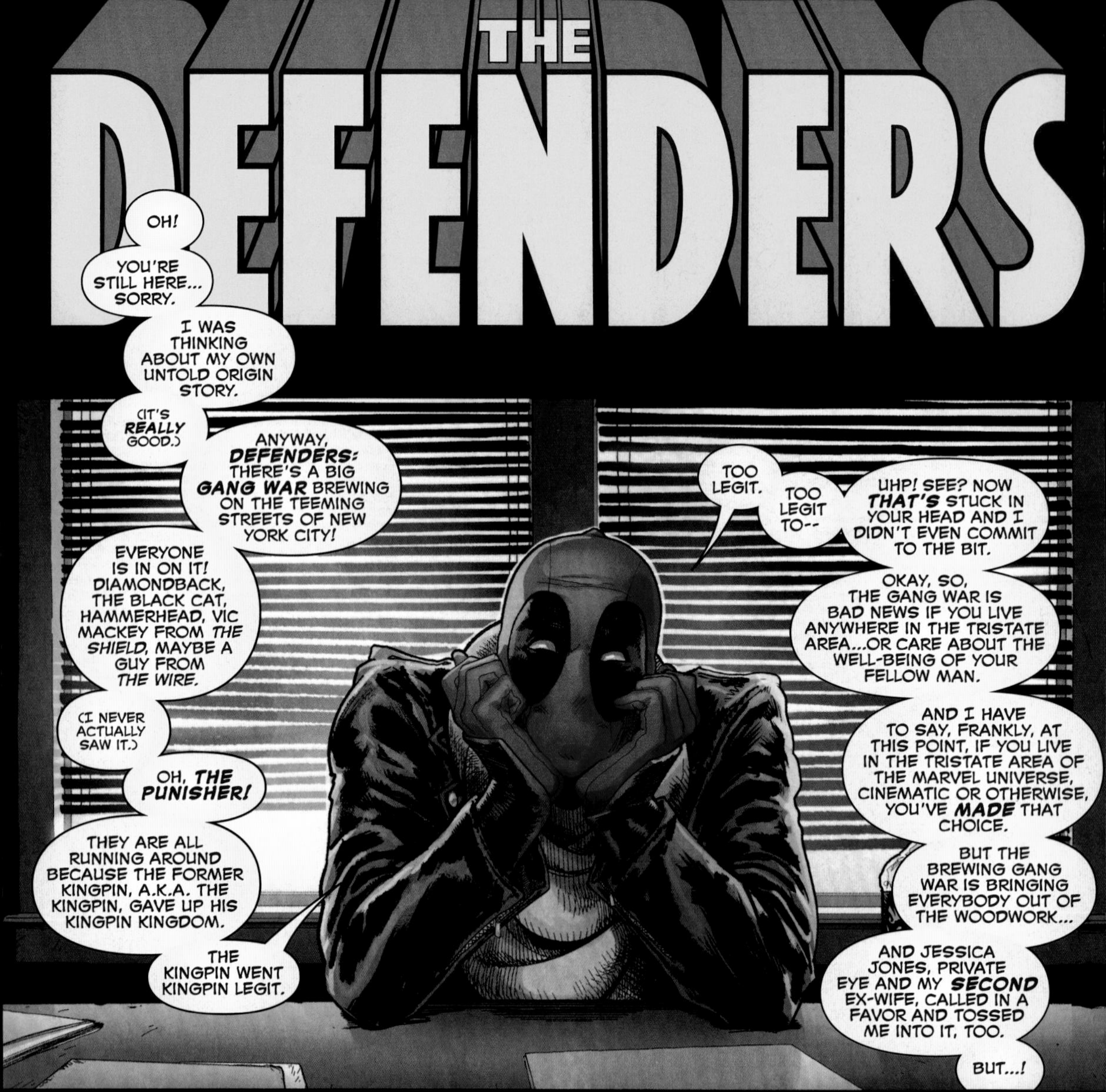

THE DEFENDERS
OH!
YOU'RE STILL HERE... SORRY.
I WAS THINKING ABOUT MY OWN UNTOLD ORIGIN STORY.
(IT'S *REALLY* GOOD.)
ANYWAY, *DEFENDERS:* THERE'S A BIG *GANG WAR* BREWING ON THE TEEMING STREETS OF NEW YORK CITY!
EVERYONE IS IN ON IT! DIAMONDBACK, THE BLACK CAT, HAMMERHEAD, VIC MACKEY FROM *THE SHIELD,* MAYBE A GUY FROM *THE WIRE.*
(I NEVER ACTUALLY SAW IT.)
OH, *THE PUNISHER!*
THEY ARE ALL RUNNING AROUND BECAUSE THE FORMER KINGPIN, A.K.A. THE KINGPIN, GAVE UP HIS KINGPIN KINGDOM.
THE KINGPIN WENT KINGPIN LEGIT.
TOO LEGIT.
TOO LEGIT TO--
UHP! SEE? NOW *THAT'S* STUCK IN YOUR HEAD AND I DIDN'T EVEN COMMIT TO THE BIT.
OKAY, SO, THE GANG WAR IS BAD NEWS IF YOU LIVE ANYWHERE IN THE TRISTATE AREA...OR CARE ABOUT THE WELL-BEING OF YOUR FELLOW MAN.
AND I HAVE TO SAY, FRANKLY, AT THIS POINT, IF YOU LIVE IN THE TRISTATE AREA OF THE MARVEL UNIVERSE, CINEMATIC OR OTHERWISE, YOU'VE *MADE* THAT CHOICE.
BUT THE BREWING GANG WAR IS BRINGING EVERYBODY OUT OF THE WOODWORK...
AND JESSICA JONES, PRIVATE EYE AND MY *SECOND* EX-WIFE, CALLED IN A FAVOR AND TOSSED ME INTO IT, TOO.
BUT...!

WRITER
BRIAN MICHAEL BENDIS
<3s LuKE CAGE

ARTIST
DAVID MARQUEZ
ACTUALLY DAREDEVIL?

COLOR ARTISTS
JUSTIN PONSOR
with PAUL MOUNTS

LETTERER
VC's CORY PETIT

COVER ARTISTS
DAVID MARQUEZ & JUSTIN PONSOR

ASSISTANT EDITOR
~~ALANNA SMITH~~
DEADPOOL

EDITOR
~~TOM BREVOORT~~
also DEADPOOL

EDITOR IN CHIEF
~~AXEL ALONSO~~
DEADPOOL
DEADPOOL

CHIEF CREATIVE OFFICER
JOE QUESADA

PRESIDENT
DAN BUCKLEY

EXECUTIVE PRODUCER
ALAN FINE

WHAT IS THIS???

DEFENDERS No. 7, Ja[illegible] Published Monthly except in [illegible] WORLDWID[illegible], a sub[illegible] of MARVEL [illegible] PUBLICA[illegible]: 135 [illegible] Str[illegible] PO[illegible] AT NE[illegible] ADDITIONAL MAILING OF[illegible]. © 2017 MARVEL [illegible] milarity [illegible] any of the names, characters, [illegible] or instit[illegible] in this magazine with th[illegible] any liv[illegible] dead [illegible] [illegible] intended, and any [illegible] similarity wh[illegible] exist is purely coincidental. $3.[illegible] per copy in the U.S. (GST #R12702[illegible]) in the [illegible] Agreement [illegible]668537. [illegible] POSTMASTER: SEND [illegible] ADDRESS CHANGES TO DEFEN[illegible], C/O M[illegible] BOX 727 [illegible] HYDE [illegible] NY 11[illegible] TELEPHO[illegible] (888) [illegible] DAN BUCKLEY, President, Marvel Entertainment; JOE QUESADA, Chief Creative Officer; T[illegible] BREVOOR[illegible] of Publis[illegible]; DAVID [illegible]ART, SVP of Business Affairs & [illegible] Brand Management & Development[illegible], SVP of Sales & Marketing, Publishing; [illegible] YOUN[illegible] Production & Special Projects; DAN CARR, Executive Director of Publishing Technology; AL[illegible] of Publishing Operations; SUSA[illegible] Production Manager; STAN LEE, Chairman Emeritus. For information regarding advertising in Marvel Comics or on Marvel.com, please contact Jonathan Parkhideh, VP of Digital Media & Marketing Solutions, at jparkhideh@marvel.com. For Marvel subscription inquiries, please call 888-511-5480. **Manufactured between 10/20/2017 and 10/31/2017 by LSC COMMUNICATIONS INC., GLASGOW, KY, USA.**

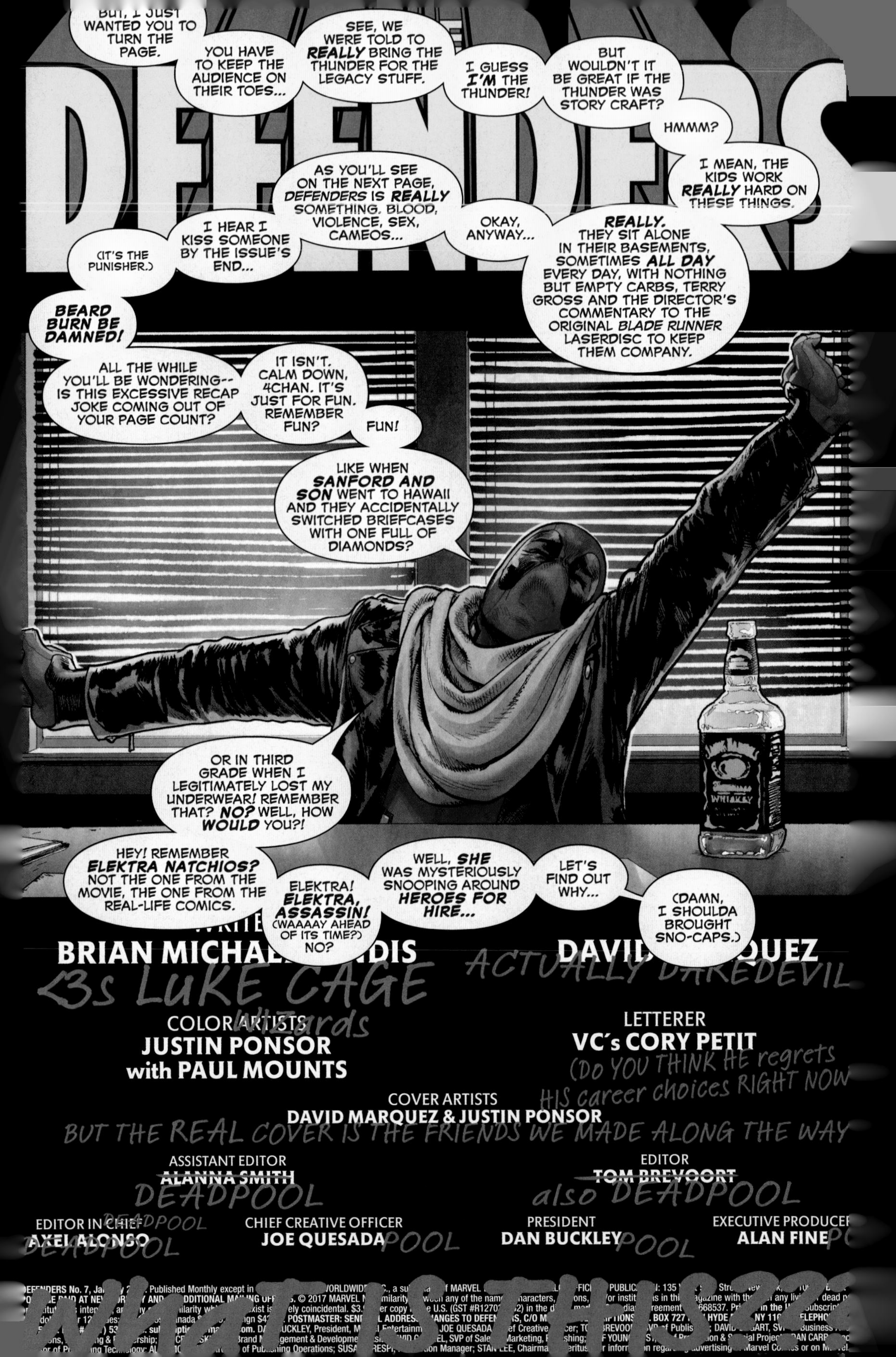
BUT, I JUST WANTED YOU TO TURN THE PAGE.
YOU HAVE TO KEEP THE AUDIENCE ON THEIR TOES...
SEE, WE WERE TOLD TO *REALLY* BRING THE THUNDER FOR THE LEGACY STUFF.
I GUESS *I'M* THE THUNDER!
BUT WOULDN'T IT BE GREAT IF THE THUNDER WAS STORY CRAFT?
HMMM?
I MEAN, THE KIDS WORK *REALLY* HARD ON THESE THINGS.
REALLY. THEY SIT ALONE IN THEIR BASEMENTS, SOMETIMES *ALL DAY* EVERY DAY, WITH NOTHING BUT EMPTY CARBS, TERRY GROSS AND THE DIRECTOR'S COMMENTARY TO THE ORIGINAL *BLADE RUNNER* LASERDISC TO KEEP THEM COMPANY.
OKAY, ANYWAY...
AS YOU'LL SEE ON THE NEXT PAGE, *DEFENDERS* IS *REALLY* SOMETHING. BLOOD, VIOLENCE, SEX, CAMEOS...
I HEAR I KISS SOMEONE BY THE ISSUE'S END...
(IT'S THE PUNISHER.)
BEARD BURN BE DAMNED!
ALL THE WHILE YOU'LL BE WONDERING-- IS THIS EXCESSIVE RECAP JOKE COMING OUT OF YOUR PAGE COUNT?
IT ISN'T. CALM DOWN, 4CHAN. IT'S JUST FOR FUN. REMEMBER FUN?
FUN!
LIKE WHEN *SANFORD AND SON* WENT TO HAWAII AND THEY ACCIDENTALLY SWITCHED BRIEFCASES WITH ONE FULL OF DIAMONDS?
OR IN THIRD GRADE WHEN I LEGITIMATELY LOST MY UNDERWEAR! REMEMBER THAT? *NO?* WELL, HOW *WOULD* YOU?!
HEY! REMEMBER *ELEKTRA NATCHIOS?* NOT THE ONE FROM THE MOVIE, THE ONE FROM THE REAL-LIFE COMICS.
ELEKTRA! *ELEKTRA, ASSASSIN!* (WAAAAY AHEAD OF ITS TIME?) NO?
WELL, *SHE* WAS MYSTERIOUSLY SNOOPING AROUND *HEROES FOR HIRE...*
LET'S FIND OUT WHY...
(DAMN, I SHOULDA BROUGHT SNO-CAPS.)

BRIAN MICHAEL BENDIS
<3s LuKE CAGE

DAVID MARQUEZ
ACTUALLY DAREDEVIL

COLOR ARTISTS Wizards
JUSTIN PONSOR with PAUL MOUNTS

LETTERER
VC's CORY PETIT
(DO YOU THINK HE regrets HIS career choices RIGHT NOW

COVER ARTISTS
DAVID MARQUEZ & JUSTIN PONSOR
BUT THE REAL COVER IS THE FRIENDS WE MADE ALONG THE WAY

ASSISTANT EDITOR
~~ALANNA SMITH~~
DEADPOOL

EDITOR
~~TOM BREVOORT~~
also DEADPOOL

EDITOR IN CHIEF DEADPOOL
AXEL ALONSO DEADPOOL

CHIEF CREATIVE OFFICER
JOE QUESADA POOL

PRESIDENT
DAN BUCKLEY POOL

EXECUTIVE PRODUCER
ALAN FINE

WHAT IS THIS???

DEFENDERS No. 7, Ja... Published Monthly except in ... WORLDWIDE ..., a su... of MARVEL ... PUBLIC... 135 ... POSTAGE PAID AT NEW ... AND ... ADDITIONAL MAILING OFF... © 2017 MARVEL ... milarity ... ween any of the names, characters, ... ons, ... or instit... in this magazine with those of any living or dead p... itut... ... inten... ilarity wh... xist is ... ely coincidental. $3.9... er copy ... e U.S. (GST #R12702...) in the ... dian ... reement ... 668537. Pri... in the ... Subscri... POSTMASTER: SEND ... ADDRESS ... ANGES TO DEFEN... S, C/O M... PTIONS ... BOX 727 ... HYDE ... NY 110... ELEPHO... ... subscripti... om. DAN BUCKLEY, President, M... Entertainm... JOE QUESADA, ... ef Creative ... cer; TOM BREVOORT, SVP of Publis...; DAVID ... GART, SVP ... Business ... ons, ... ng & ... ership; ... Brand M... gement & Developme... ... EL, SVP of Sales ... Marketing, ... shing; ... F YOUNG... ... ion & S... ial Projects; DAN CARR... ... of Publishing Operations; SUSA... RESPI, ... ion Manager; STAN LEE, Chairman ... eritus. ... r inform... on regar... ... advertising ... Marvel Comics or on Marvel...

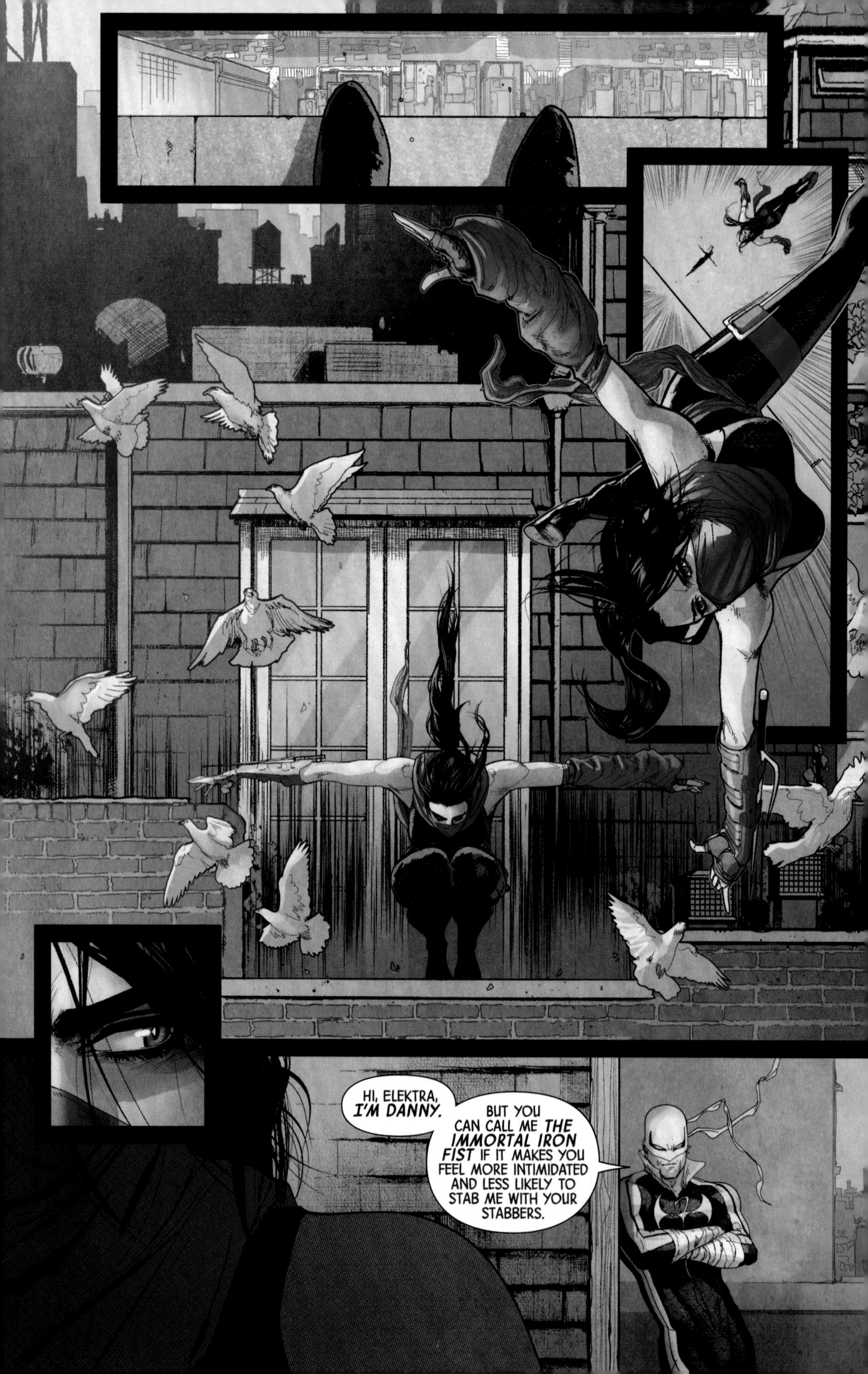
HI, ELEKTRA, *I'M DANNY.*
BUT YOU CAN CALL ME *THE IMMORTAL IRON FIST* IF IT MAKES YOU FEEL MORE INTIMIDATED AND LESS LIKELY TO STAB ME WITH YOUR STABBERS.

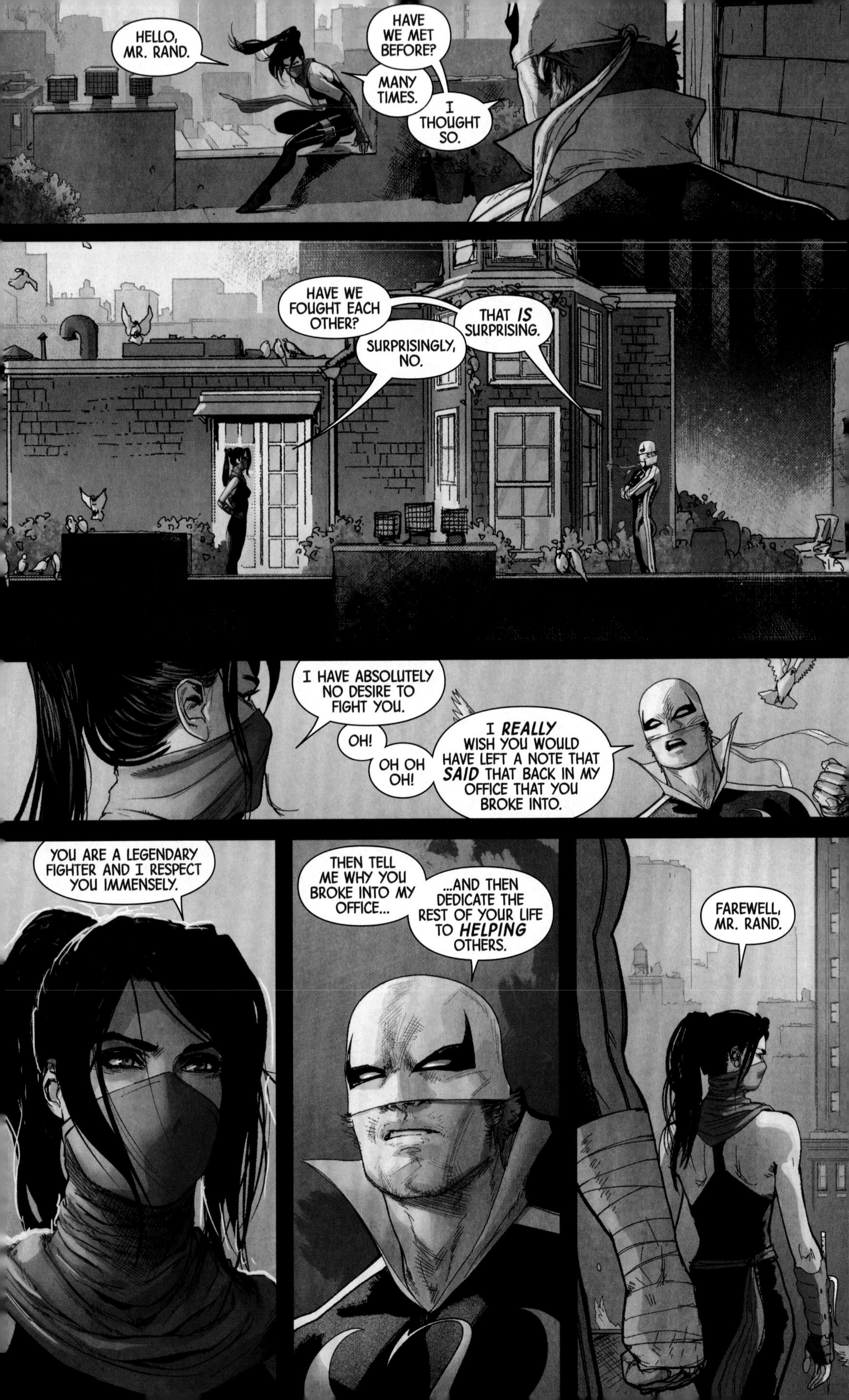
HELLO, MR. RAND.
HAVE WE MET BEFORE?
MANY TIMES.
I THOUGHT SO.
HAVE WE FOUGHT EACH OTHER?
SURPRISINGLY, NO.
THAT *IS* SURPRISING.
I HAVE ABSOLUTELY NO DESIRE TO FIGHT YOU.
OH!
OH OH OH!
I *REALLY* WISH YOU WOULD HAVE LEFT A NOTE THAT *SAID* THAT BACK IN MY OFFICE THAT YOU BROKE INTO.
YOU ARE A LEGENDARY FIGHTER AND I RESPECT YOU IMMENSELY.
THEN TELL ME WHY YOU BROKE INTO MY OFFICE...
...AND THEN DEDICATE THE REST OF YOUR LIFE TO *HELPING* OTHERS.
FAREWELL, MR. RAND.

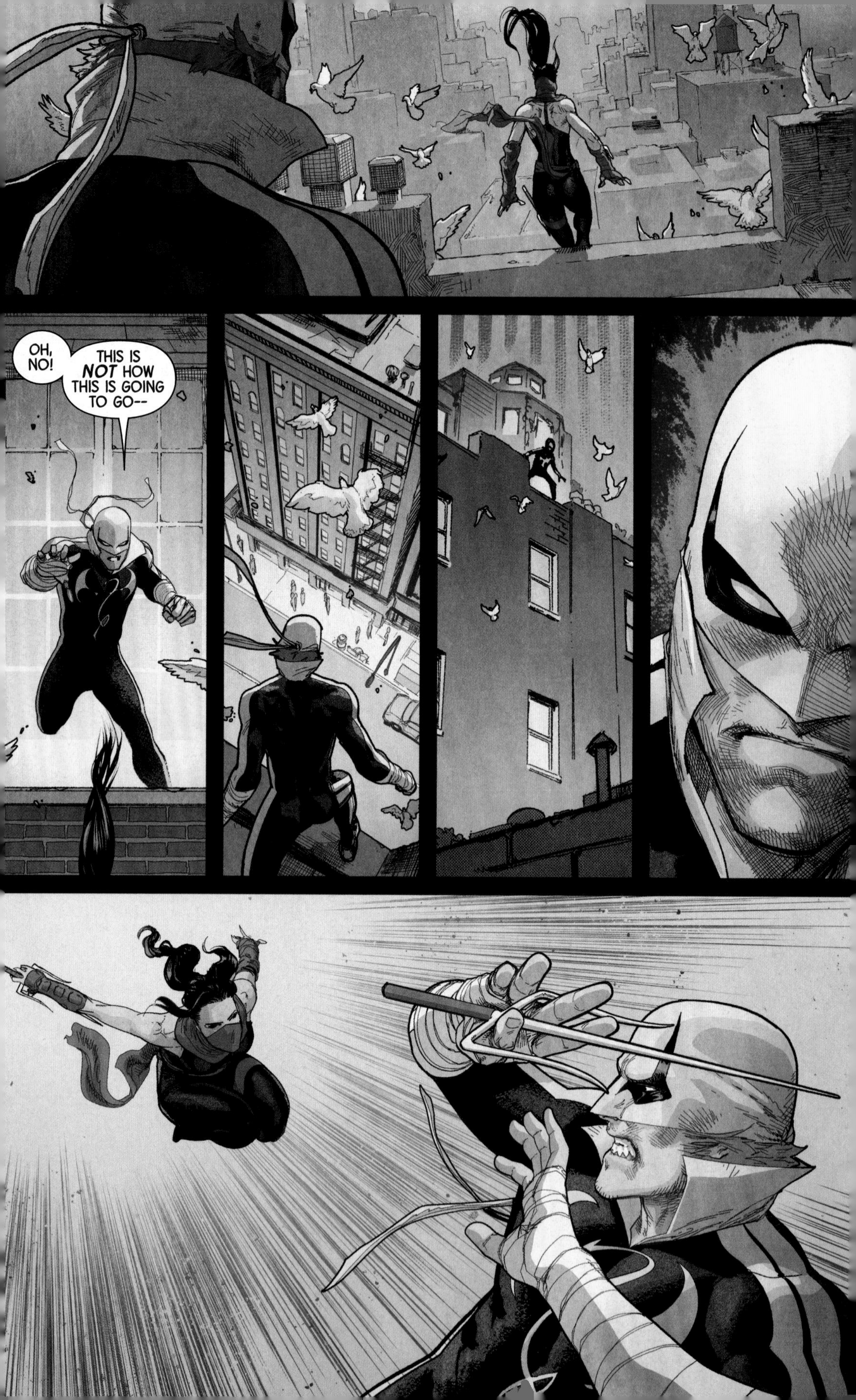
OH, NO!
THIS IS **NOT** HOW THIS IS GOING TO GO--

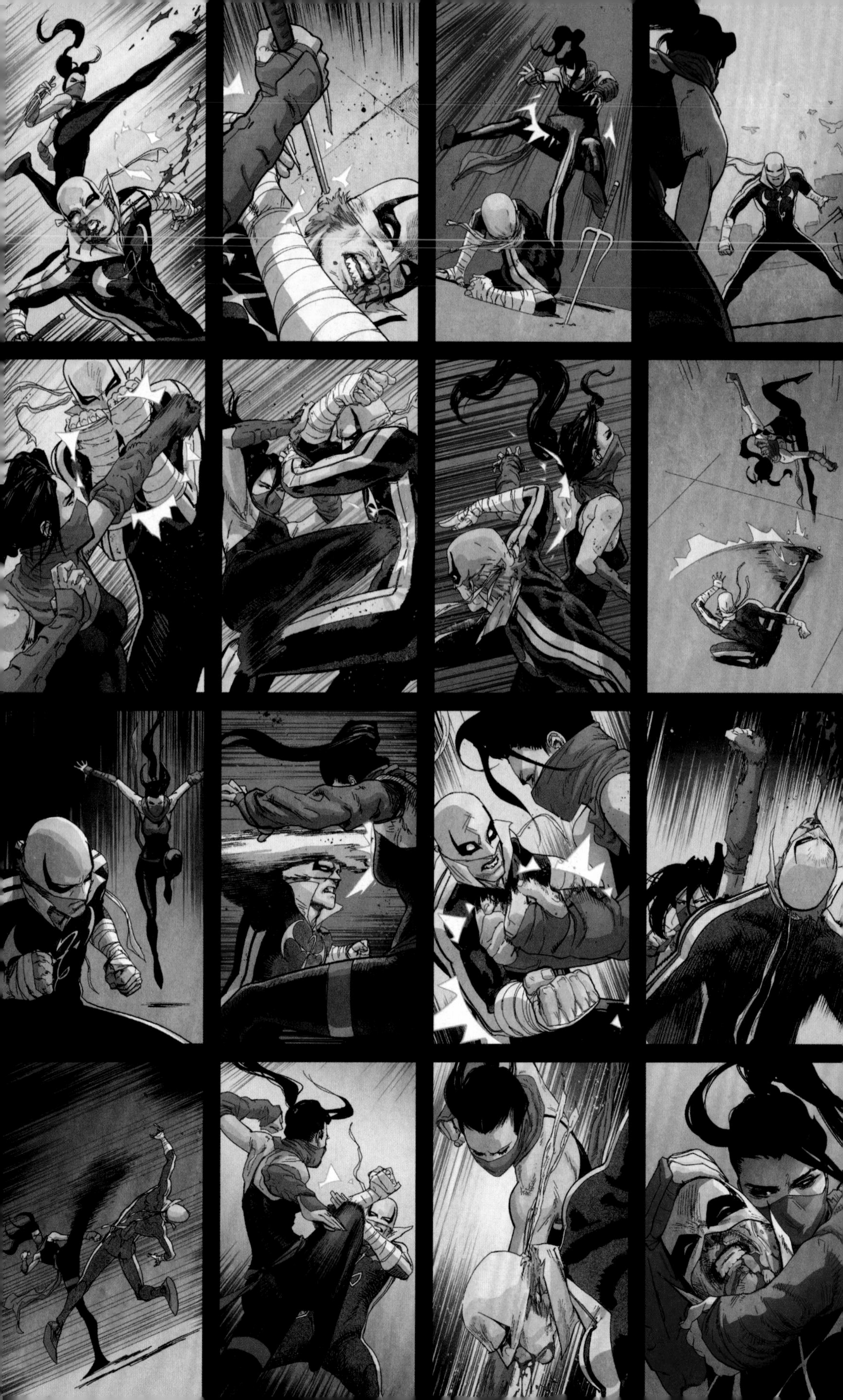

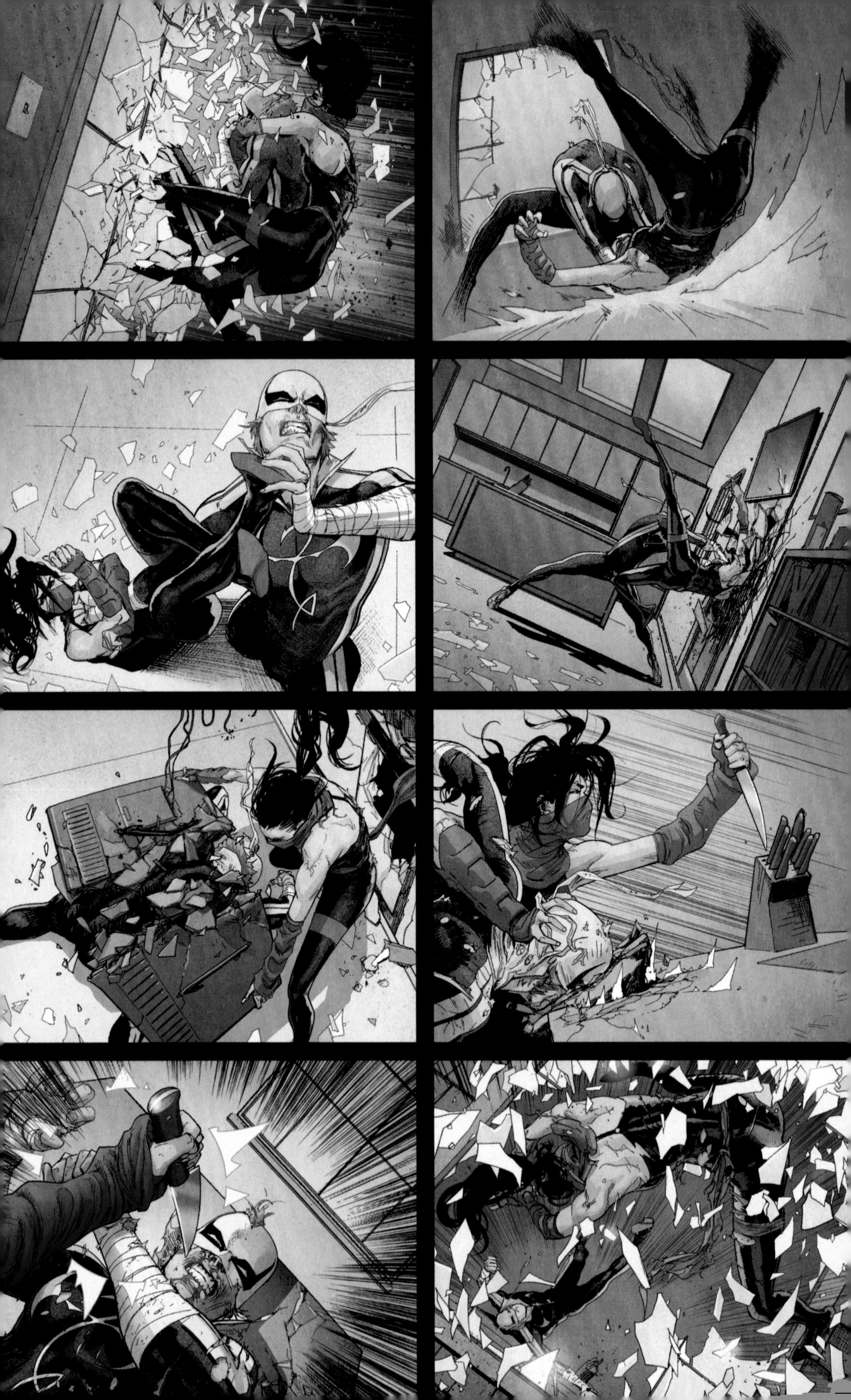

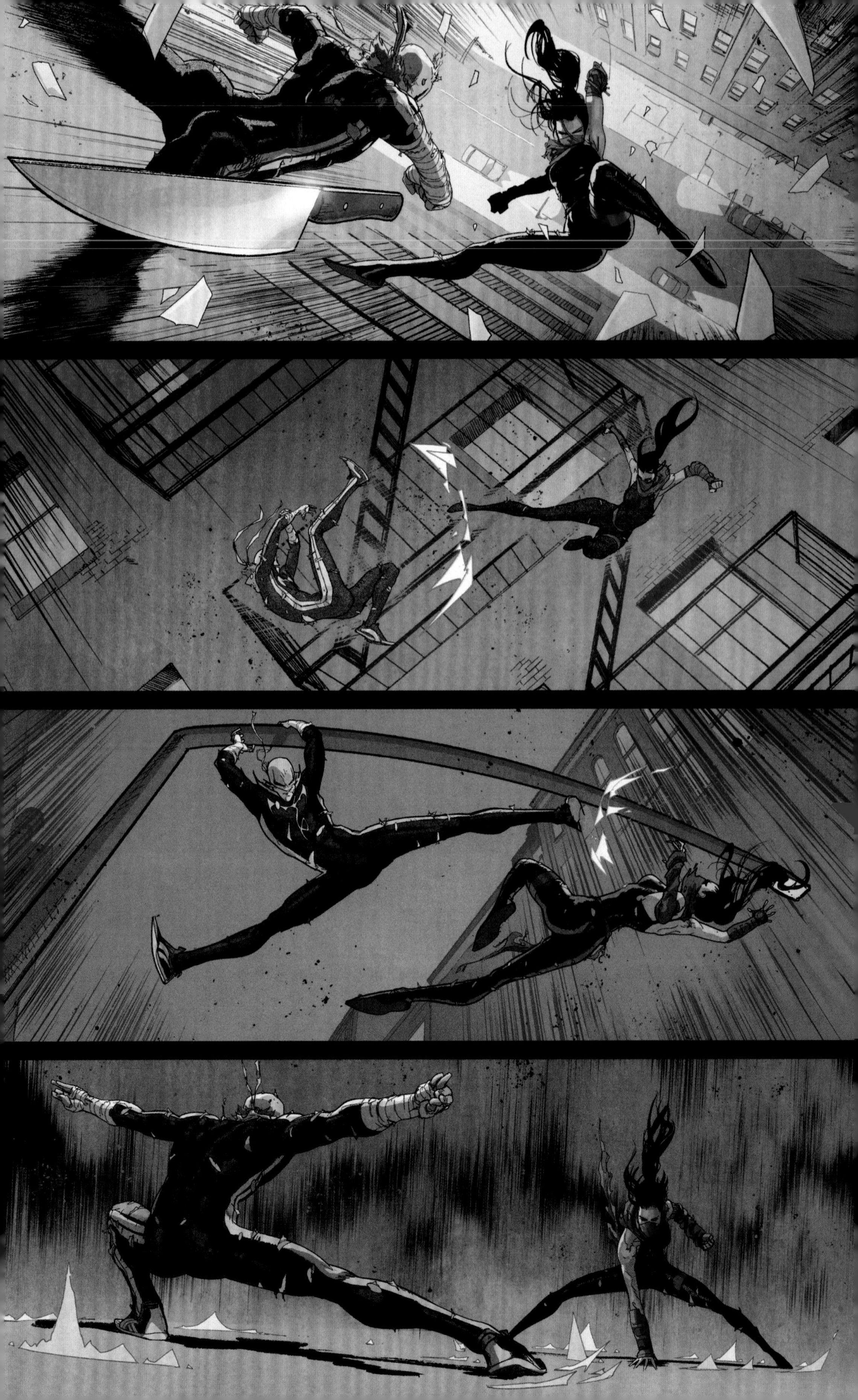

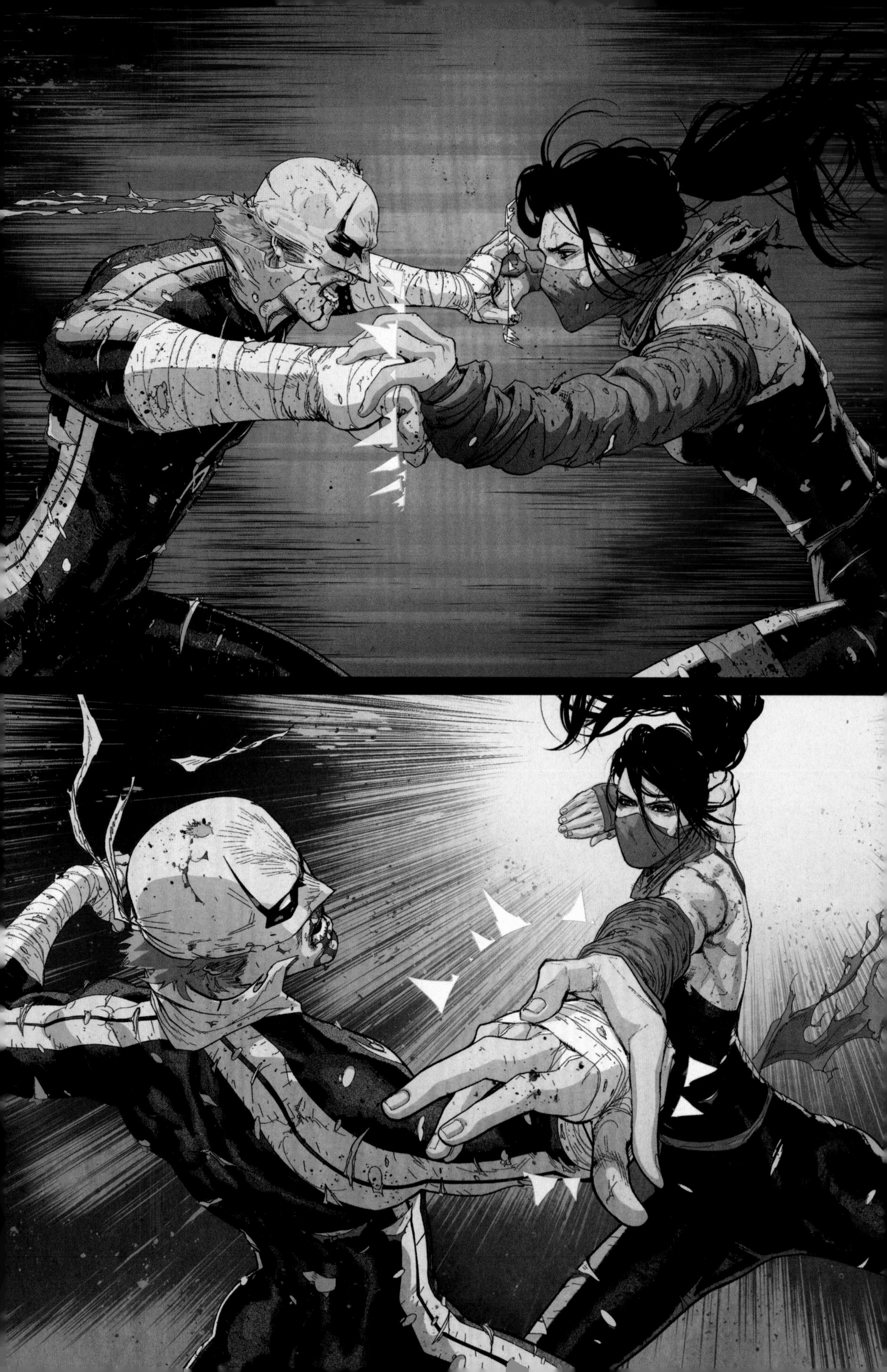

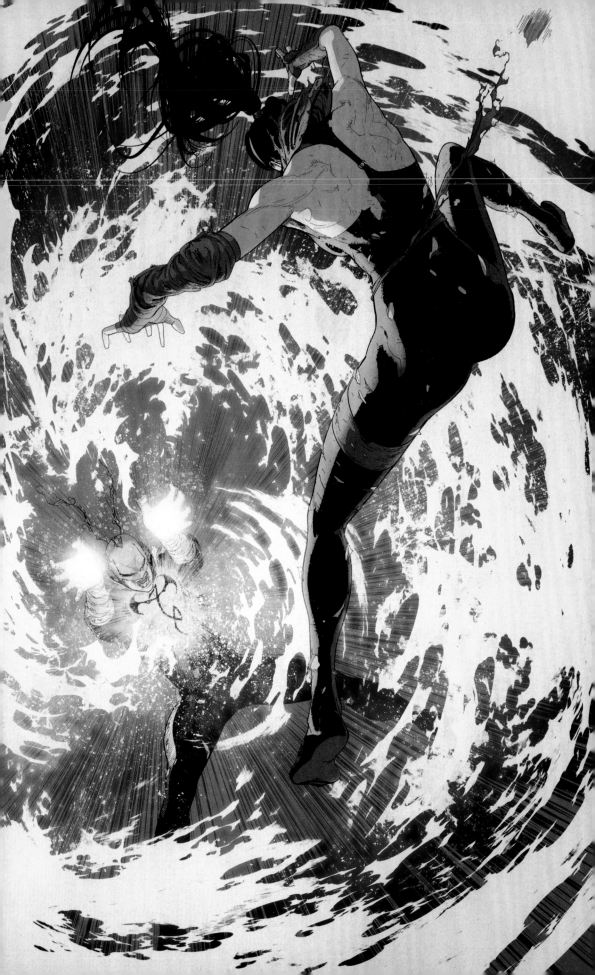

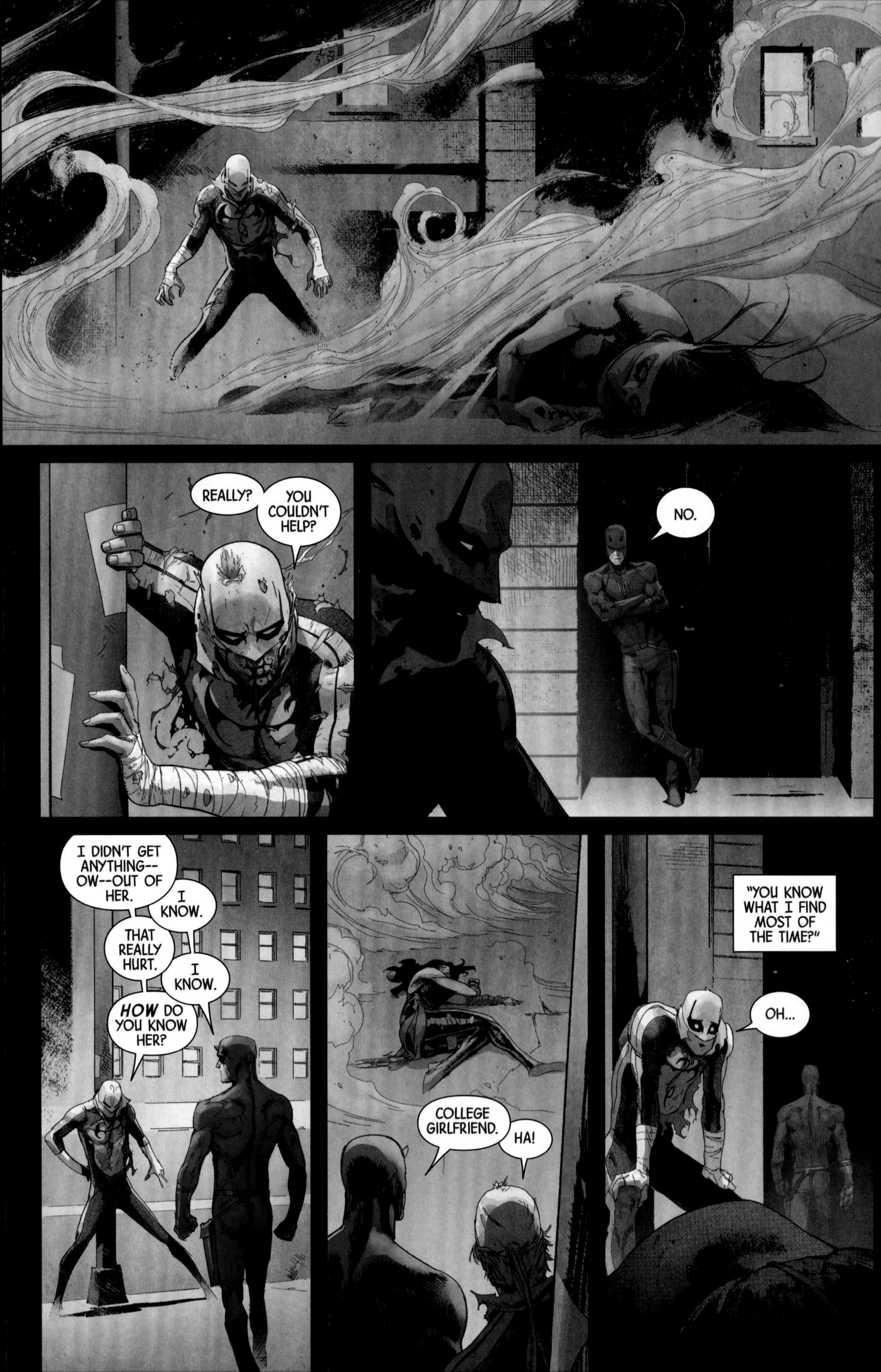
REALLY?
YOU COULDN'T HELP?
NO.
I DIDN'T GET ANYTHING--OW--OUT OF HER.
I KNOW.
THAT REALLY HURT.
I KNOW.
HOW DO YOU KNOW HER?
COLLEGE GIRLFRIEND.
HA!
"YOU KNOW WHAT I FIND MOST OF THE TIME?"
OH...

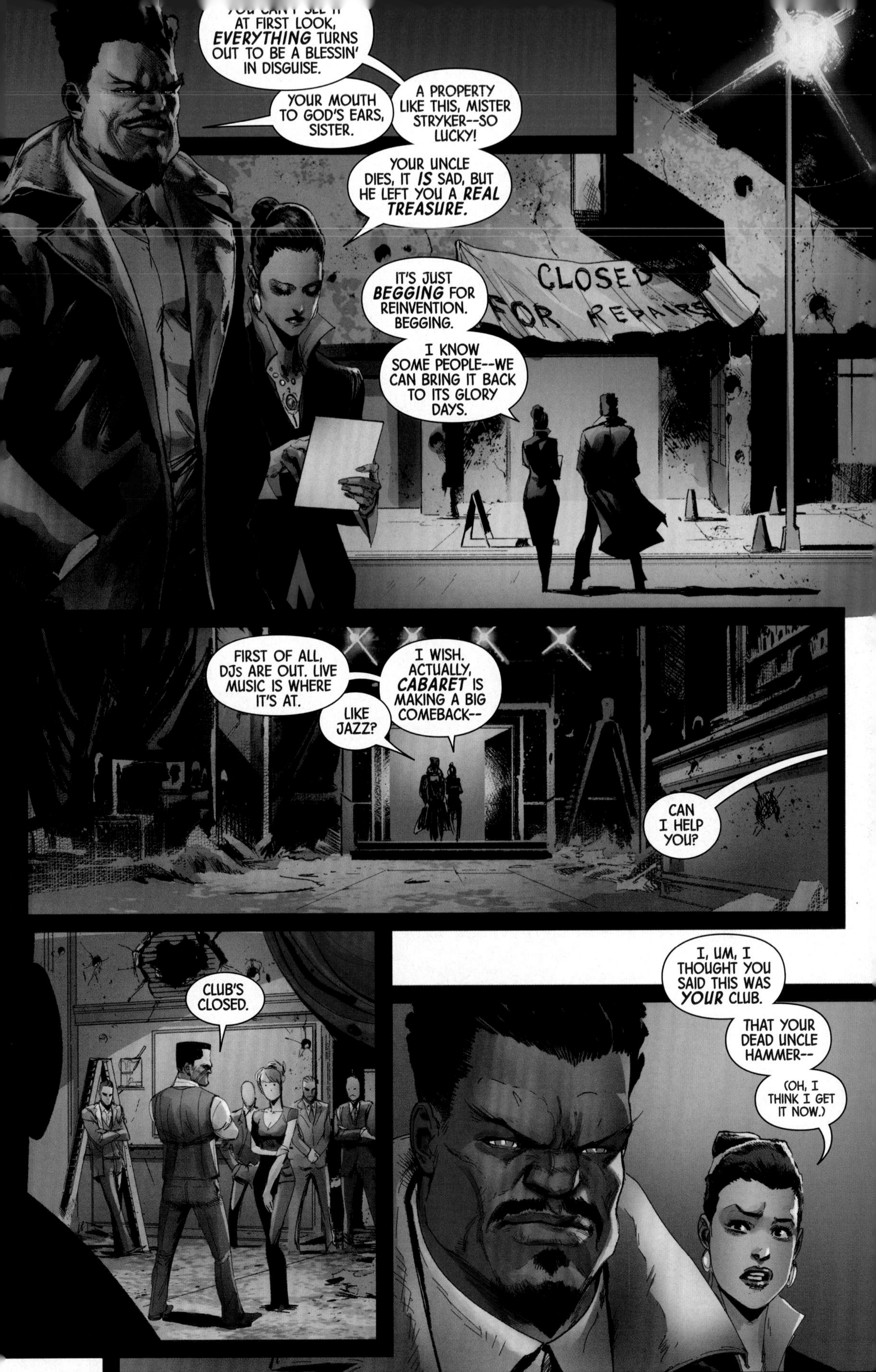
AT FIRST LOOK, EVERYTHING TURNS OUT TO BE A BLESSIN' IN DISGUISE.
YOUR MOUTH TO GOD'S EARS, SISTER.
A PROPERTY LIKE THIS, MISTER STRYKER--SO LUCKY!
YOUR UNCLE DIES, IT IS SAD, BUT HE LEFT YOU A REAL TREASURE.
CLOSED FOR REPAIRS
IT'S JUST BEGGING FOR REINVENTION. BEGGING.
I KNOW SOME PEOPLE--WE CAN BRING IT BACK TO ITS GLORY DAYS.
FIRST OF ALL, DJs ARE OUT. LIVE MUSIC IS WHERE IT'S AT.
LIKE JAZZ?
I WISH. ACTUALLY, CABARET IS MAKING A BIG COMEBACK--
CAN I HELP YOU?
CLUB'S CLOSED.
I, UM, I THOUGHT YOU SAID THIS WAS YOUR CLUB.
THAT YOUR DEAD UNCLE HAMMER--
(OH, I THINK I GET IT NOW.)

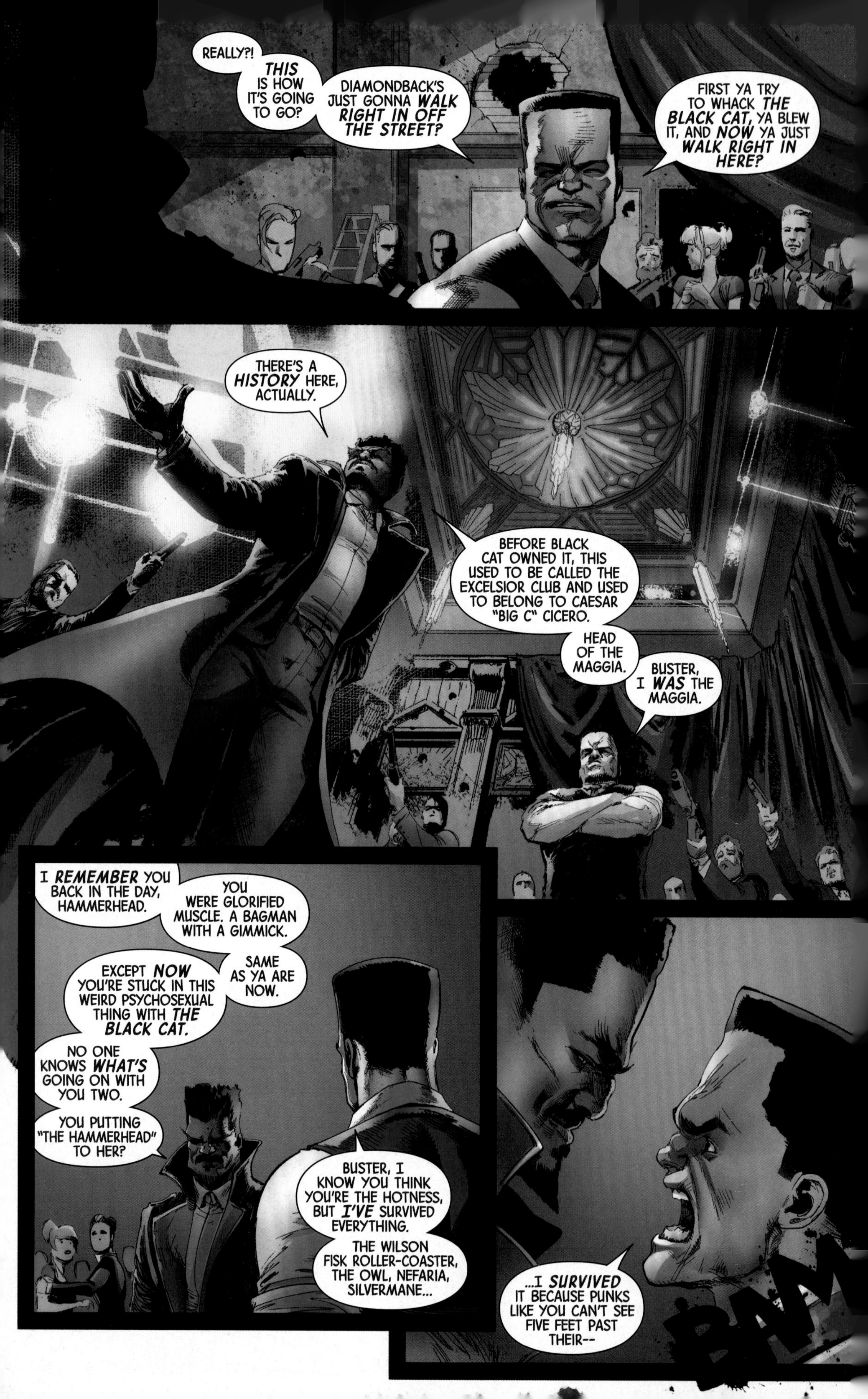
REALLY?! THIS IS HOW IT'S GOING TO GO?
DIAMONDBACK'S JUST GONNA WALK RIGHT IN OFF THE STREET?
FIRST YA TRY TO WHACK THE BLACK CAT, YA BLEW IT, AND NOW YA JUST WALK RIGHT IN HERE?
THERE'S A HISTORY HERE, ACTUALLY.
BEFORE BLACK CAT OWNED IT, THIS USED TO BE CALLED THE EXCELSIOR CLUB AND USED TO BELONG TO CAESAR "BIG C" CICERO.
HEAD OF THE MAGGIA.
BUSTER, I WAS THE MAGGIA.
I REMEMBER YOU BACK IN THE DAY, HAMMERHEAD.
YOU WERE GLORIFIED MUSCLE. A BAGMAN WITH A GIMMICK.
SAME AS YA ARE NOW.
EXCEPT NOW YOU'RE STUCK IN THIS WEIRD PSYCHOSEXUAL THING WITH THE BLACK CAT.
NO ONE KNOWS WHAT'S GOING ON WITH YOU TWO.
YOU PUTTING "THE HAMMERHEAD" TO HER?
BUSTER, I KNOW YOU THINK YOU'RE THE HOTNESS, BUT I'VE SURVIVED EVERYTHING.
THE WILSON FISK ROLLER-COASTER, THE OWL, NEFARIA, SILVERMANE...
...I SURVIVED IT BECAUSE PUNKS LIKE YOU CAN'T SEE FIVE FEET PAST THEIR--

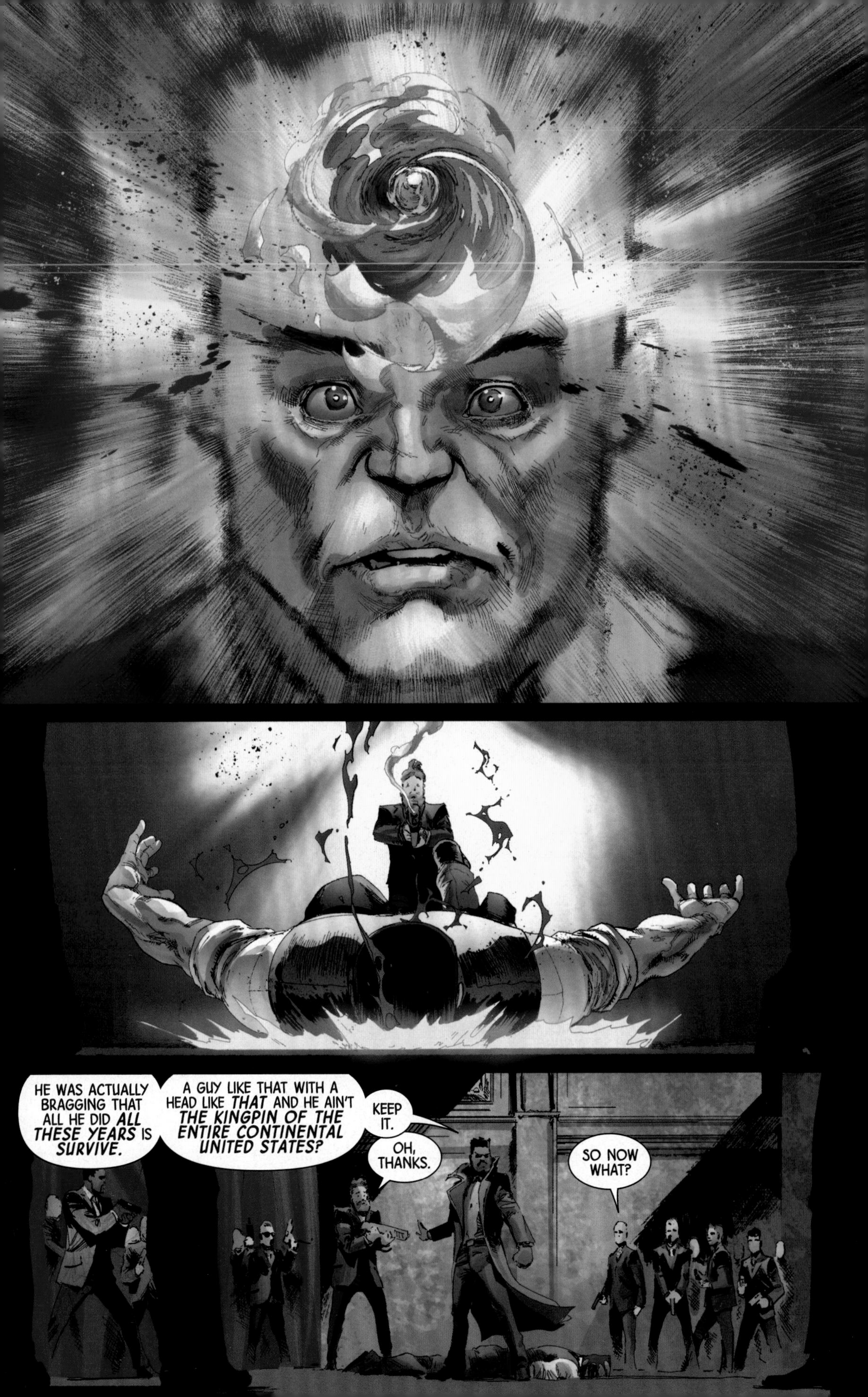
HE WAS ACTUALLY BRAGGING THAT ALL HE DID *ALL THESE YEARS* IS *SURVIVE.*
A GUY LIKE THAT WITH A HEAD LIKE *THAT* AND HE AIN'T *THE KINGPIN OF THE ENTIRE CONTINENTAL UNITED STATES?*
KEEP IT.
OH, THANKS.
SO NOW WHAT?

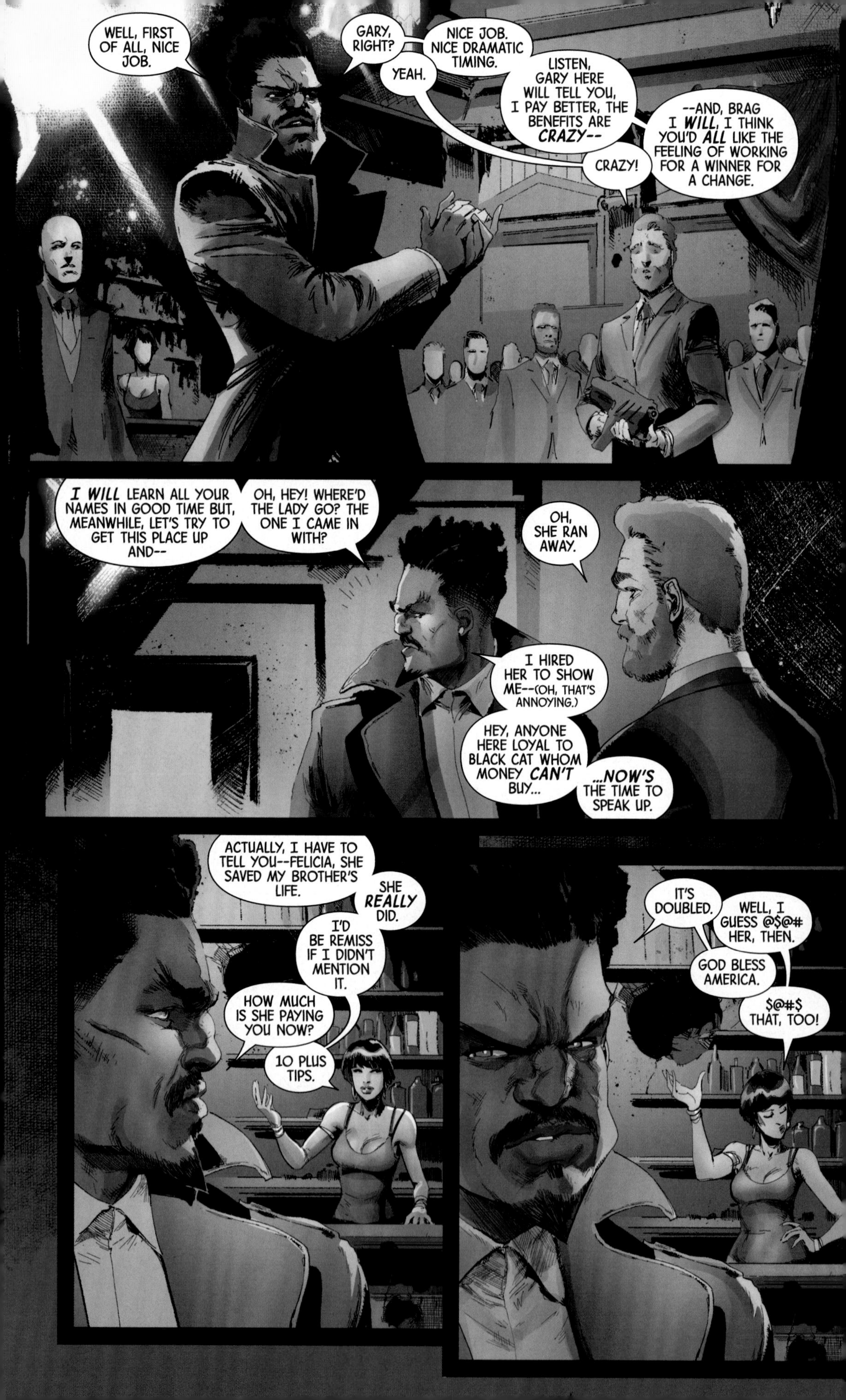
WELL, FIRST OF ALL, NICE JOB.
GARY, RIGHT?
NICE JOB. NICE DRAMATIC TIMING.
YEAH.
LISTEN, GARY HERE WILL TELL YOU, I PAY BETTER, THE BENEFITS ARE CRAZY--
CRAZY!
--AND, BRAG I WILL, I THINK YOU'D ALL LIKE THE FEELING OF WORKING FOR A WINNER FOR A CHANGE.
I WILL LEARN ALL YOUR NAMES IN GOOD TIME BUT, MEANWHILE, LET'S TRY TO GET THIS PLACE UP AND--
OH, HEY! WHERE'D THE LADY GO? THE ONE I CAME IN WITH?
OH, SHE RAN AWAY.
I HIRED HER TO SHOW ME--(OH, THAT'S ANNOYING.)
HEY, ANYONE HERE LOYAL TO BLACK CAT WHOM MONEY CAN'T BUY...
...NOW'S THE TIME TO SPEAK UP.
ACTUALLY, I HAVE TO TELL YOU--FELICIA, SHE SAVED MY BROTHER'S LIFE.
SHE REALLY DID.
I'D BE REMISS IF I DIDN'T MENTION IT.
HOW MUCH IS SHE PAYING YOU NOW?
10 PLUS TIPS.
IT'S DOUBLED.
WELL, I GUESS @$@# HER, THEN.
GOD BLESS AMERICA.
$@#$ THAT, TOO!

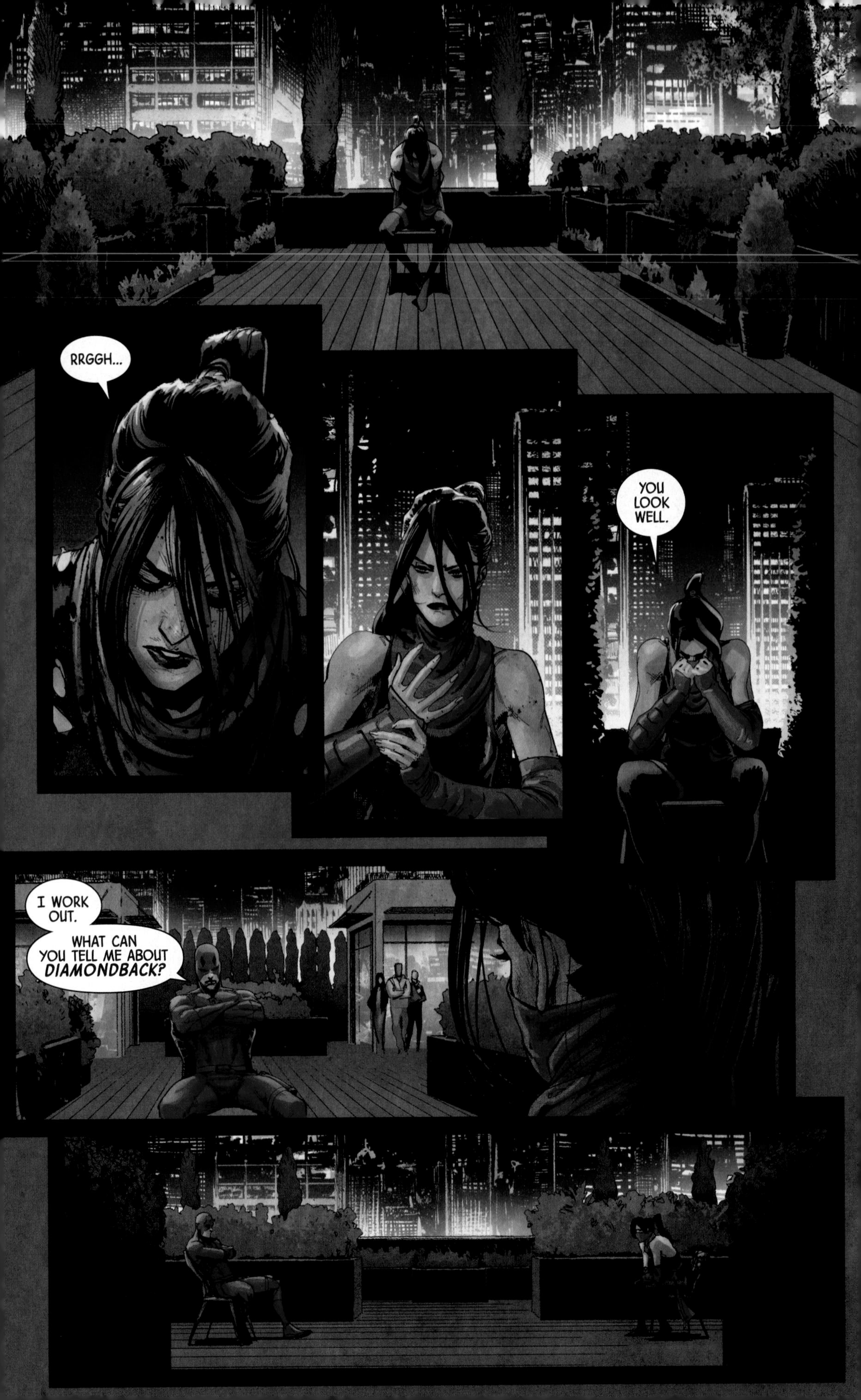
RRGGH...
YOU LOOK WELL.
I WORK OUT.
WHAT CAN YOU TELL ME ABOUT *DIAMONDBACK?*

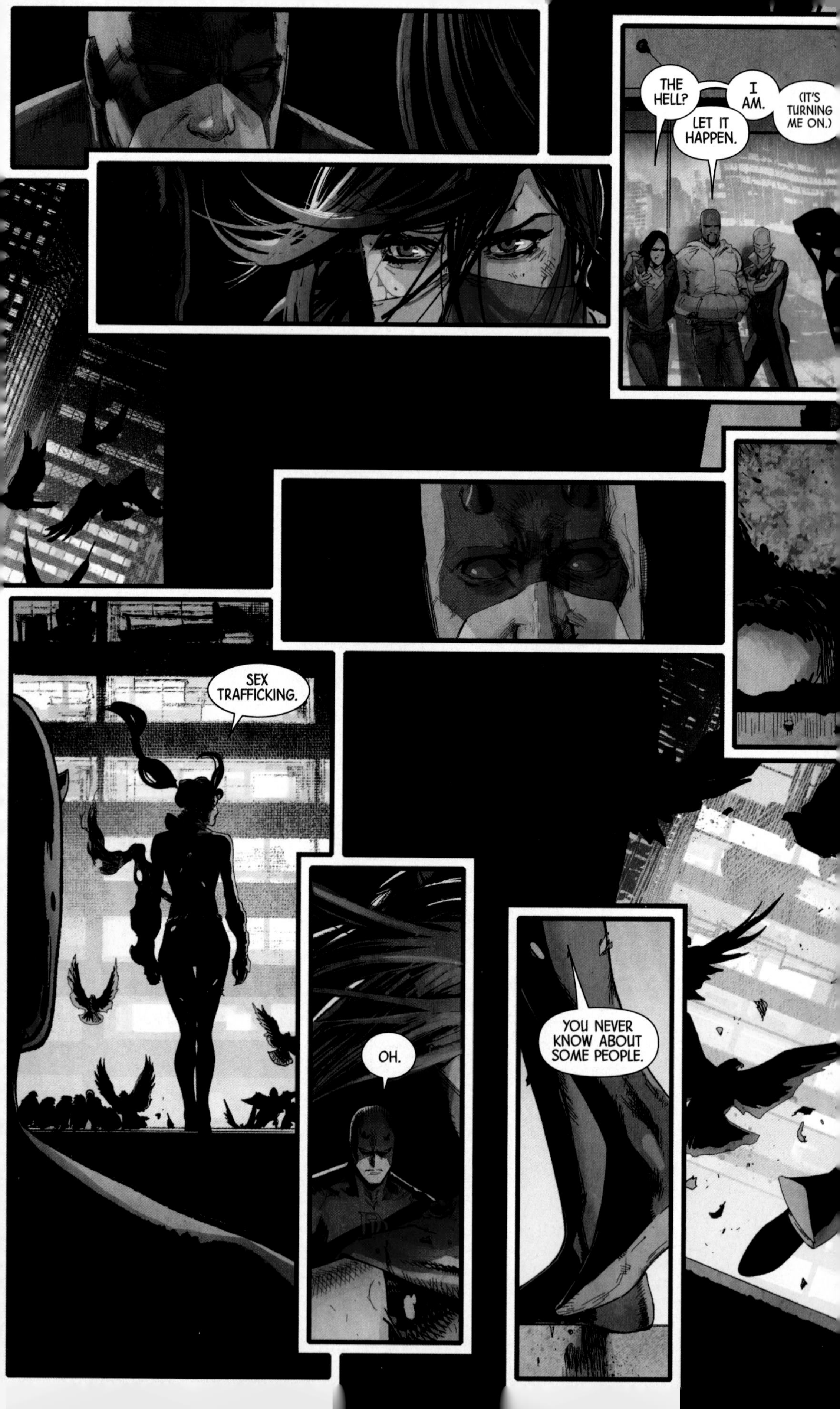
THE HELL?
I AM.
LET IT HAPPEN.
(IT'S TURNING ME ON.)
SEX TRAFFICKING.
OH.
YOU NEVER KNOW ABOUT SOME PEOPLE.

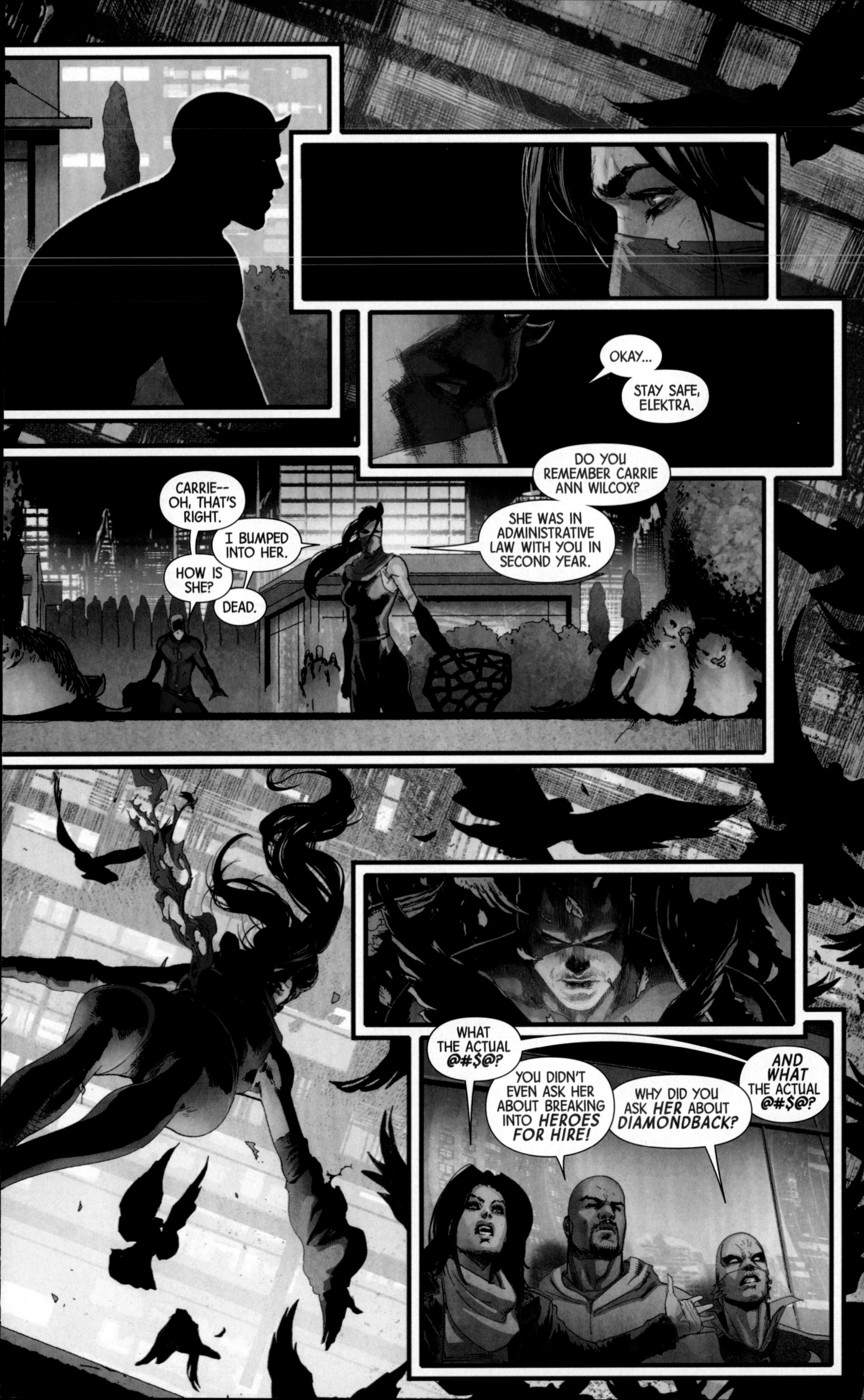
OKAY...
STAY SAFE, ELEKTRA.
DO YOU REMEMBER CARRIE ANN WILCOX?
SHE WAS IN ADMINISTRATIVE LAW WITH YOU IN SECOND YEAR.
CARRIE-- OH, THAT'S RIGHT.
I BUMPED INTO HER.
HOW IS SHE?
DEAD.
WHAT THE ACTUAL @#$@?
YOU DIDN'T EVEN ASK HER ABOUT BREAKING INTO HEROES FOR HIRE!
WHY DID YOU ASK HER ABOUT DIAMONDBACK?
AND WHAT THE ACTUAL @#$@?

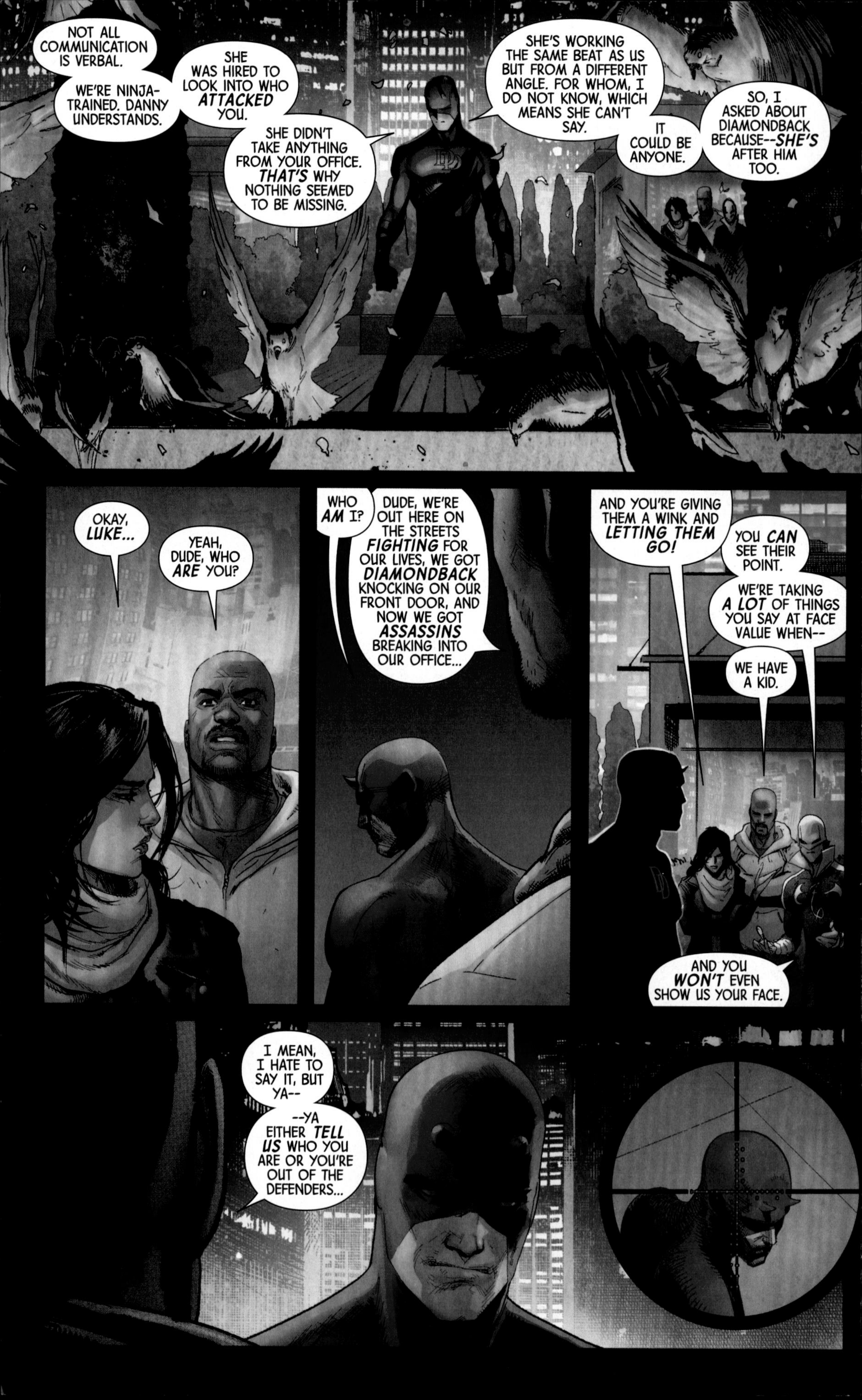
NOT ALL COMMUNICATION IS VERBAL.
WE'RE NINJA-TRAINED. DANNY UNDERSTANDS.
SHE WAS HIRED TO LOOK INTO WHO ATTACKED YOU.
SHE DIDN'T TAKE ANYTHING FROM YOUR OFFICE. THAT'S WHY NOTHING SEEMED TO BE MISSING.
SHE'S WORKING THE SAME BEAT AS US BUT FROM A DIFFERENT ANGLE. FOR WHOM, I DO NOT KNOW, WHICH MEANS SHE CAN'T SAY.
IT COULD BE ANYONE.
SO, I ASKED ABOUT DIAMONDBACK BECAUSE--SHE'S AFTER HIM TOO.
OKAY, LUKE...
YEAH, DUDE, WHO ARE YOU?
WHO AM I?
DUDE, WE'RE OUT HERE ON THE STREETS FIGHTING FOR OUR LIVES, WE GOT DIAMONDBACK KNOCKING ON OUR FRONT DOOR, AND NOW WE GOT ASSASSINS BREAKING INTO OUR OFFICE...
AND YOU'RE GIVING THEM A WINK AND LETTING THEM GO!
YOU CAN SEE THEIR POINT.
WE'RE TAKING A LOT OF THINGS YOU SAY AT FACE VALUE WHEN--
WE HAVE A KID.
AND YOU WON'T EVEN SHOW US YOUR FACE.
I MEAN, I HATE TO SAY IT, BUT YA--
--YA EITHER TELL US WHO YOU ARE OR YOU'RE OUT OF THE DEFENDERS...

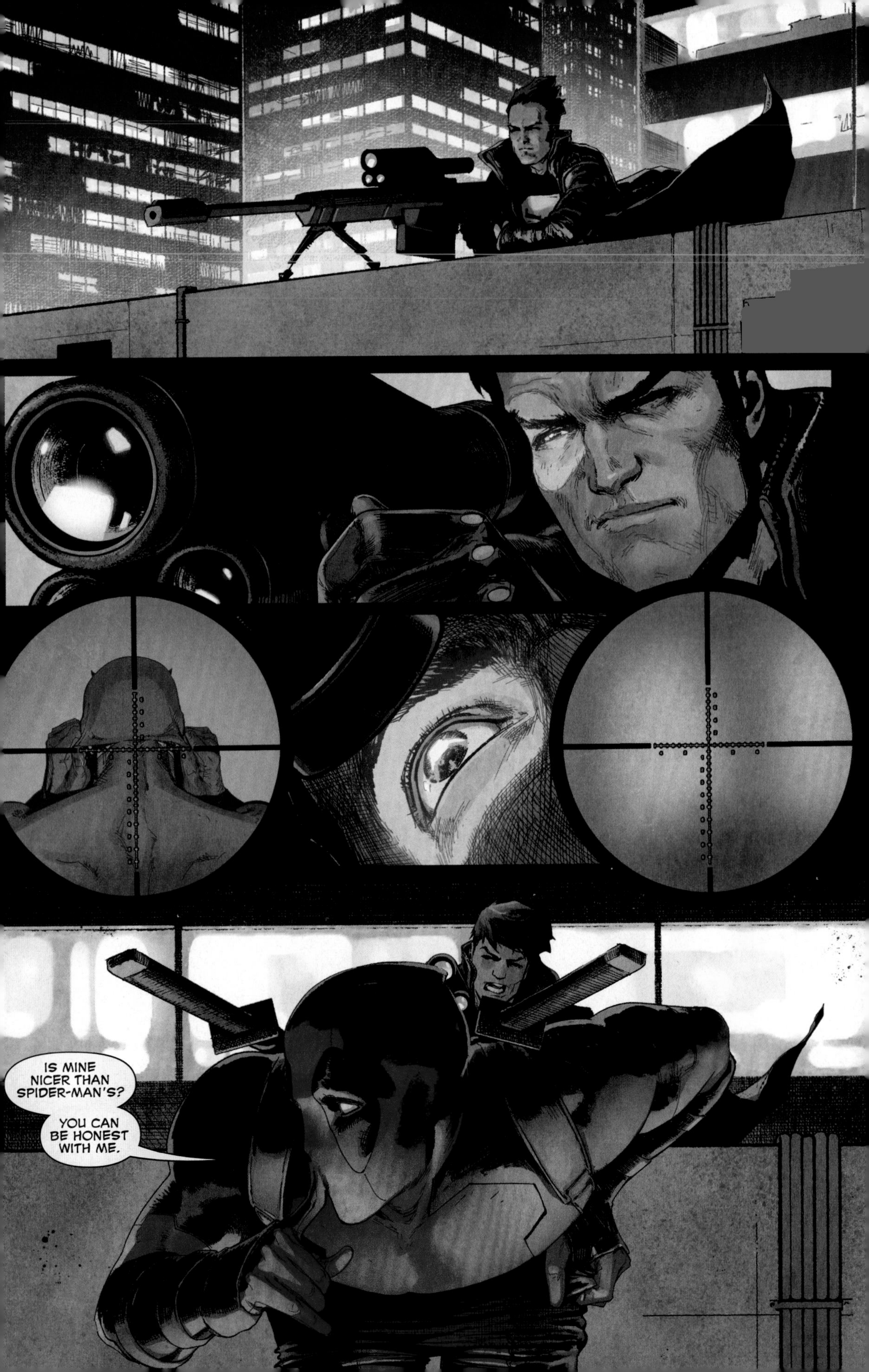
IS MINE NICER THAN SPIDER-MAN'S?
YOU CAN BE HONEST WITH ME.

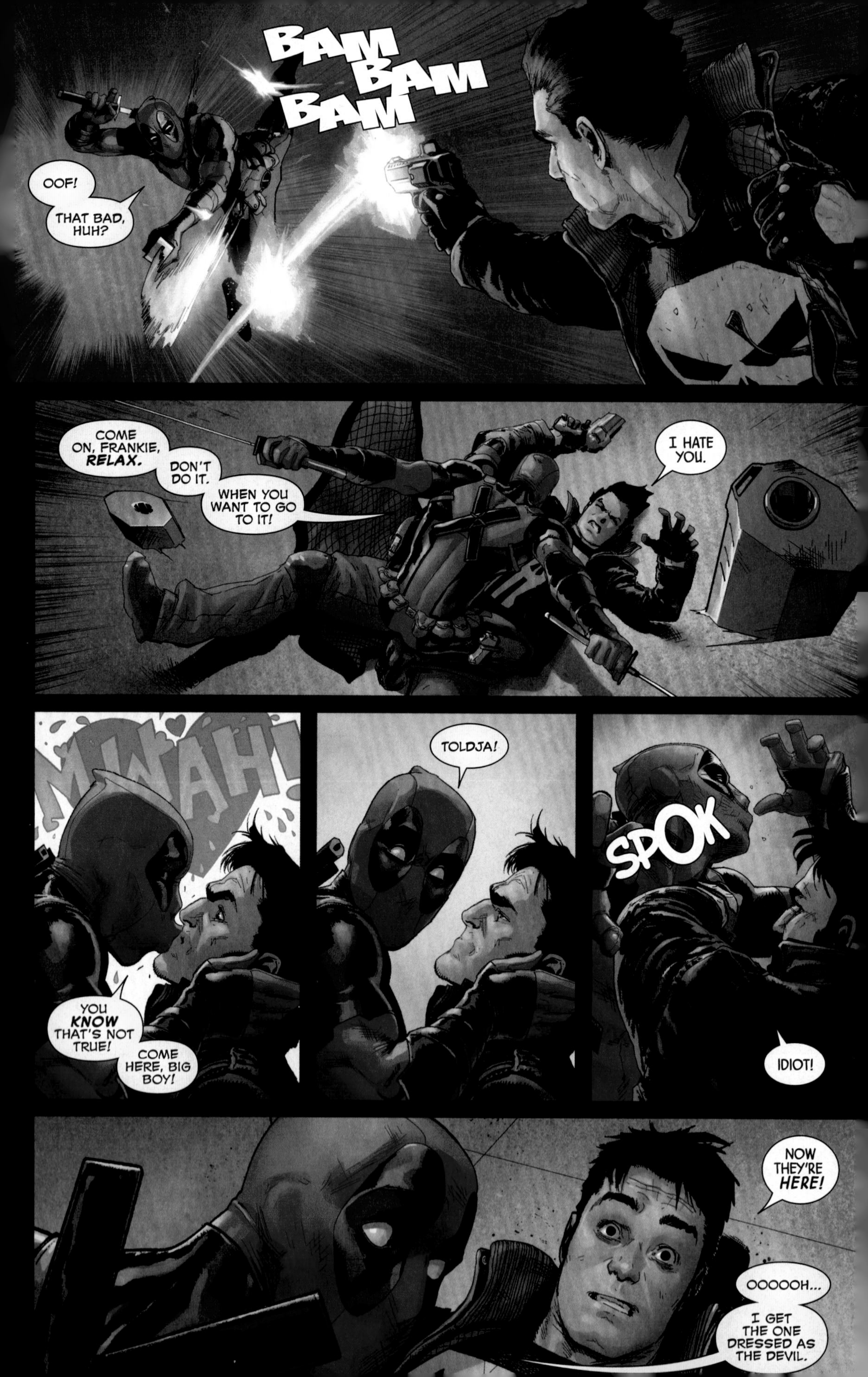
BAM BAM BAM
OOF!
THAT BAD, HUH?
COME ON, FRANKIE, **RELAX.**
DON'T DO IT.
WHEN YOU WANT TO GO TO IT!
I HATE YOU.
MWAH!
YOU **KNOW** THAT'S NOT TRUE!
COME HERE, BIG BOY!
TOLDJA!
SPOK
IDIOT!
NOW THEY'RE ***HERE!***
OOOOOH...
I GET THE ONE DRESSED AS THE DEVIL.

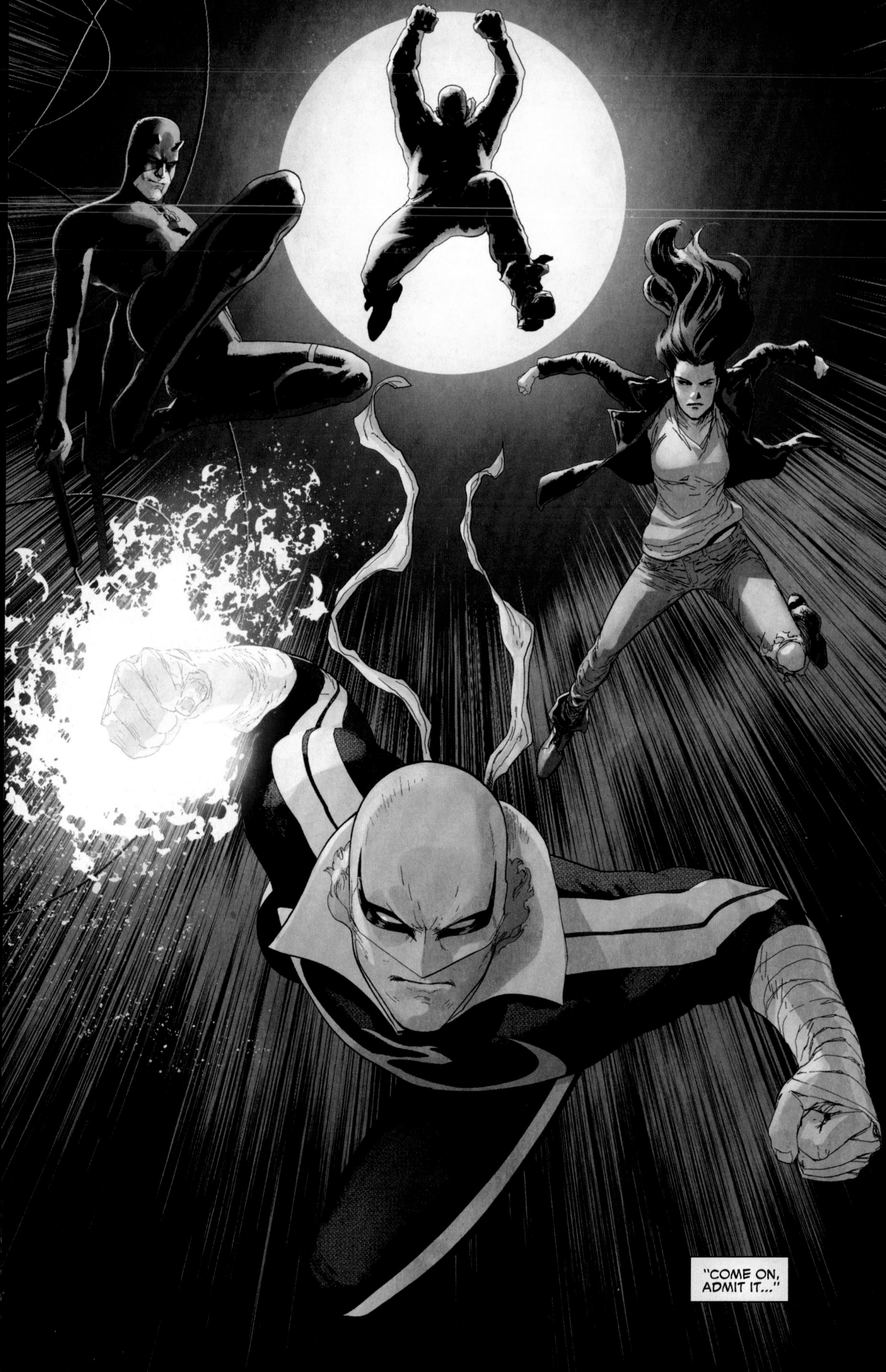
"COME ON, ADMIT IT..."

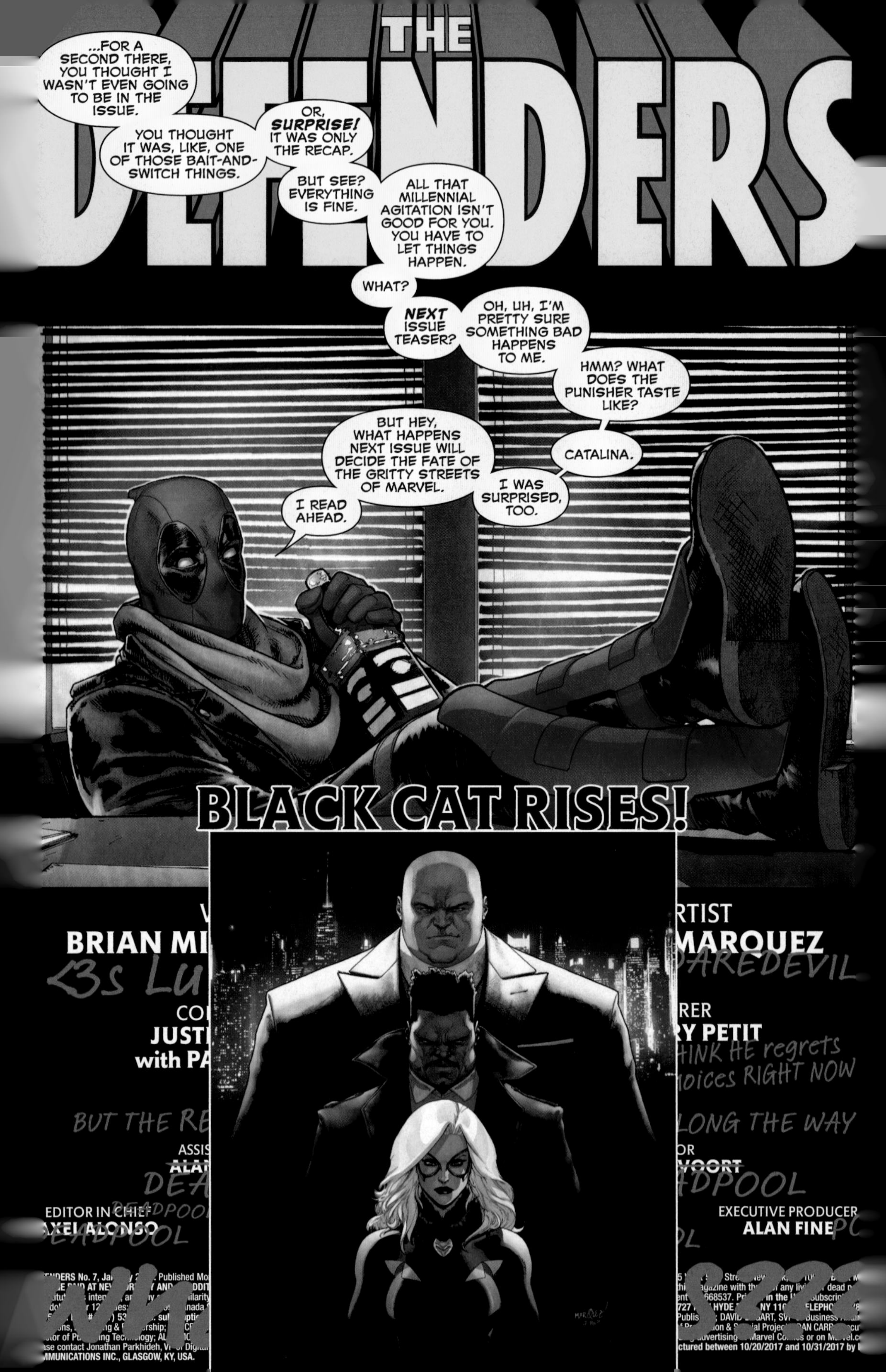
THE DEFENDERS
...FOR A SECOND THERE, YOU THOUGHT I WASN'T EVEN GOING TO BE IN THE ISSUE.
YOU THOUGHT IT WAS, LIKE, ONE OF THOSE BAIT-AND-SWITCH THINGS.
OR, SURPRISE! IT WAS ONLY THE RECAP.
BUT SEE? EVERYTHING IS FINE.
ALL THAT MILLENNIAL AGITATION ISN'T GOOD FOR YOU. YOU HAVE TO LET THINGS HAPPEN.
WHAT?
NEXT ISSUE TEASER?
OH, UH, I'M PRETTY SURE SOMETHING BAD HAPPENS TO ME.
HMM? WHAT DOES THE PUNISHER TASTE LIKE?
CATALINA.
I WAS SURPRISED, TOO.
BUT HEY, WHAT HAPPENS NEXT ISSUE WILL DECIDE THE FATE OF THE GRITTY STREETS OF MARVEL.
I READ AHEAD.
BLACK CAT RISES!
BRIAN MI
MARQUEZ
<3s Lu
DAREDEVIL
JUSTI
with PA
RY PETIT
HINK HE regrets
hoices RIGHT NOW
BUT THE RE
LONG THE WAY
DEA
DPOOL
EDITOR IN CHIEF
AXEL ALONSO
EXECUTIVE PRODUCER
ALAN FINE
DEADPOOL
Wh
$???

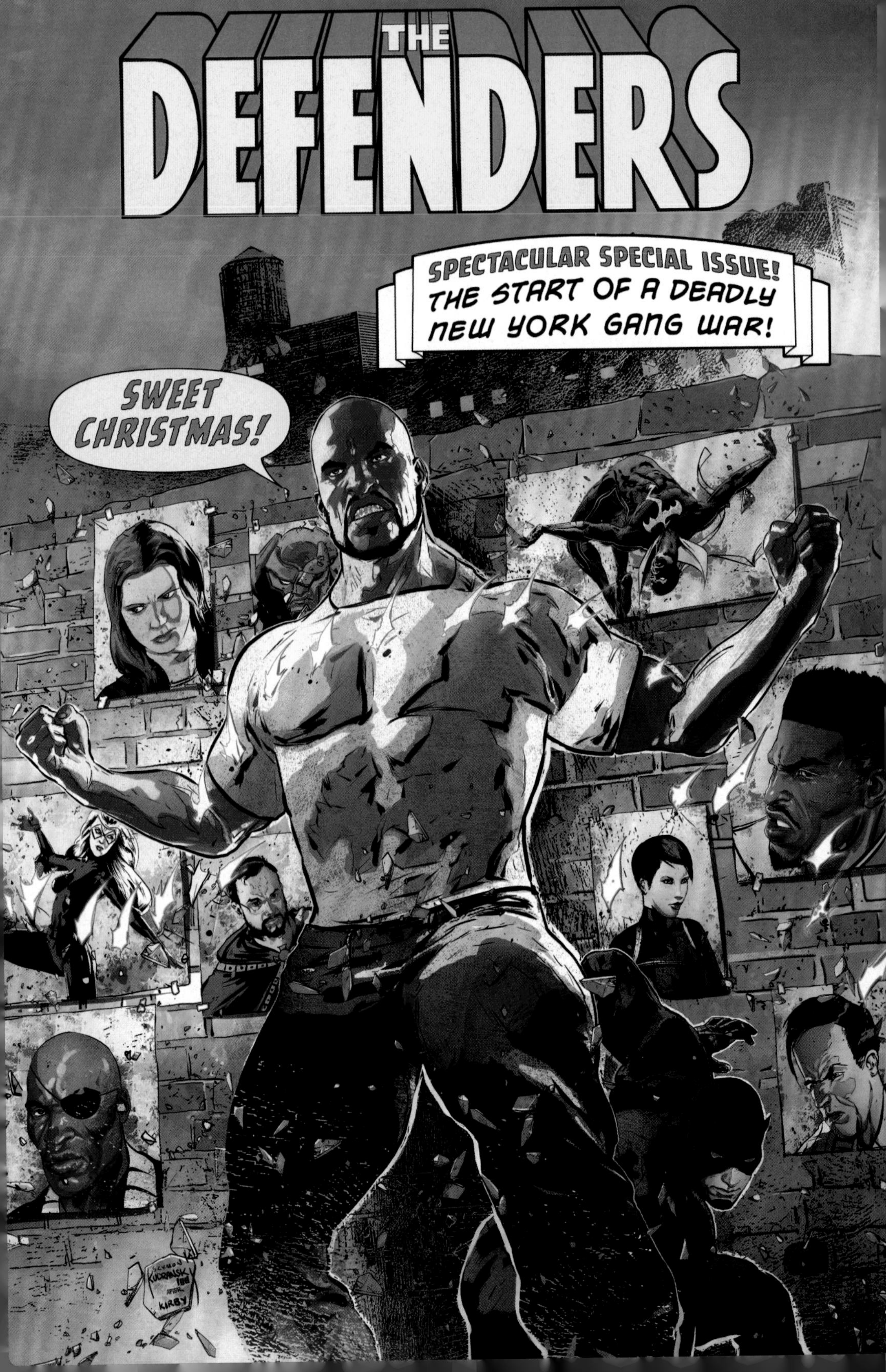
THE DEFENDERS
SPECTACULAR SPECIAL ISSUE!
THE START OF A DEADLY NEW YORK GANG WAR!
SWEET CHRISTMAS!

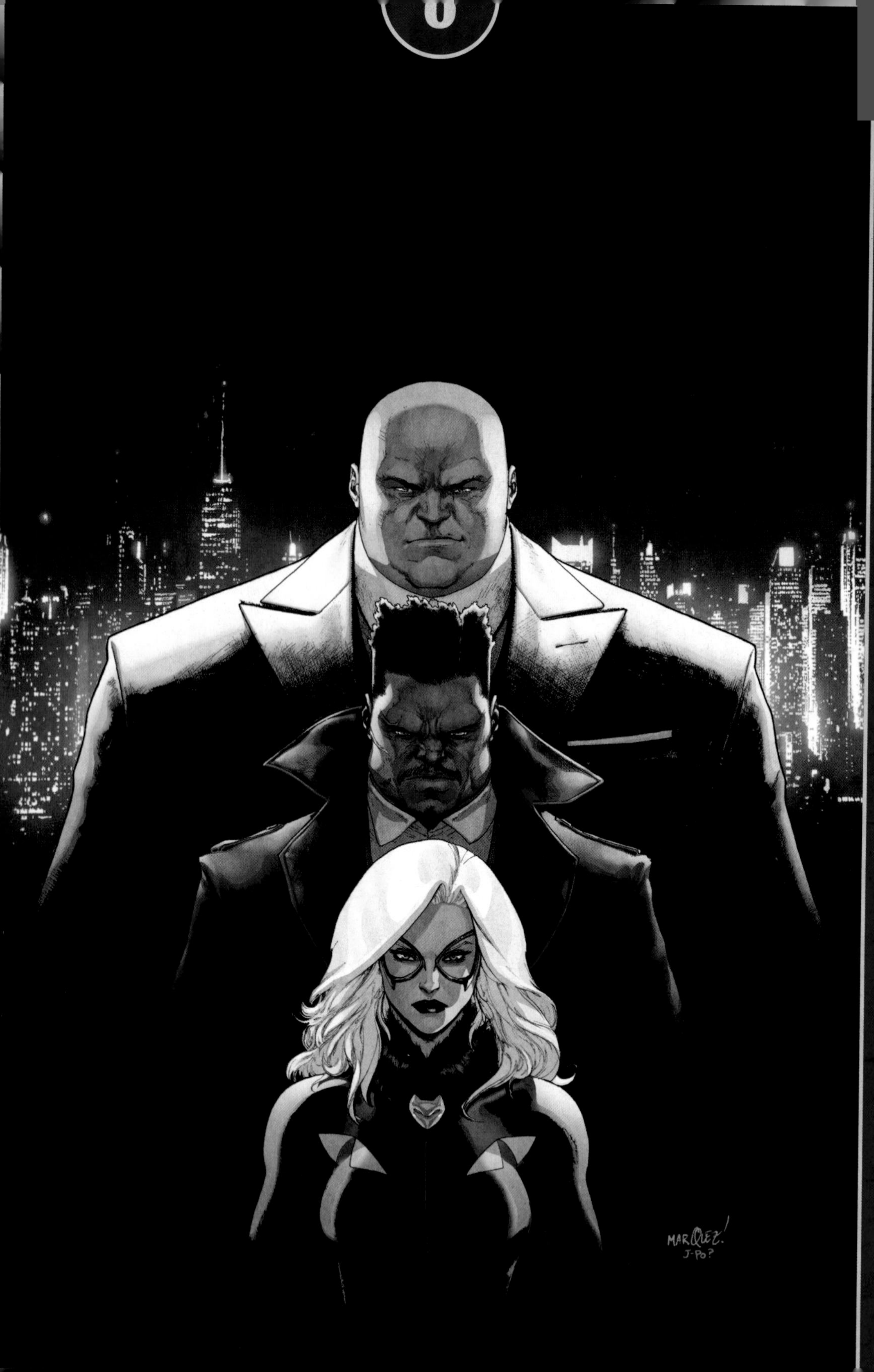
MARQUEZ!
J-Po?

THE DEFENDERS

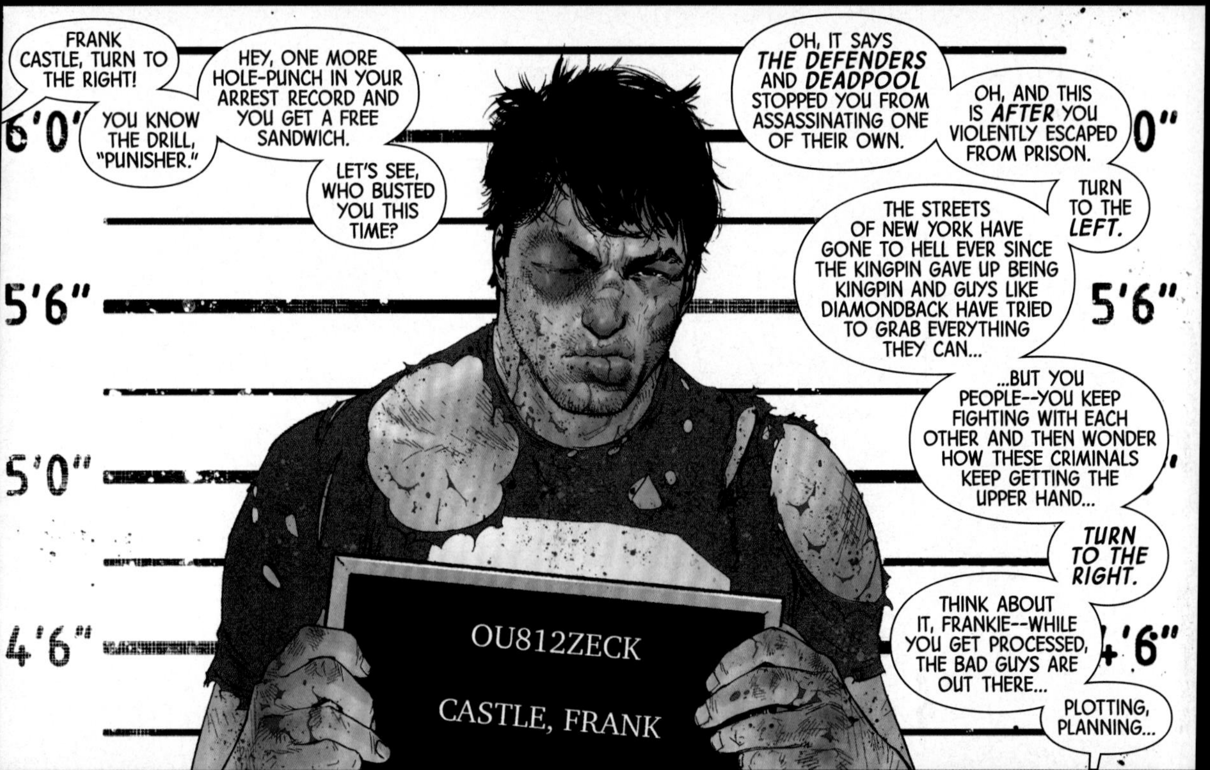
FRANK CASTLE, TURN TO THE RIGHT!
YOU KNOW THE DRILL, "PUNISHER."
HEY, ONE MORE HOLE-PUNCH IN YOUR ARREST RECORD AND YOU GET A FREE SANDWICH.
LET'S SEE, WHO BUSTED YOU THIS TIME?
OH, IT SAYS *THE DEFENDERS* AND *DEADPOOL* STOPPED YOU FROM ASSASSINATING ONE OF THEIR OWN.
OH, AND THIS IS *AFTER* YOU VIOLENTLY ESCAPED FROM PRISON.
TURN TO THE *LEFT.*
THE STREETS OF NEW YORK HAVE GONE TO HELL EVER SINCE THE KINGPIN GAVE UP BEING KINGPIN AND GUYS LIKE DIAMONDBACK HAVE TRIED TO GRAB EVERYTHING THEY CAN...
...BUT YOU PEOPLE--YOU KEEP FIGHTING WITH EACH OTHER AND THEN WONDER HOW THESE CRIMINALS KEEP GETTING THE UPPER HAND...
TURN TO THE RIGHT.
THINK ABOUT IT, FRANKIE--WHILE YOU GET PROCESSED, THE BAD GUYS ARE OUT THERE...
PLOTTING, PLANNING...
OU812ZECK
CASTLE, FRANK
6'0"
5'6"
5'0"
4'6"

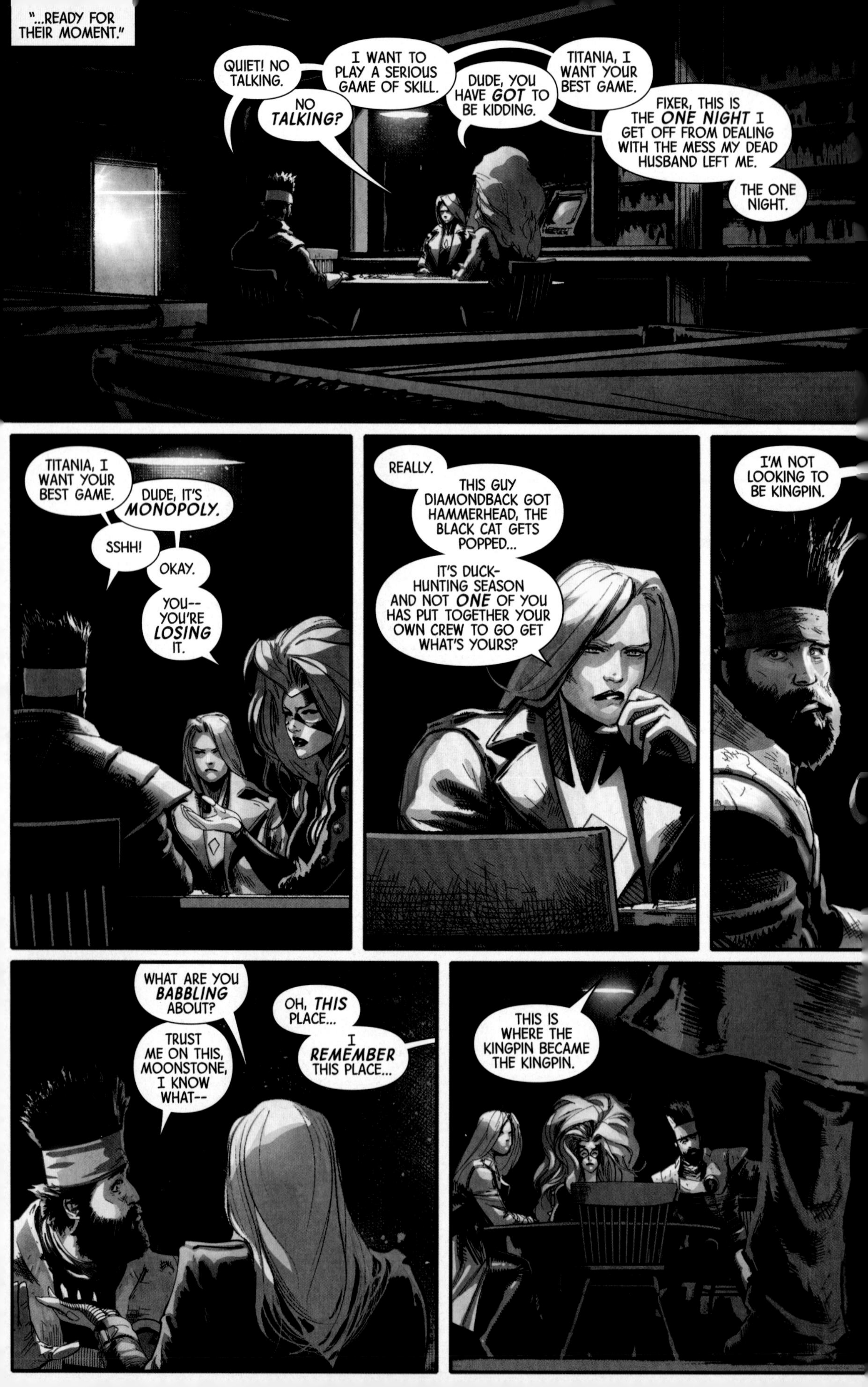
"...READY FOR THEIR MOMENT."
QUIET! NO TALKING.
I WANT TO PLAY A SERIOUS GAME OF SKILL.
NO TALKING?
DUDE, YOU HAVE GOT TO BE KIDDING.
TITANIA, I WANT YOUR BEST GAME.
FIXER, THIS IS THE ONE NIGHT I GET OFF FROM DEALING WITH THE MESS MY DEAD HUSBAND LEFT ME.
THE ONE NIGHT.
TITANIA, I WANT YOUR BEST GAME.
DUDE, IT'S MONOPOLY.
SSHH!
OKAY.
YOU-- YOU'RE LOSING IT.
REALLY.
THIS GUY DIAMONDBACK GOT HAMMERHEAD, THE BLACK CAT GETS POPPED...
IT'S DUCK-HUNTING SEASON AND NOT ONE OF YOU HAS PUT TOGETHER YOUR OWN CREW TO GO GET WHAT'S YOURS?
I'M NOT LOOKING TO BE KINGPIN.
WHAT ARE YOU BABBLING ABOUT?
TRUST ME ON THIS, MOONSTONE, I KNOW WHAT--
OH, THIS PLACE...
I REMEMBER THIS PLACE...
THIS IS WHERE THE KINGPIN BECAME THE KINGPIN.

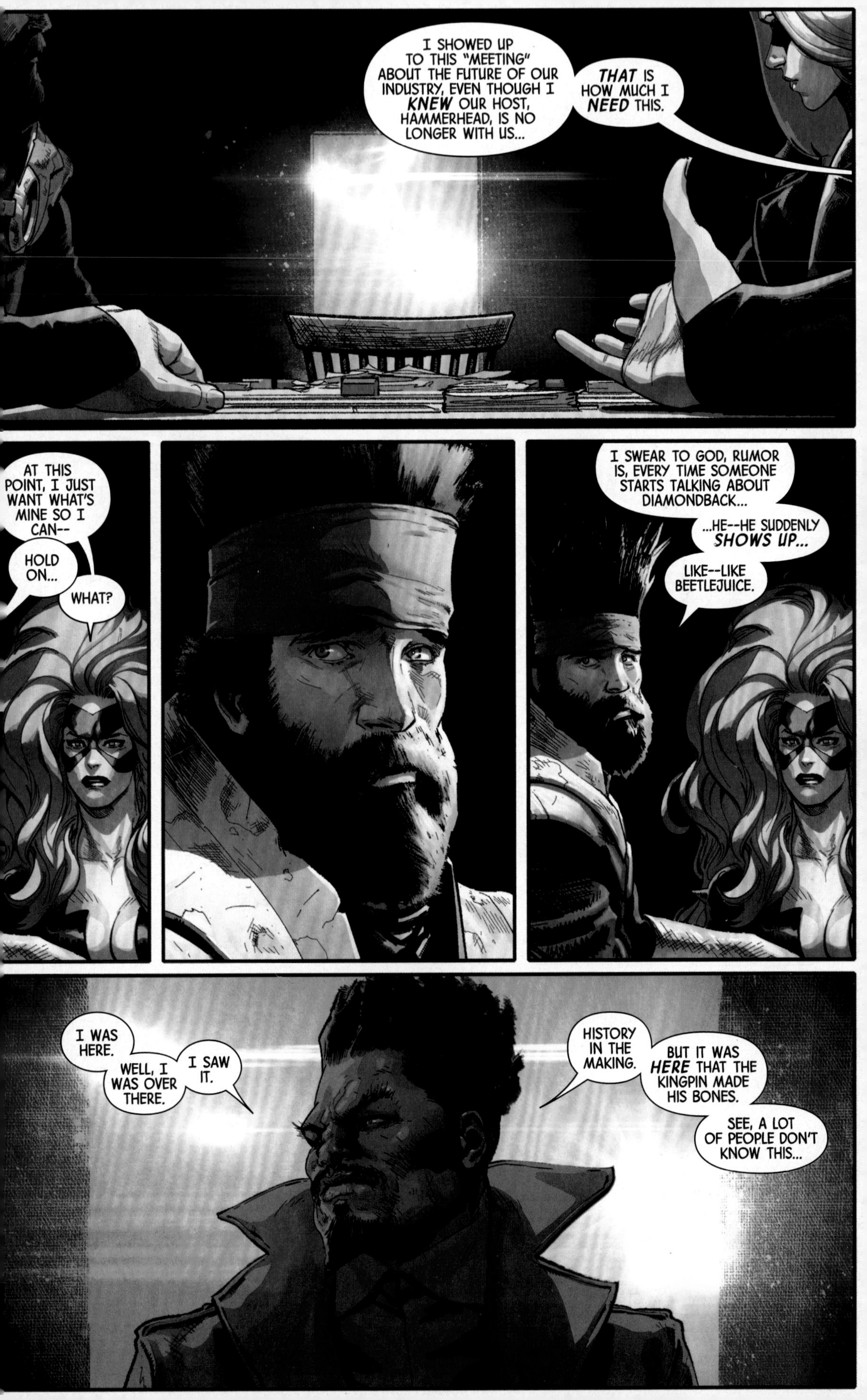

I SHOWED UP TO THIS "MEETING" ABOUT THE FUTURE OF OUR INDUSTRY, EVEN THOUGH I *KNEW* OUR HOST, HAMMERHEAD, IS NO LONGER WITH US...
THAT IS HOW MUCH I *NEED* THIS.
AT THIS POINT, I JUST WANT WHAT'S MINE SO I CAN--
HOLD ON...
WHAT?
I SWEAR TO GOD, RUMOR IS, EVERY TIME SOMEONE STARTS TALKING ABOUT DIAMONDBACK...
...HE--HE SUDDENLY *SHOWS UP...*
LIKE--LIKE BEETLEJUICE.
I WAS HERE.
WELL, I WAS OVER THERE.
I SAW IT.
HISTORY IN THE MAKING.
BUT IT WAS *HERE* THAT THE KINGPIN MADE HIS BONES.
SEE, A LOT OF PEOPLE DON'T KNOW THIS...

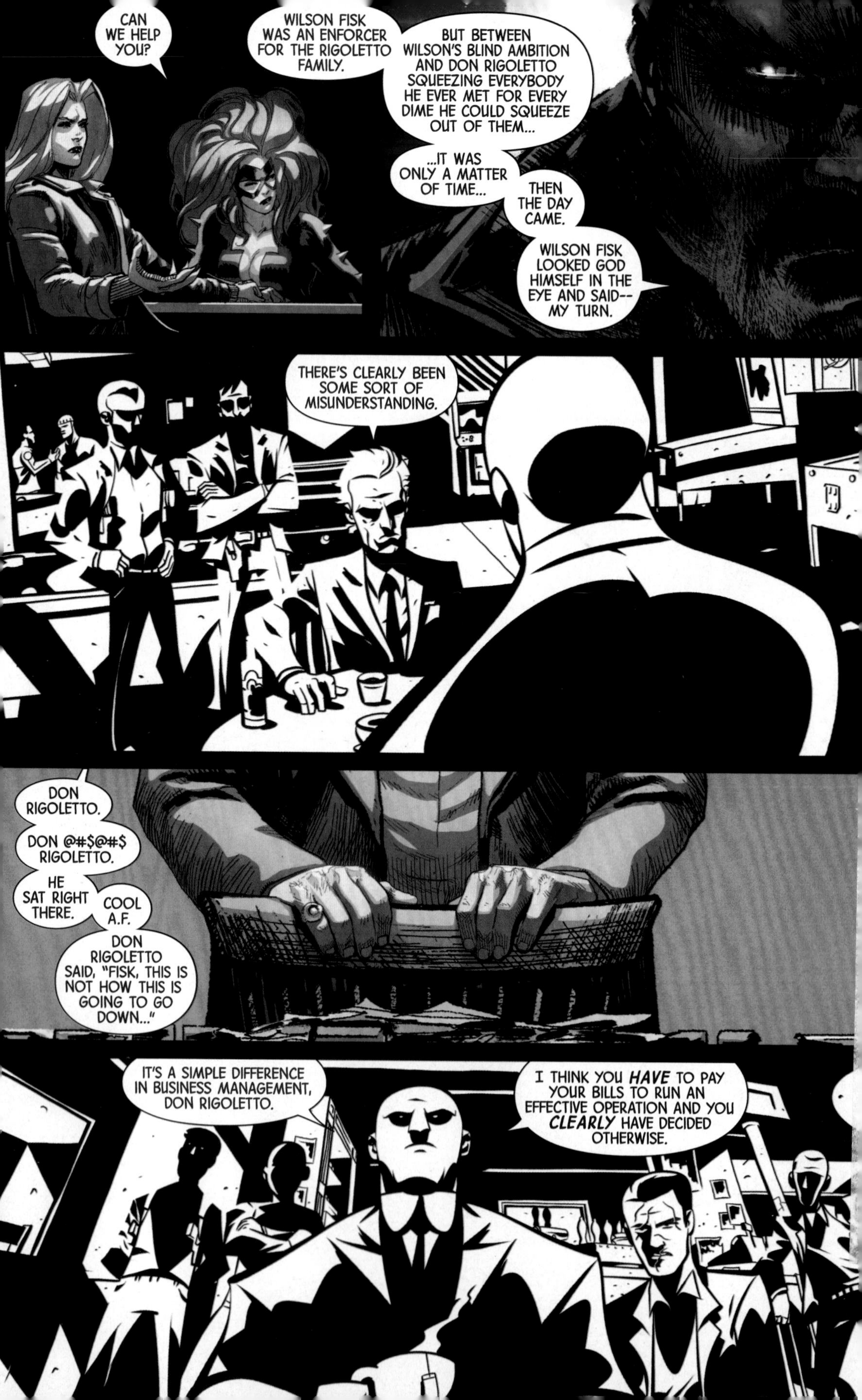
CAN WE HELP YOU?
WILSON FISK WAS AN ENFORCER FOR THE RIGOLETTO FAMILY.
BUT BETWEEN WILSON'S BLIND AMBITION AND DON RIGOLETTO SQUEEZING EVERYBODY HE EVER MET FOR EVERY DIME HE COULD SQUEEZE OUT OF THEM...
...IT WAS ONLY A MATTER OF TIME...
THEN THE DAY CAME.
WILSON FISK LOOKED GOD HIMSELF IN THE EYE AND SAID-- MY TURN.
THERE'S CLEARLY BEEN SOME SORT OF MISUNDERSTANDING.
DON RIGOLETTO.
DON @#$@#$ RIGOLETTO.
HE SAT RIGHT THERE.
COOL A.F.
DON RIGOLETTO SAID, "FISK, THIS IS NOT HOW THIS IS GOING TO GO DOWN..."
IT'S A SIMPLE DIFFERENCE IN BUSINESS MANAGEMENT, DON RIGOLETTO.
I THINK YOU HAVE TO PAY YOUR BILLS TO RUN AN EFFECTIVE OPERATION AND YOU CLEARLY HAVE DECIDED OTHERWISE.

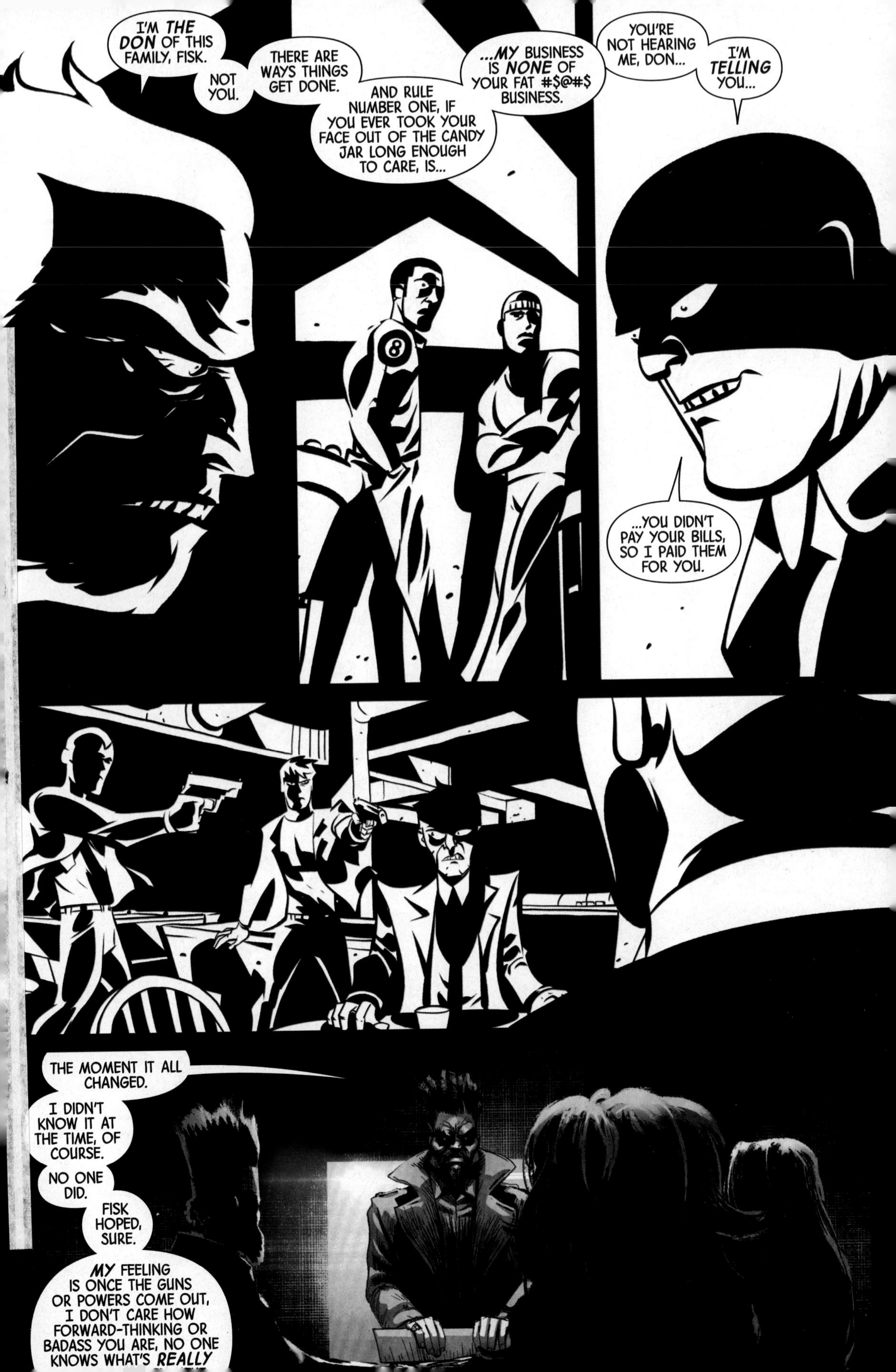
I'M THE DON OF THIS FAMILY, FISK.
NOT YOU.
THERE ARE WAYS THINGS GET DONE.
AND RULE NUMBER ONE, IF YOU EVER TOOK YOUR FACE OUT OF THE CANDY JAR LONG ENOUGH TO CARE, IS...
...MY BUSINESS IS NONE OF YOUR FAT #$@#$ BUSINESS.
YOU'RE NOT HEARING ME, DON...
I'M TELLING YOU...
...YOU DIDN'T PAY YOUR BILLS, SO I PAID THEM FOR YOU.
THE MOMENT IT ALL CHANGED.
I DIDN'T KNOW IT AT THE TIME, OF COURSE.
NO ONE DID.
FISK HOPED, SURE.
MY FEELING IS ONCE THE GUNS OR POWERS COME OUT, I DON'T CARE HOW FORWARD-THINKING OR BADASS YOU ARE, NO ONE KNOWS WHAT'S REALLY

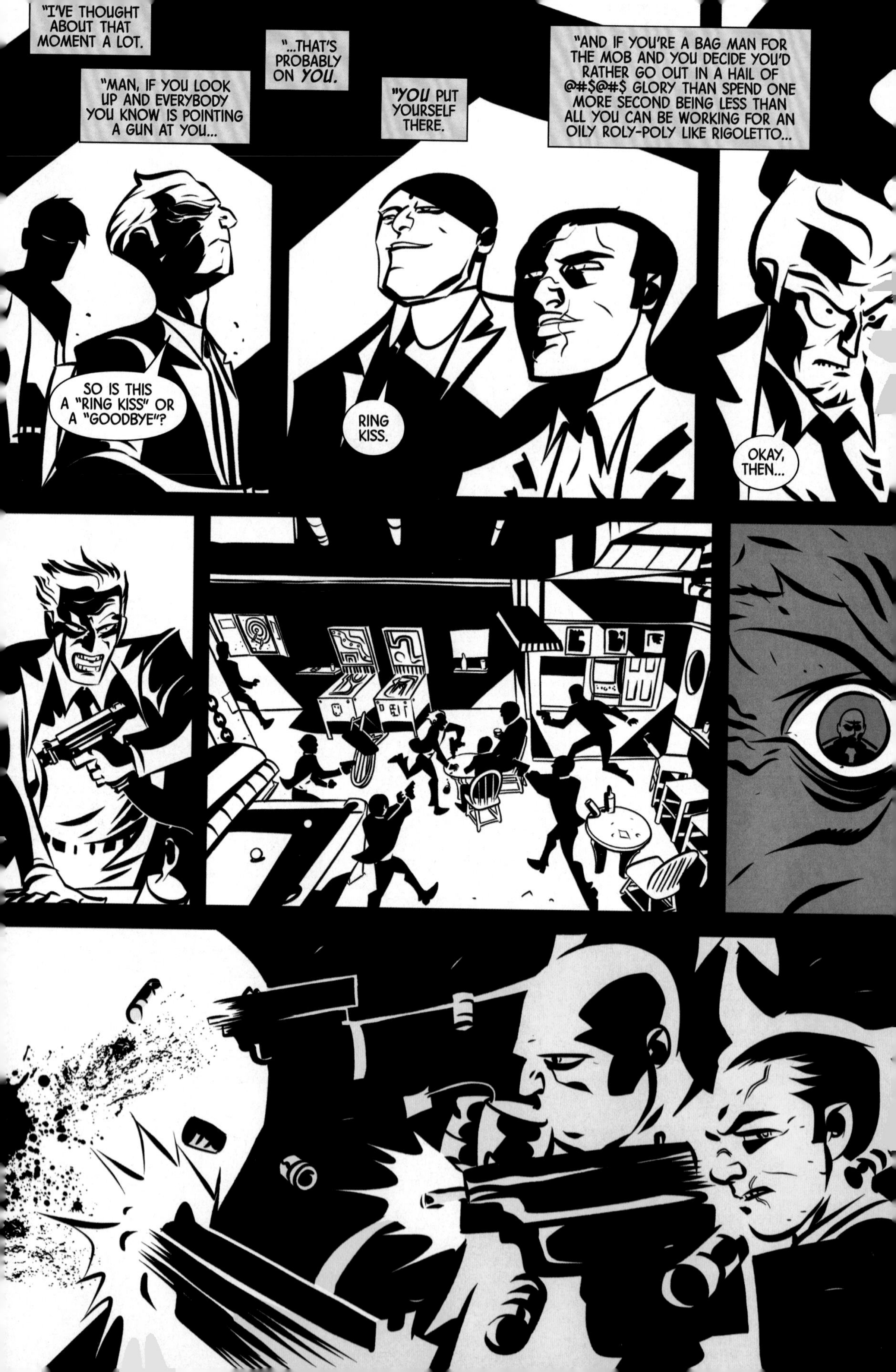
"I'VE THOUGHT ABOUT THAT MOMENT A LOT.
"MAN, IF YOU LOOK UP AND EVERYBODY YOU KNOW IS POINTING A GUN AT YOU...
"...THAT'S PROBABLY ON *YOU.*
"*YOU* PUT YOURSELF THERE.
"AND IF YOU'RE A BAG MAN FOR THE MOB AND YOU DECIDE YOU'D RATHER GO OUT IN A HAIL OF @#$@#$ GLORY THAN SPEND ONE MORE SECOND BEING LESS THAN ALL YOU CAN BE WORKING FOR AN OILY ROLY-POLY LIKE RIGOLETTO...
SO IS THIS A "RING KISS" OR A "GOODBYE"?
RING KISS.
OKAY, THEN...

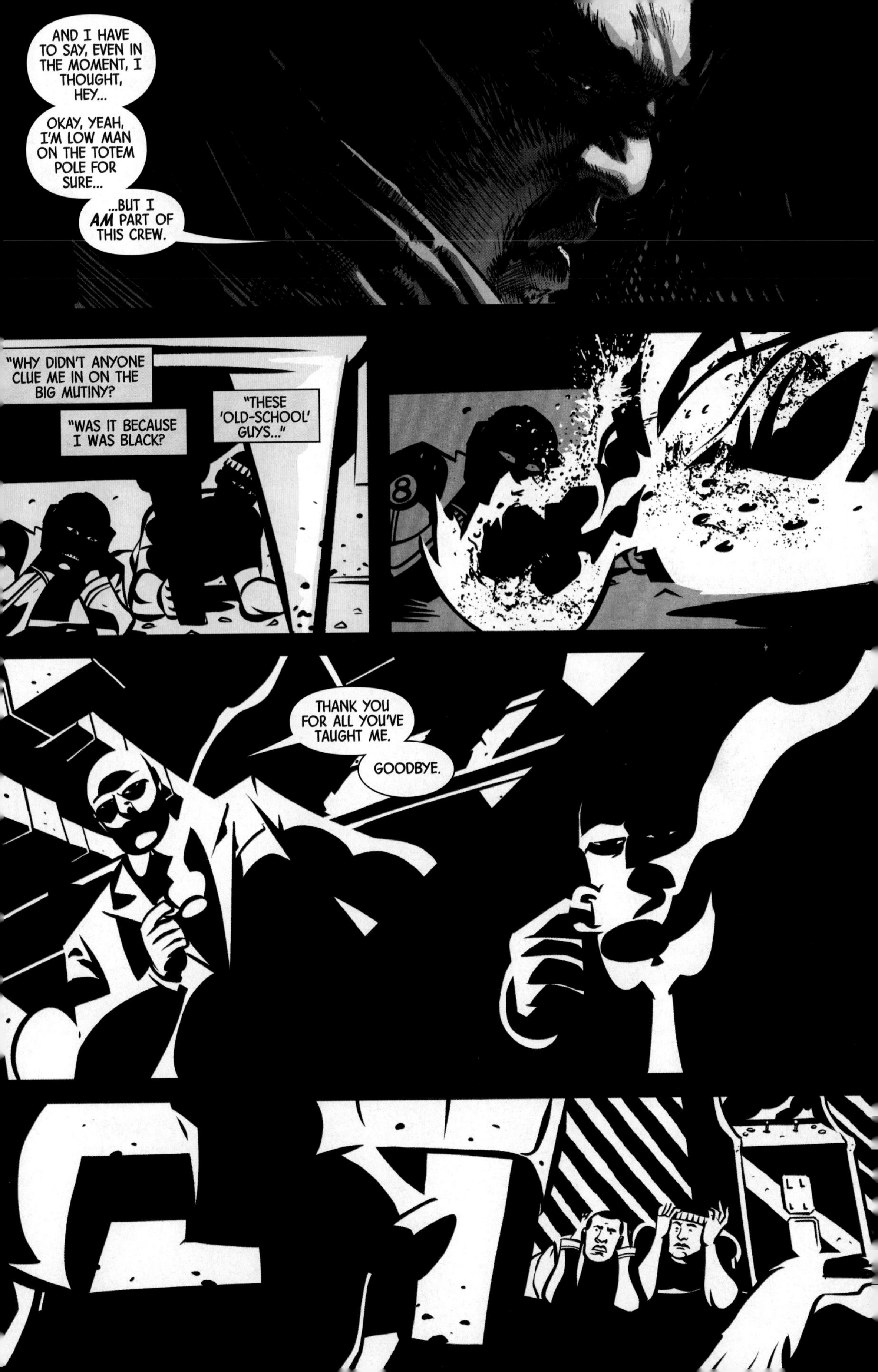
AND I HAVE TO SAY, EVEN IN THE MOMENT, I THOUGHT, HEY...
OKAY, YEAH, I'M LOW MAN ON THE TOTEM POLE FOR SURE...
...BUT I *AM* PART OF THIS CREW.
"WHY DIDN'T ANYONE CLUE ME IN ON THE BIG MUTINY?
"WAS IT BECAUSE I WAS BLACK?
"THESE 'OLD-SCHOOL' GUYS..."
THANK YOU FOR ALL YOU'VE TAUGHT ME.
GOODBYE.

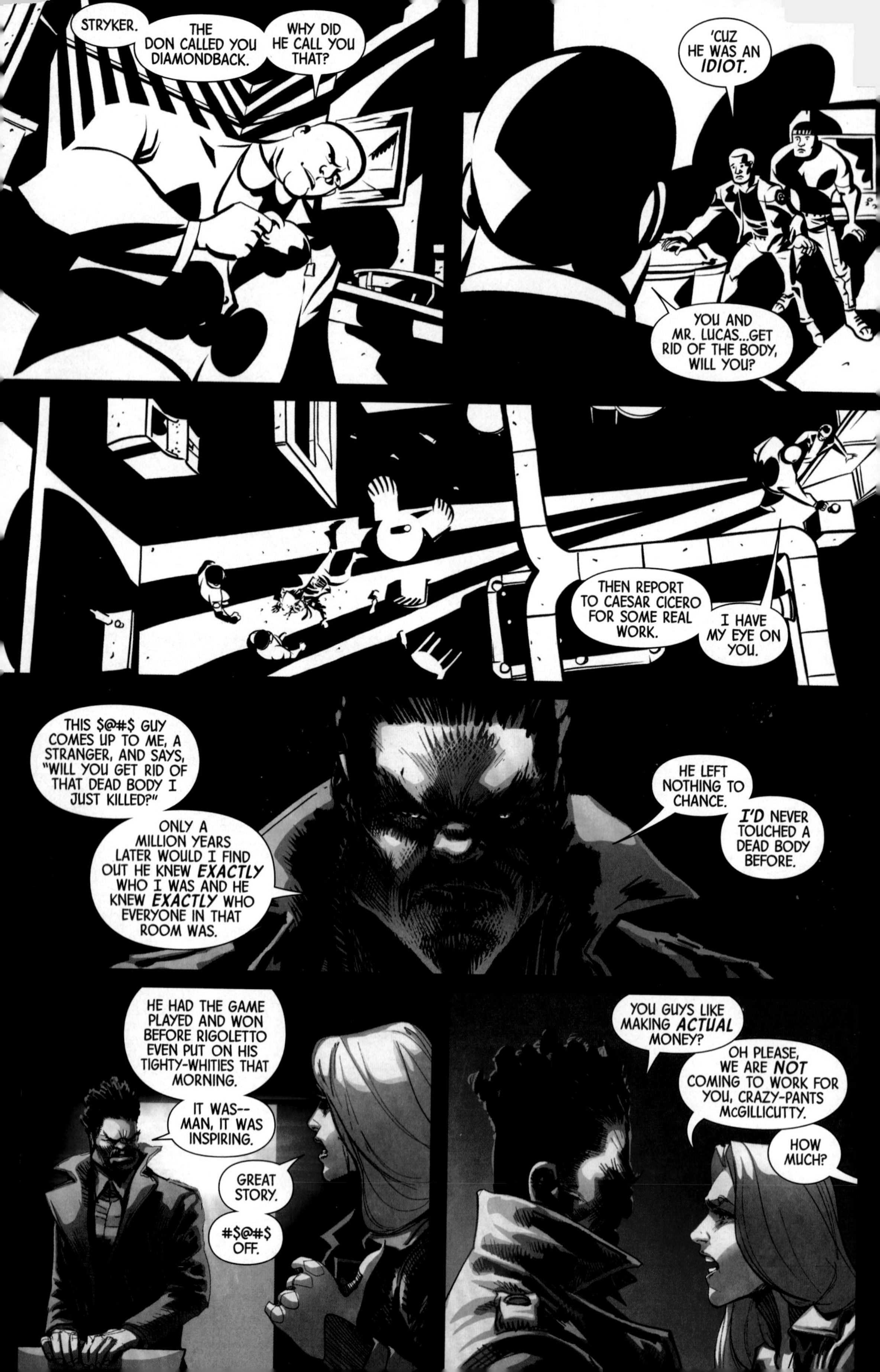
STRYKER.
THE DON CALLED YOU DIAMONDBACK.
WHY DID HE CALL YOU THAT?
'CUZ HE WAS AN IDIOT.
YOU AND MR. LUCAS...GET RID OF THE BODY, WILL YOU?
THEN REPORT TO CAESAR CICERO FOR SOME REAL WORK.
I HAVE MY EYE ON YOU.
THIS $@#$ GUY COMES UP TO ME, A STRANGER, AND SAYS, "WILL YOU GET RID OF THAT DEAD BODY I JUST KILLED?"
ONLY A MILLION YEARS LATER WOULD I FIND OUT HE KNEW EXACTLY WHO I WAS AND HE KNEW EXACTLY WHO EVERYONE IN THAT ROOM WAS.
HE LEFT NOTHING TO CHANCE.
I'D NEVER TOUCHED A DEAD BODY BEFORE.
HE HAD THE GAME PLAYED AND WON BEFORE RIGOLETTO EVEN PUT ON HIS TIGHTY-WHITIES THAT MORNING.
IT WAS-- MAN, IT WAS INSPIRING.
GREAT STORY.
#$@#$ OFF.
YOU GUYS LIKE MAKING ACTUAL MONEY?
OH PLEASE, WE ARE NOT COMING TO WORK FOR YOU, CRAZY-PANTS McGILLICUTTY.
HOW MUCH?

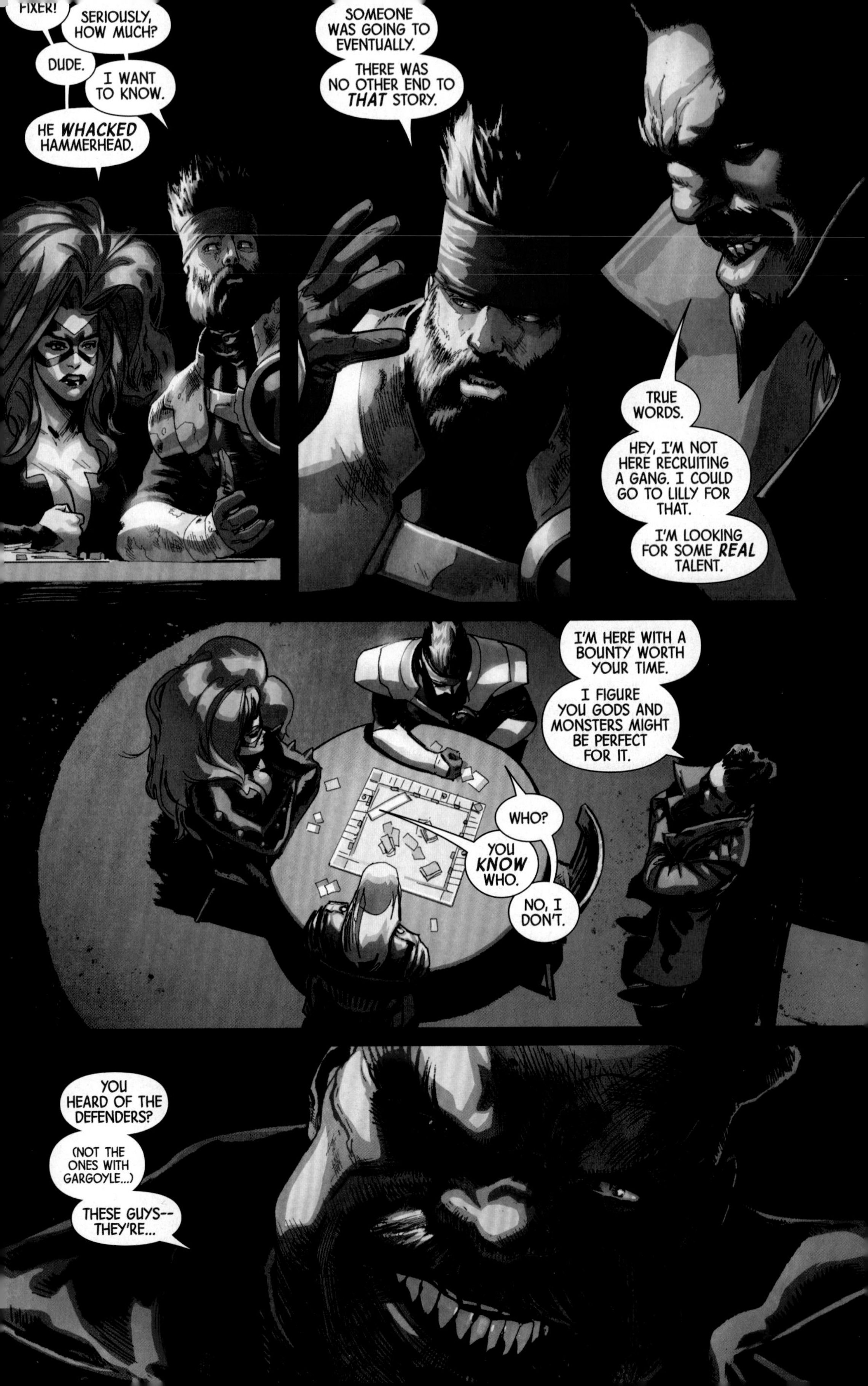
FIXER!
SERIOUSLY, HOW MUCH?
DUDE.
I WANT TO KNOW.
HE WHACKED HAMMERHEAD.
SOMEONE WAS GOING TO EVENTUALLY.
THERE WAS NO OTHER END TO THAT STORY.
TRUE WORDS.
HEY, I'M NOT HERE RECRUITING A GANG. I COULD GO TO LILLY FOR THAT.
I'M LOOKING FOR SOME REAL TALENT.
I'M HERE WITH A BOUNTY WORTH YOUR TIME.
I FIGURE YOU GODS AND MONSTERS MIGHT BE PERFECT FOR IT.
WHO?
YOU KNOW WHO.
NO, I DON'T.
YOU HEARD OF THE DEFENDERS?
(NOT THE ONES WITH GARGOYLE...)
THESE GUYS-- THEY'RE...

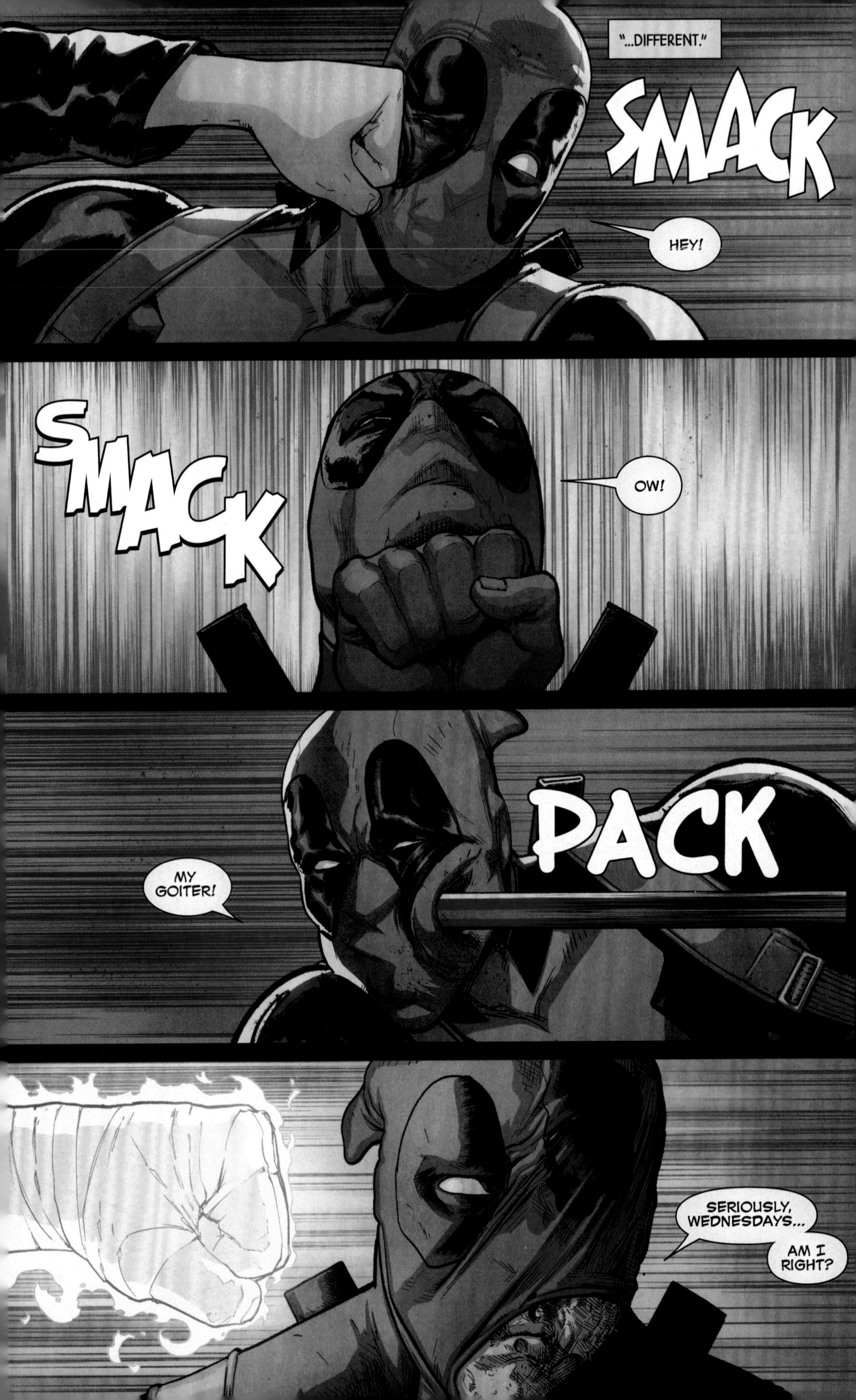
"...DIFFERENT."
SMACK
HEY!
SMACK
OW!
PACK
MY GOITER!
SERIOUSLY, WEDNESDAYS...
AM I RIGHT?

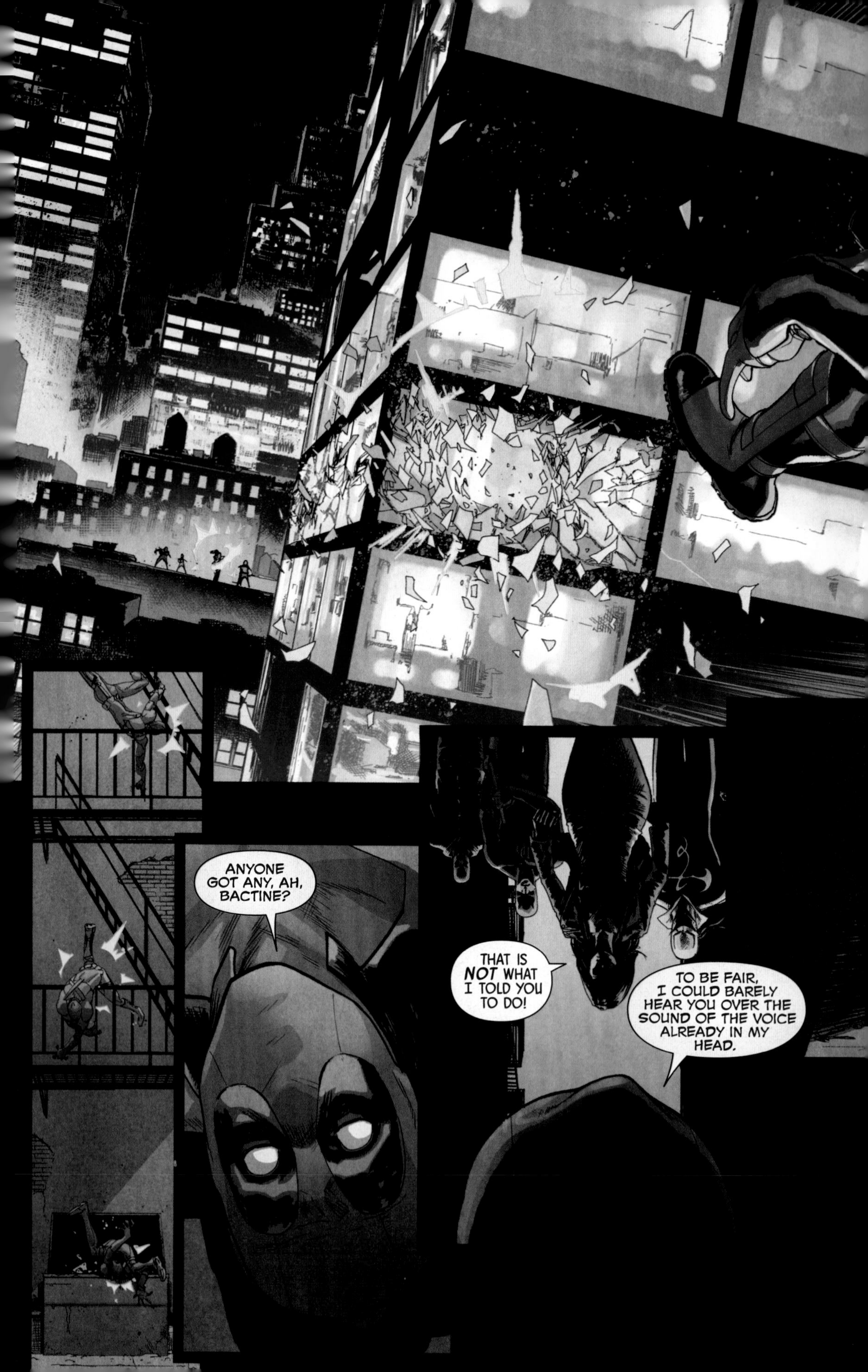
ANYONE GOT ANY, AH, BACTINE?
THAT IS NOT WHAT I TOLD YOU TO DO!
TO BE FAIR, I COULD BARELY HEAR YOU OVER THE SOUND OF THE VOICE ALREADY IN MY HEAD.

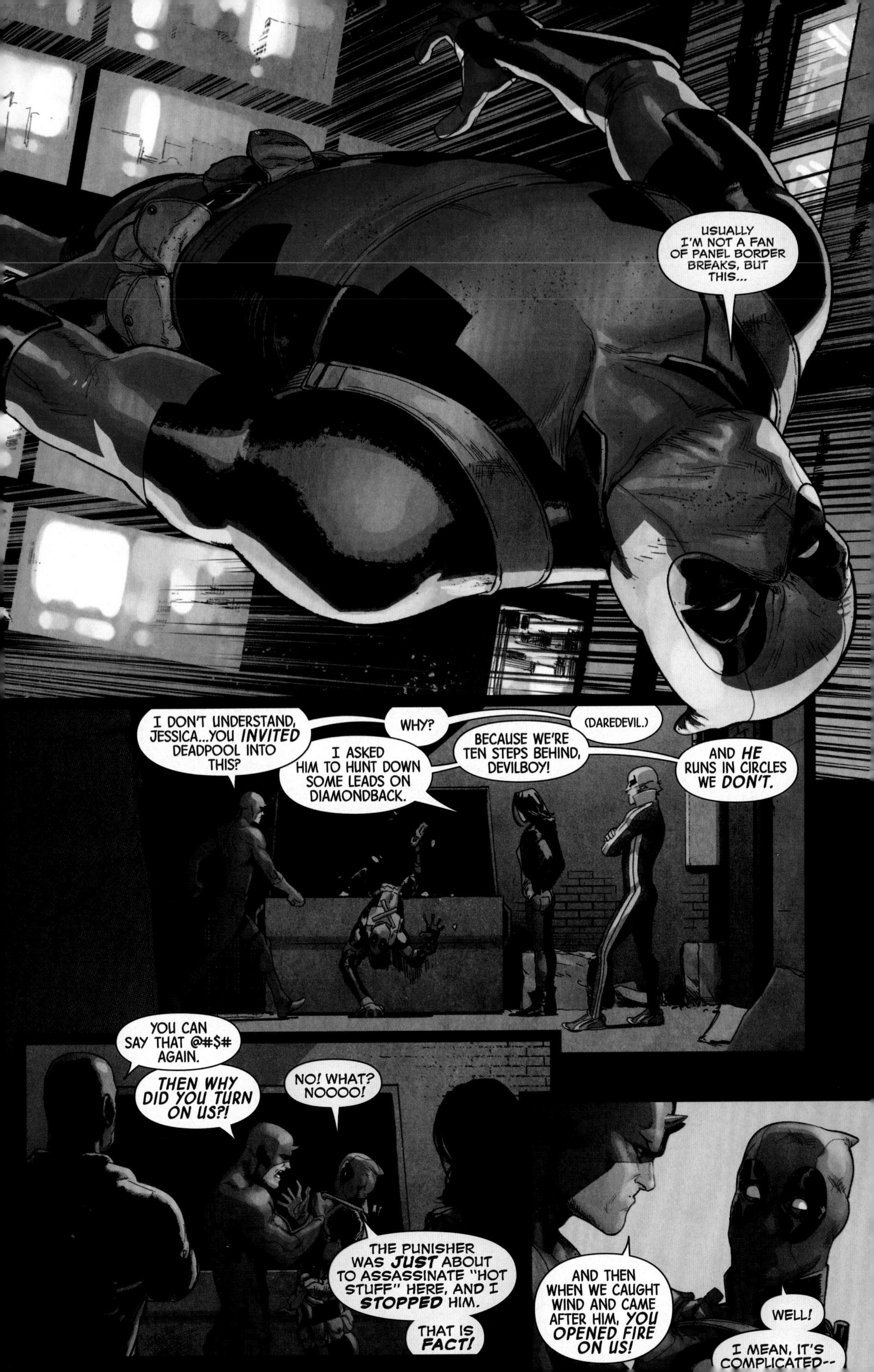
USUALLY I'M NOT A FAN OF PANEL BORDER BREAKS, BUT THIS...
I DON'T UNDERSTAND, JESSICA...YOU INVITED DEADPOOL INTO THIS?
WHY?
(DAREDEVIL.)
I ASKED HIM TO HUNT DOWN SOME LEADS ON DIAMONDBACK.
BECAUSE WE'RE TEN STEPS BEHIND, DEVILBOY!
AND HE RUNS IN CIRCLES WE DON'T.
YOU CAN SAY THAT @#$# AGAIN.
THEN WHY DID YOU TURN ON US?!
NO! WHAT? NOOOO!
THE PUNISHER WAS JUST ABOUT TO ASSASSINATE "HOT STUFF" HERE, AND I STOPPED HIM.
THAT IS FACT!
AND THEN WHEN WE CAUGHT WIND AND CAME AFTER HIM, YOU OPENED FIRE ON US!
WELL!
I MEAN, IT'S COMPLICATED--

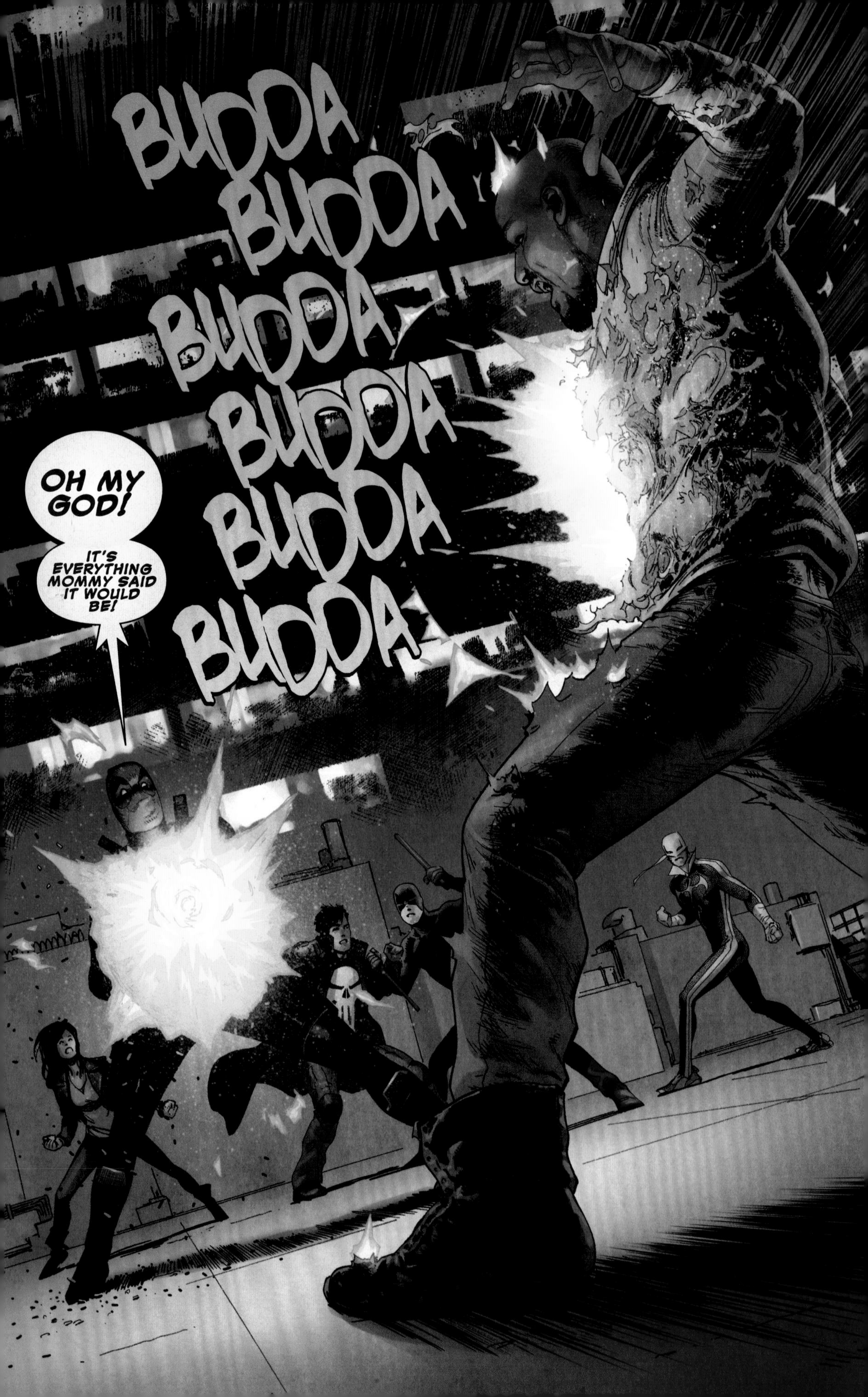
BUDDA BUDDA BUDDA BUDDA BUDDA BUDDA
OH MY GOD!
IT'S EVERYTHING MOMMY SAID IT WOULD BE!

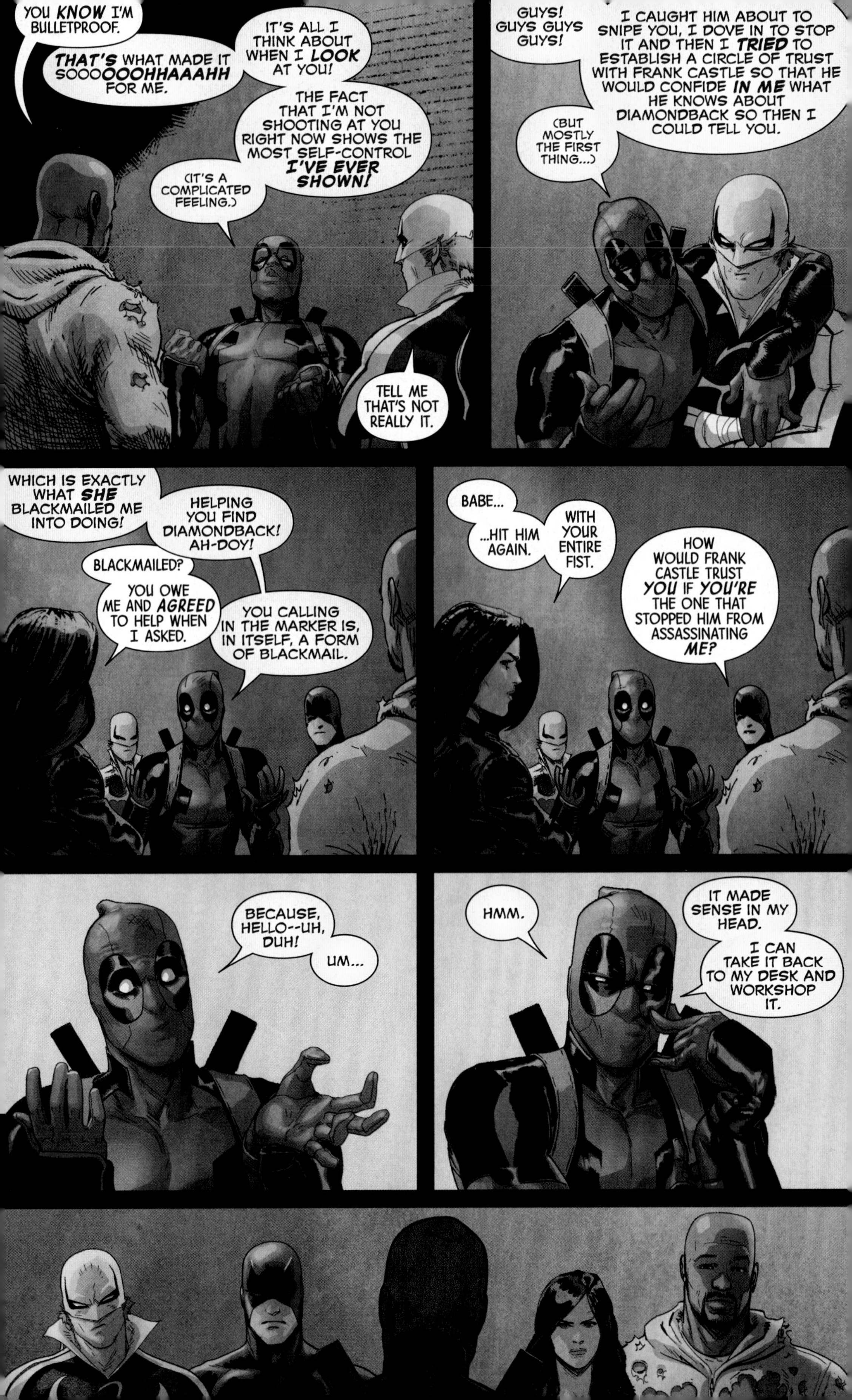
YOU KNOW I'M BULLETPROOF.
THAT'S WHAT MADE IT SOOOOOOOHHAAAAHH FOR ME.
IT'S ALL I THINK ABOUT WHEN I LOOK AT YOU!
THE FACT THAT I'M NOT SHOOTING AT YOU RIGHT NOW SHOWS THE MOST SELF-CONTROL I'VE EVER SHOWN!
(IT'S A COMPLICATED FEELING.)
TELL ME THAT'S NOT REALLY IT.
GUYS! GUYS GUYS GUYS!
I CAUGHT HIM ABOUT TO SNIPE YOU, I DOVE IN TO STOP IT AND THEN I TRIED TO ESTABLISH A CIRCLE OF TRUST WITH FRANK CASTLE SO THAT HE WOULD CONFIDE IN ME WHAT HE KNOWS ABOUT DIAMONDBACK SO THEN I COULD TELL YOU.
(BUT MOSTLY THE FIRST THING...)
WHICH IS EXACTLY WHAT SHE BLACKMAILED ME INTO DOING!
HELPING YOU FIND DIAMONDBACK! AH-DOY!
BLACKMAILED?
YOU OWE ME AND AGREED TO HELP WHEN I ASKED.
YOU CALLING IN THE MARKER IS, IN ITSELF, A FORM OF BLACKMAIL.
BABE...
...HIT HIM AGAIN.
WITH YOUR ENTIRE FIST.
HOW WOULD FRANK CASTLE TRUST YOU IF YOU'RE THE ONE THAT STOPPED HIM FROM ASSASSINATING ME?
BECAUSE, HELLO--UH, DUH!
UM...
HMM.
IT MADE SENSE IN MY HEAD.
I CAN TAKE IT BACK TO MY DESK AND WORKSHOP IT.

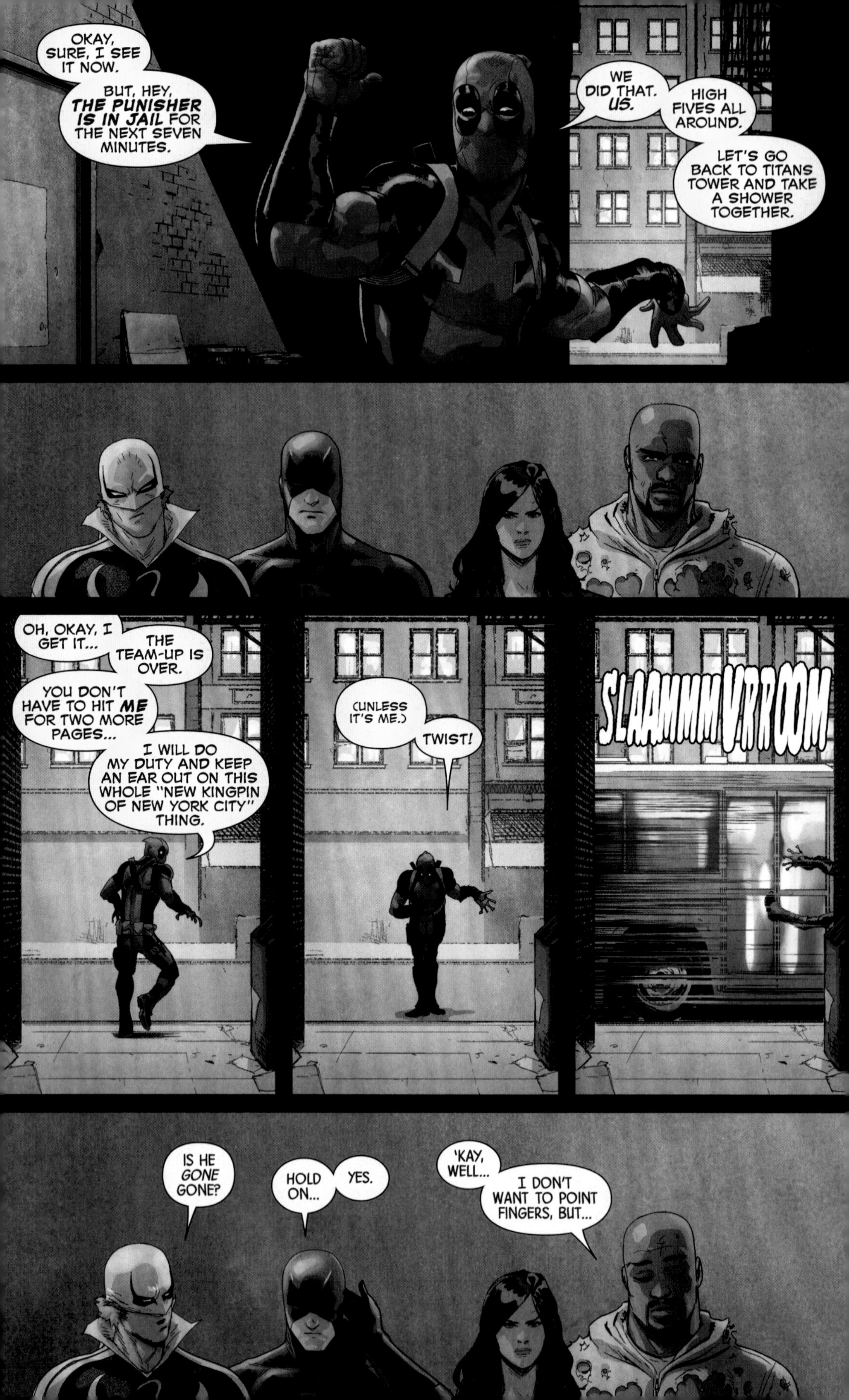
OKAY, SURE, I SEE IT NOW.
BUT, HEY, THE PUNISHER IS IN JAIL FOR THE NEXT SEVEN MINUTES.
WE DID THAT. US.
HIGH FIVES ALL AROUND.
LET'S GO BACK TO TITANS TOWER AND TAKE A SHOWER TOGETHER.
OH, OKAY, I GET IT...
THE TEAM-UP IS OVER.
YOU DON'T HAVE TO HIT ME FOR TWO MORE PAGES...
I WILL DO MY DUTY AND KEEP AN EAR OUT ON THIS WHOLE "NEW KINGPIN OF NEW YORK CITY" THING.
(UNLESS IT'S ME.)
TWIST!
SLAAMMM VRROOM
IS HE GONE GONE?
HOLD ON...
YES.
'KAY, WELL...
I DON'T WANT TO POINT FINGERS, BUT...

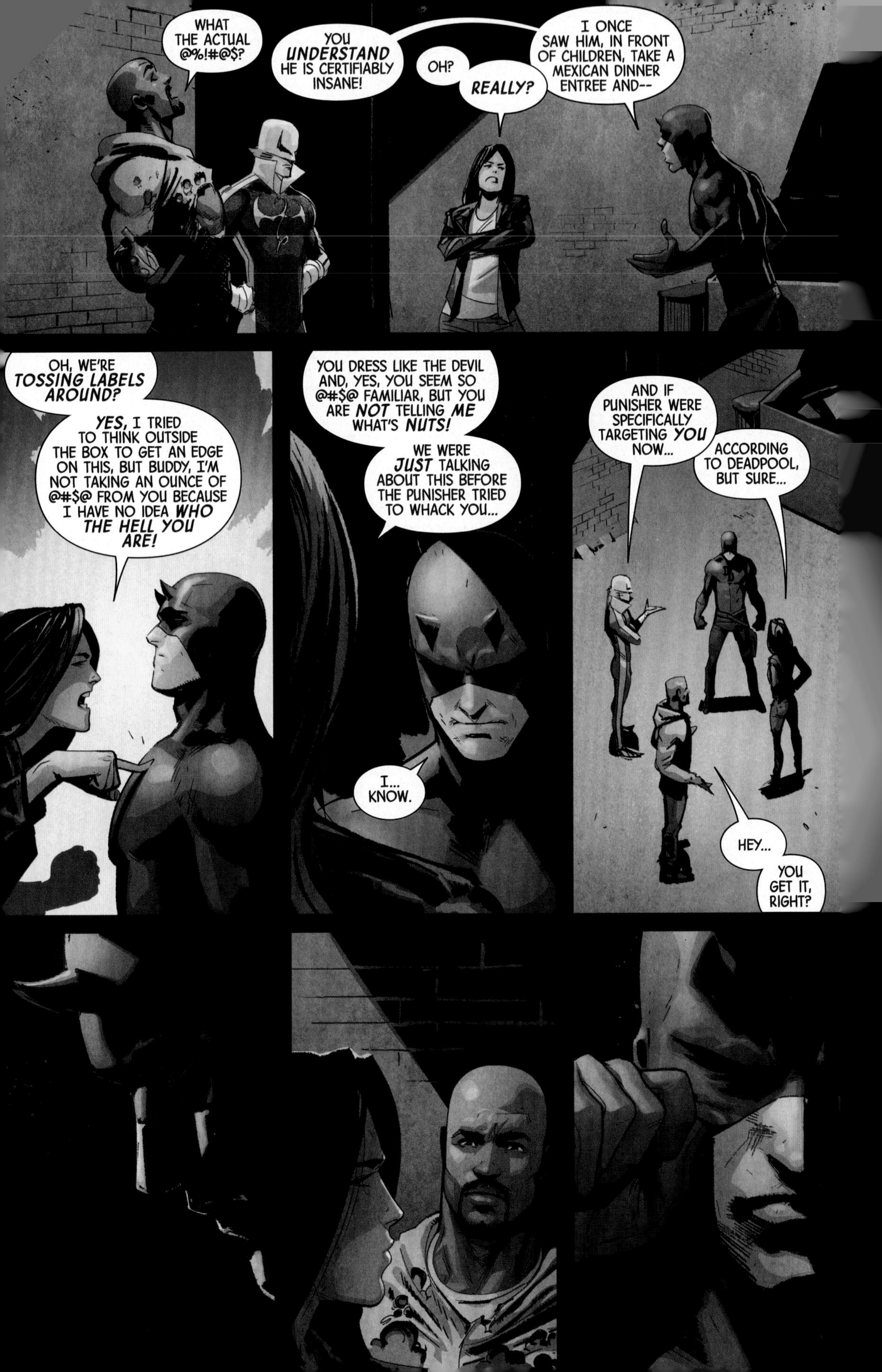
WHAT THE ACTUAL @%!#@$?
YOU UNDERSTAND HE IS CERTIFIABLY INSANE!
OH?
REALLY?
I ONCE SAW HIM, IN FRONT OF CHILDREN, TAKE A MEXICAN DINNER ENTREE AND--
OH, WE'RE TOSSING LABELS AROUND?
YES, I TRIED TO THINK OUTSIDE THE BOX TO GET AN EDGE ON THIS, BUT BUDDY, I'M NOT TAKING AN OUNCE OF @#$@ FROM YOU BECAUSE I HAVE NO IDEA WHO THE HELL YOU ARE!
YOU DRESS LIKE THE DEVIL AND, YES, YOU SEEM SO @#$@ FAMILIAR, BUT YOU ARE NOT TELLING ME WHAT'S NUTS!
WE WERE JUST TALKING ABOUT THIS BEFORE THE PUNISHER TRIED TO WHACK YOU...
I... KNOW.
AND IF PUNISHER WERE SPECIFICALLY TARGETING YOU NOW...
ACCORDING TO DEADPOOL, BUT SURE...
HEY...
YOU GET IT, RIGHT?

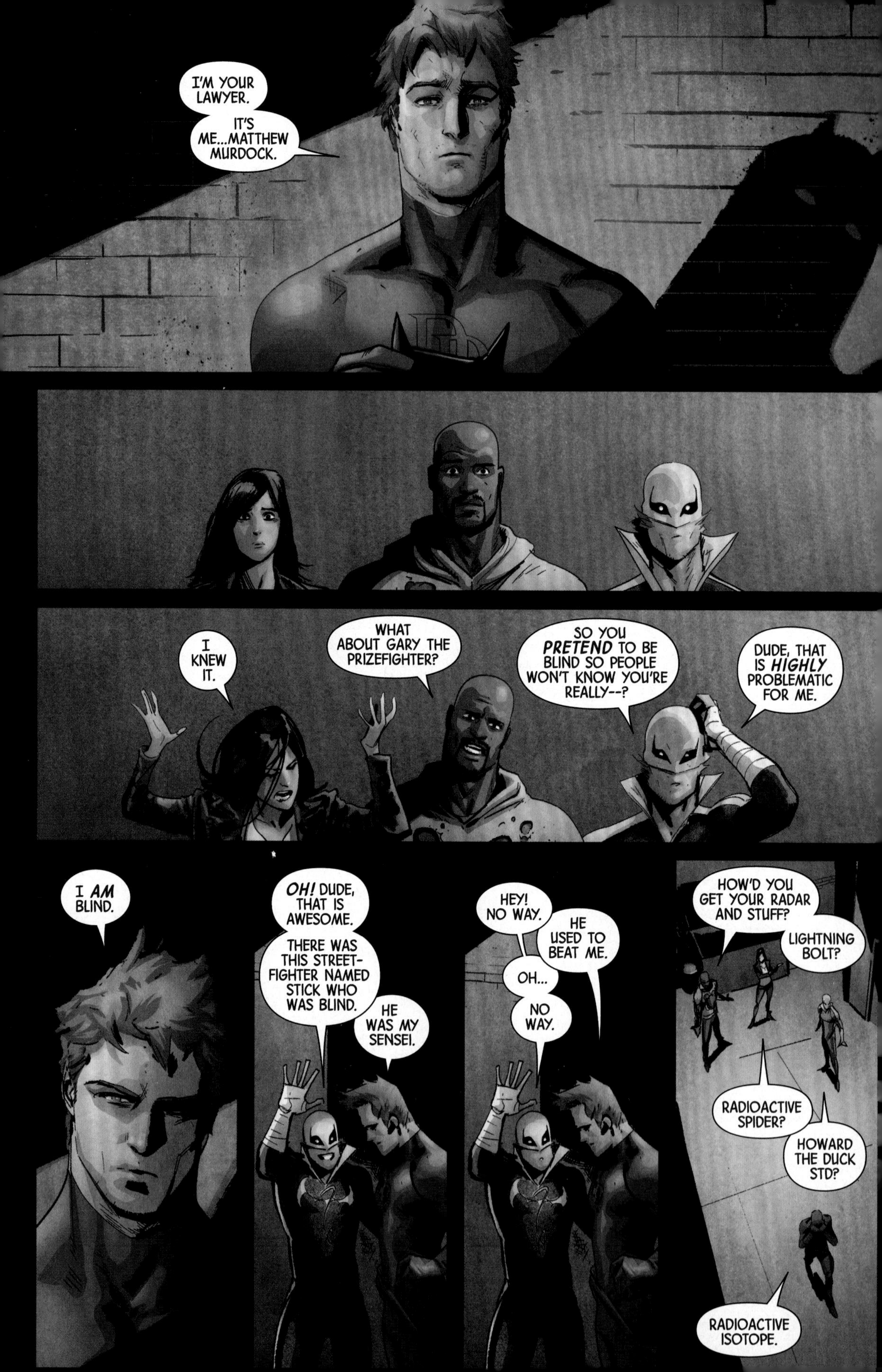

I'M YOUR LAWYER.
IT'S ME...MATTHEW MURDOCK.
I KNEW IT.
WHAT ABOUT GARY THE PRIZEFIGHTER?
SO YOU PRETEND TO BE BLIND SO PEOPLE WON'T KNOW YOU'RE REALLY--?
DUDE, THAT IS HIGHLY PROBLEMATIC FOR ME.
I AM BLIND.
OH! DUDE, THAT IS AWESOME.
THERE WAS THIS STREET-FIGHTER NAMED STICK WHO WAS BLIND.
HE WAS MY SENSEI.
HEY! NO WAY.
HE USED TO BEAT ME.
OH...
NO WAY.
HOW'D YOU GET YOUR RADAR AND STUFF?
LIGHTNING BOLT?
RADIOACTIVE SPIDER?
HOWARD THE DUCK STD?
RADIOACTIVE ISOTOPE.

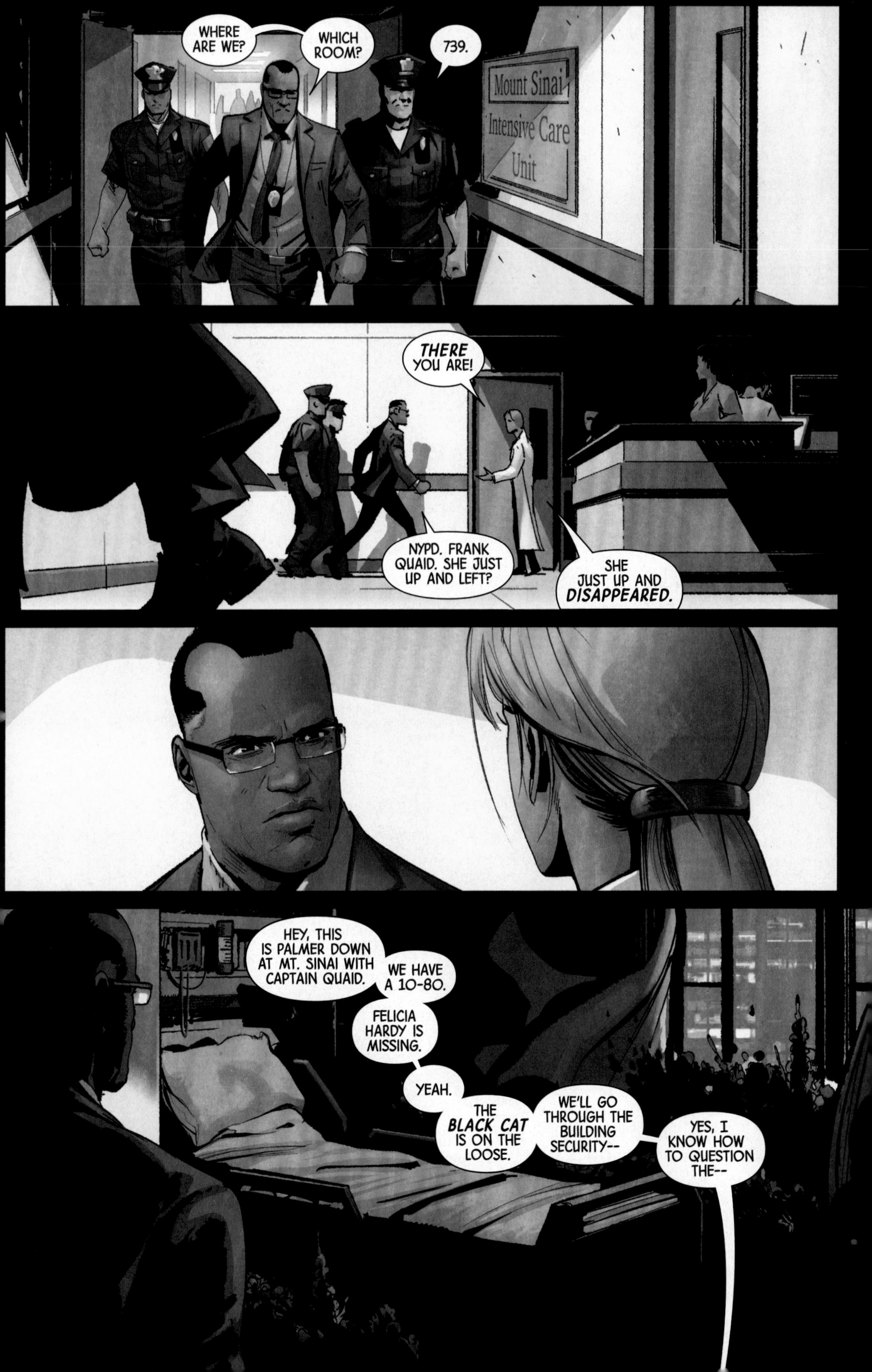
WHERE ARE WE?
WHICH ROOM?
739.
Mount Sinai Intensive Care Unit
THERE YOU ARE!
NYPD. FRANK QUAID. SHE JUST UP AND LEFT?
SHE JUST UP AND DISAPPEARED.
HEY, THIS IS PALMER DOWN AT MT. SINAI WITH CAPTAIN QUAID.
WE HAVE A 10-80.
FELICIA HARDY IS MISSING.
YEAH.
THE BLACK CAT IS ON THE LOOSE.
WE'LL GO THROUGH THE BUILDING SECURITY--
YES, I KNOW HOW TO QUESTION THE--

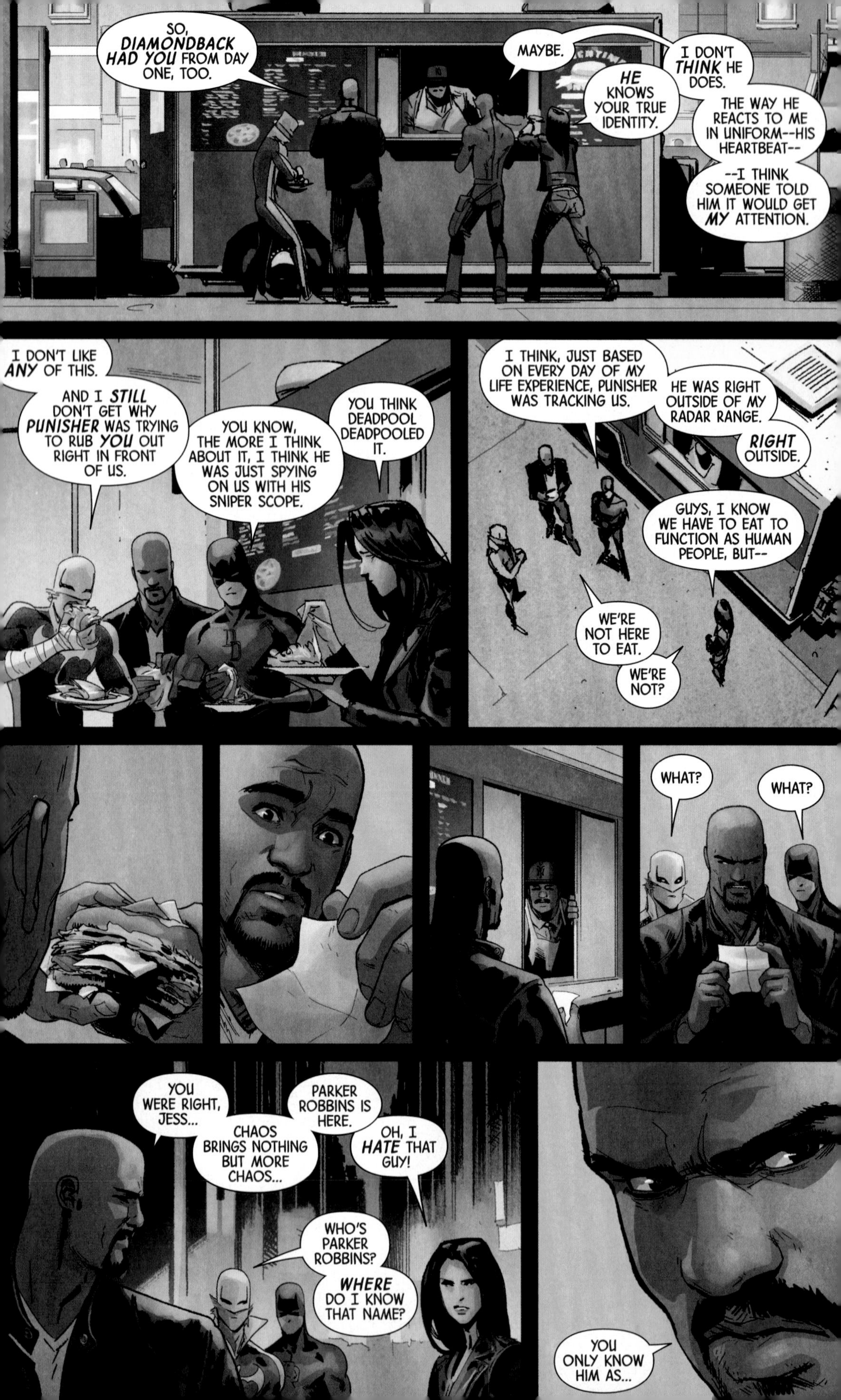
SO, DIAMONDBACK HAD YOU FROM DAY ONE, TOO.
MAYBE.
HE KNOWS YOUR TRUE IDENTITY.
I DON'T THINK HE DOES.
THE WAY HE REACTS TO ME IN UNIFORM--HIS HEARTBEAT--
--I THINK SOMEONE TOLD HIM IT WOULD GET MY ATTENTION.
I DON'T LIKE ANY OF THIS.
AND I STILL DON'T GET WHY PUNISHER WAS TRYING TO RUB YOU OUT RIGHT IN FRONT OF US.
YOU KNOW, THE MORE I THINK ABOUT IT, I THINK HE WAS JUST SPYING ON US WITH HIS SNIPER SCOPE.
YOU THINK DEADPOOL DEADPOOLED IT.
I THINK, JUST BASED ON EVERY DAY OF MY LIFE EXPERIENCE, PUNISHER WAS TRACKING US.
HE WAS RIGHT OUTSIDE OF MY RADAR RANGE.
RIGHT OUTSIDE.
GUYS, I KNOW WE HAVE TO EAT TO FUNCTION AS HUMAN PEOPLE, BUT--
WE'RE NOT HERE TO EAT.
WE'RE NOT?
WHAT?
WHAT?
YOU WERE RIGHT, JESS...
CHAOS BRINGS NOTHING BUT MORE CHAOS...
PARKER ROBBINS IS HERE.
OH, I HATE THAT GUY!
WHO'S PARKER ROBBINS?
WHERE DO I KNOW THAT NAME?
YOU ONLY KNOW HIM AS...

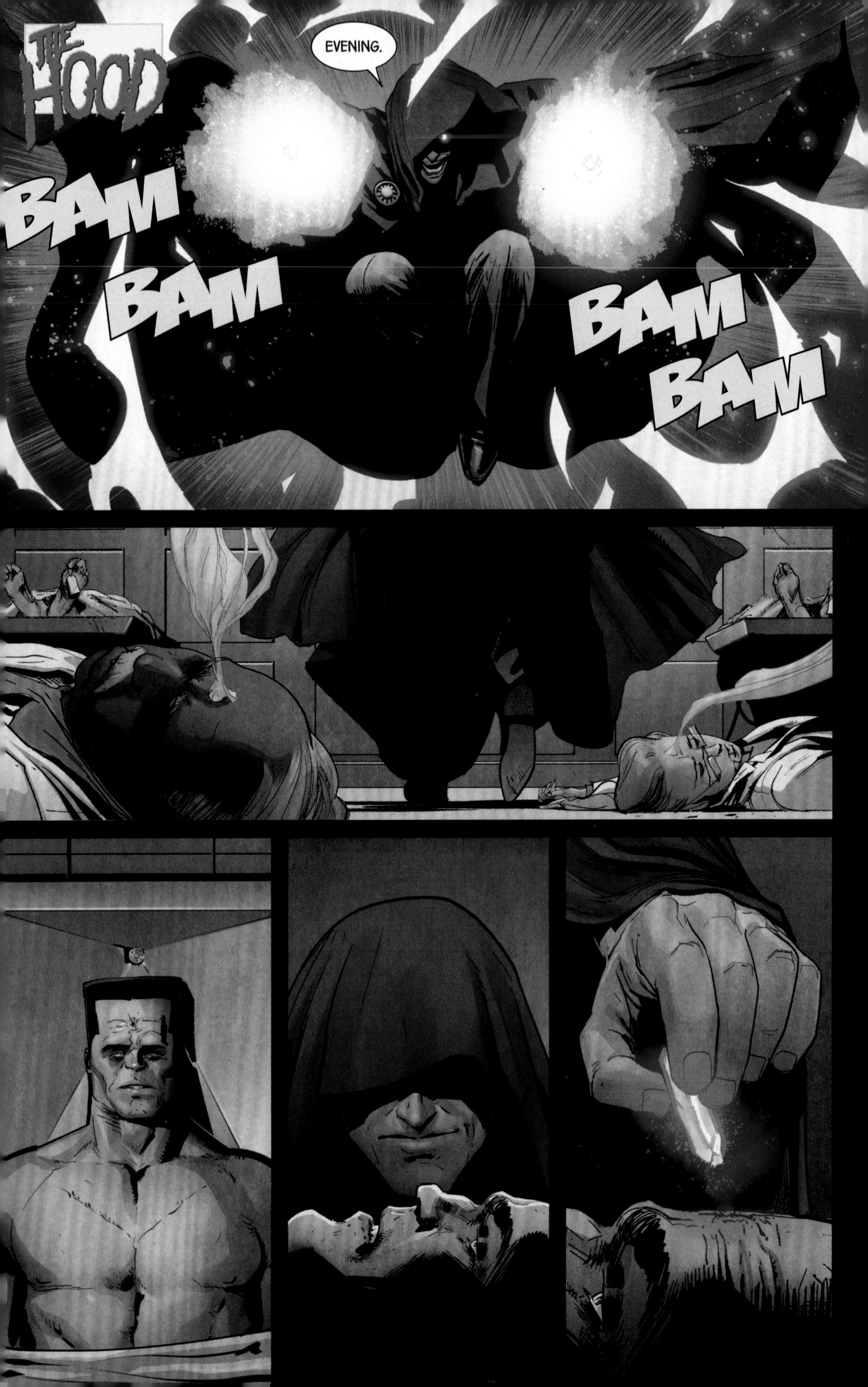
THE HOOD
EVENING.
BAM
BAM
BAM
BAM

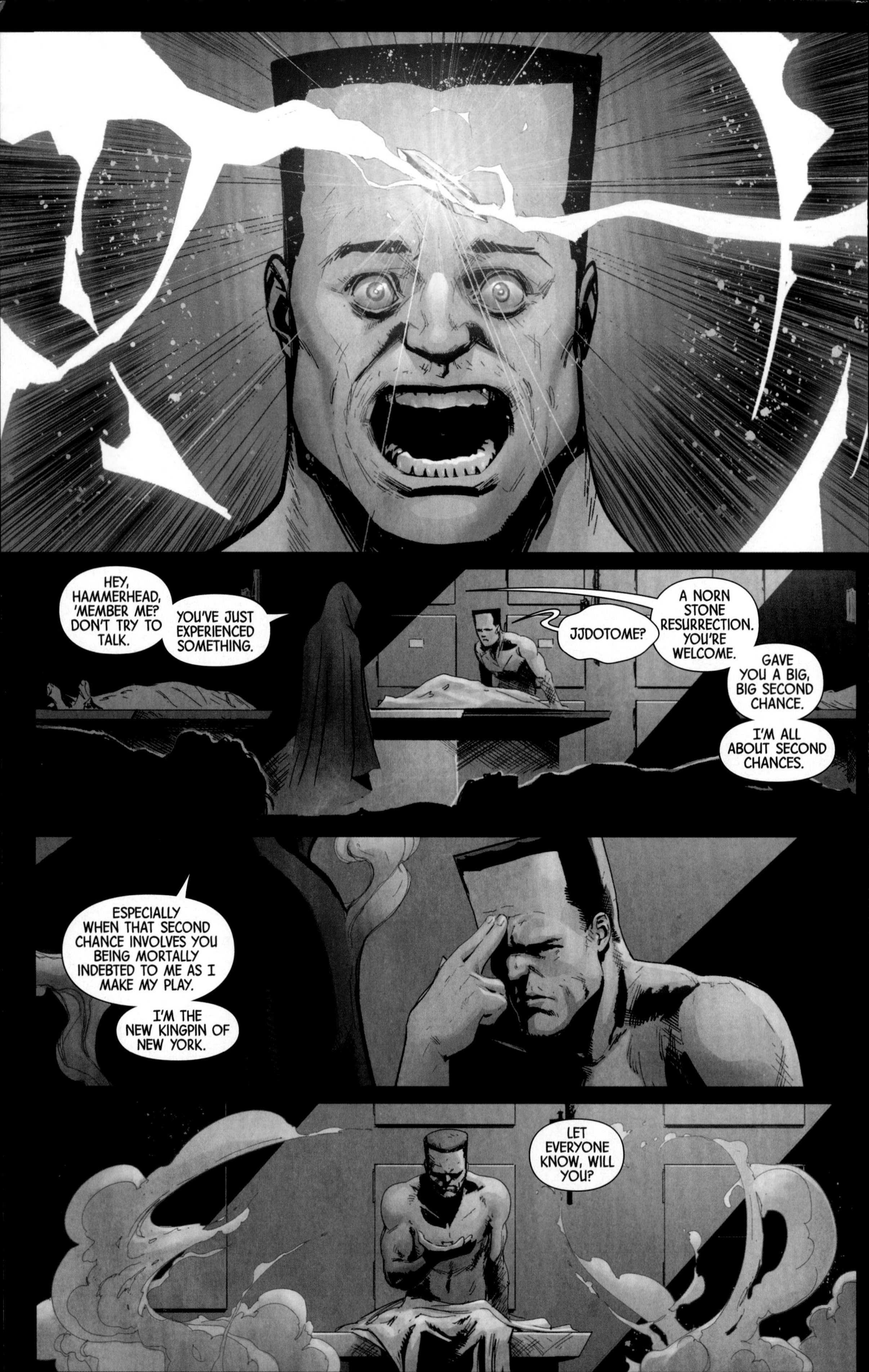
HEY, HAMMERHEAD, 'MEMBER ME? DON'T TRY TO TALK.
YOU'VE JUST EXPERIENCED SOMETHING.
JJDOTOME?
A NORN STONE RESURRECTION. YOU'RE WELCOME.
GAVE YOU A BIG, BIG SECOND CHANCE.
I'M ALL ABOUT SECOND CHANCES.
ESPECIALLY WHEN THAT SECOND CHANCE INVOLVES YOU BEING MORTALLY INDEBTED TO ME AS I MAKE MY PLAY.
I'M THE NEW KINGPIN OF NEW YORK.
LET EVERYONE KNOW, WILL YOU?

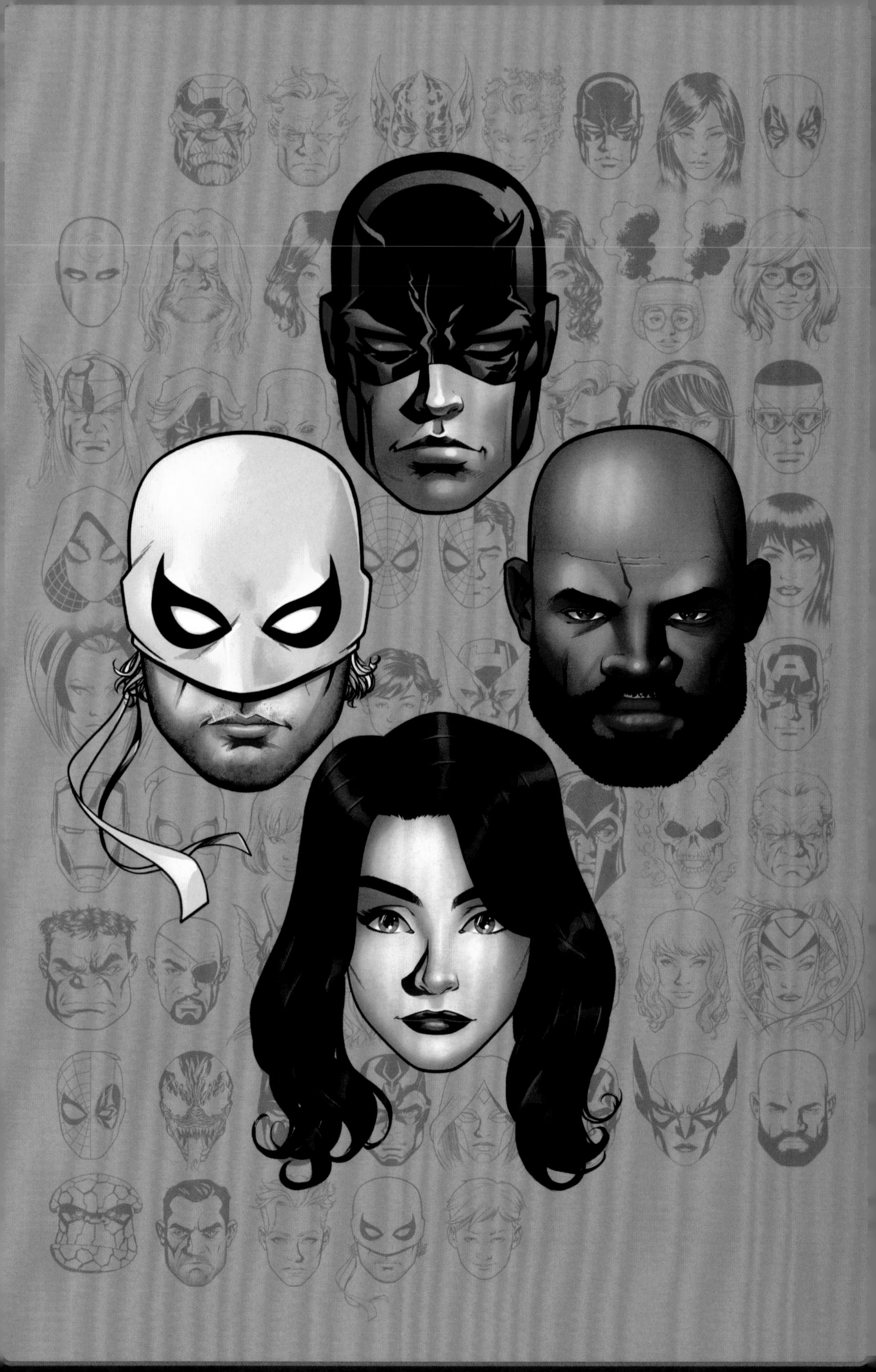

NO. 6 LEGACY HEADSHOT VARIANT BY
MIKE McKONE, ANDY TROY & RACHELLE ROSENBERG

9

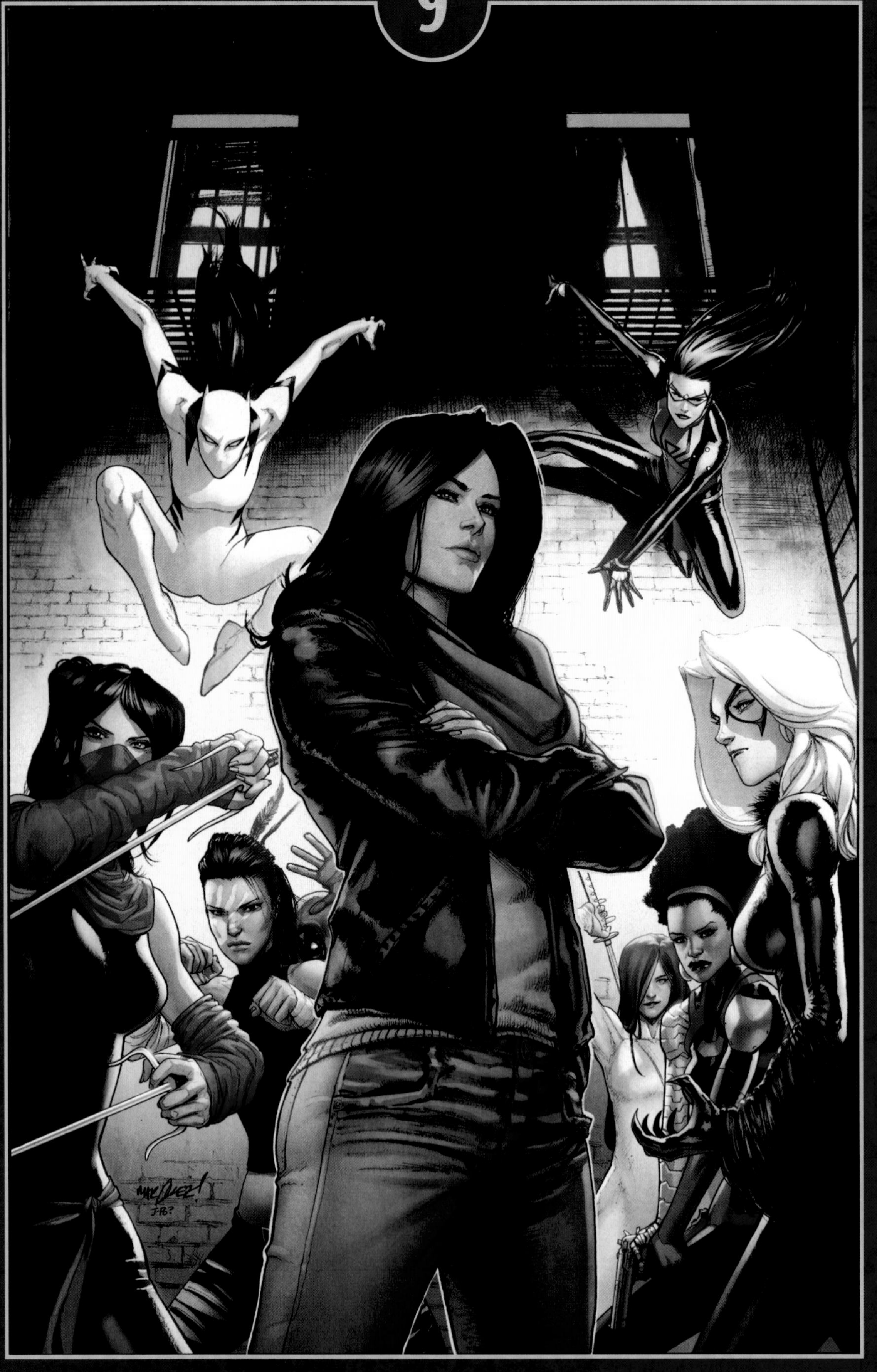

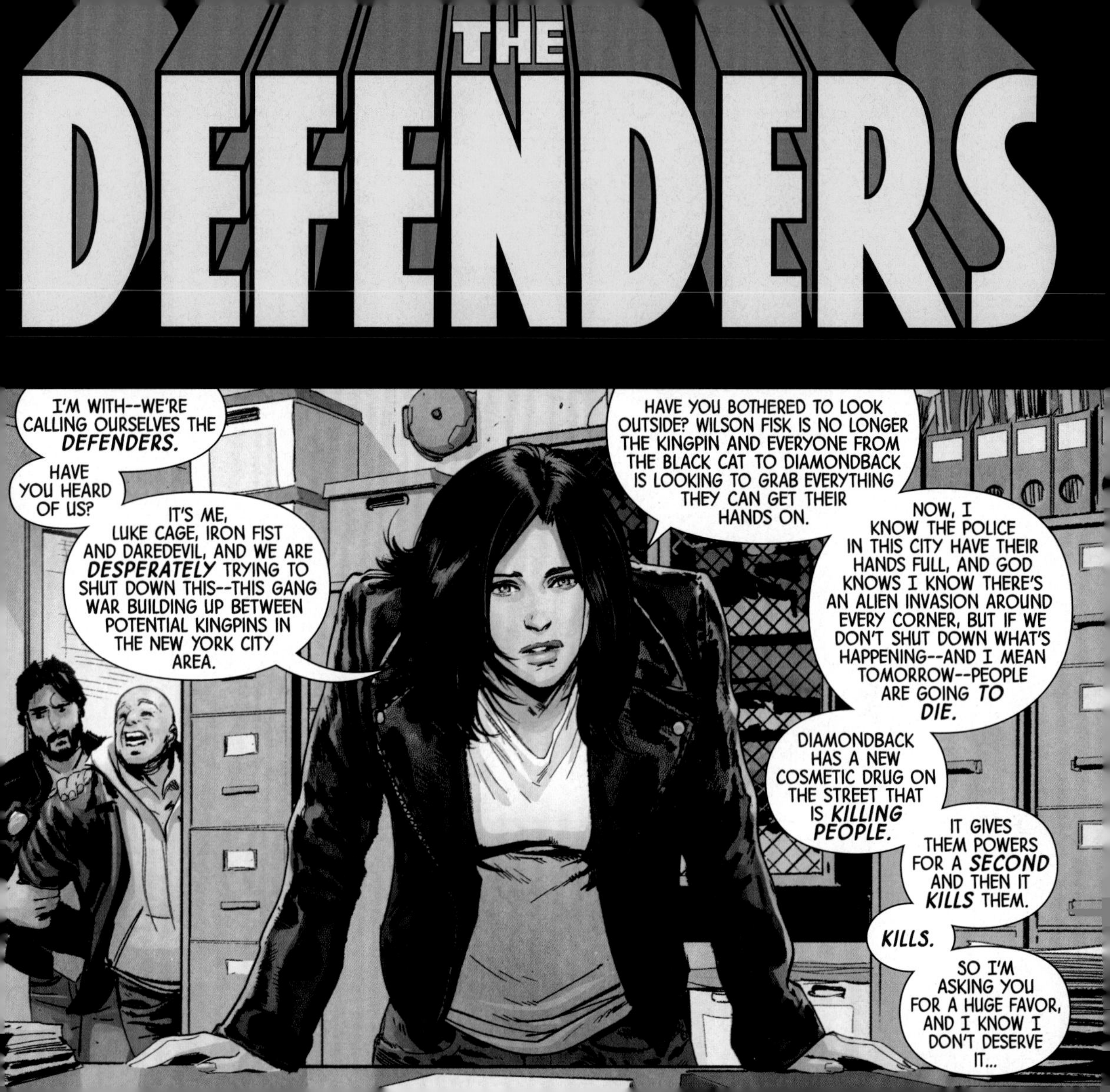
THE DEFENDERS
I'M WITH--WE'RE CALLING OURSELVES THE *DEFENDERS.*
HAVE YOU HEARD OF US?
IT'S ME, LUKE CAGE, IRON FIST AND DAREDEVIL, AND WE ARE *DESPERATELY* TRYING TO SHUT DOWN THIS--THIS GANG WAR BUILDING UP BETWEEN POTENTIAL KINGPINS IN THE NEW YORK CITY AREA.
HAVE YOU BOTHERED TO LOOK OUTSIDE? WILSON FISK IS NO LONGER THE KINGPIN AND EVERYONE FROM THE BLACK CAT TO DIAMONDBACK IS LOOKING TO GRAB EVERYTHING THEY CAN GET THEIR HANDS ON.
NOW, I KNOW THE POLICE IN THIS CITY HAVE THEIR HANDS FULL, AND GOD KNOWS I KNOW THERE'S AN ALIEN INVASION AROUND EVERY CORNER, BUT IF WE DON'T SHUT DOWN WHAT'S HAPPENING--AND I MEAN TOMORROW--PEOPLE ARE GOING *TO DIE.*
DIAMONDBACK HAS A NEW COSMETIC DRUG ON THE STREET THAT IS *KILLING PEOPLE.*
IT GIVES THEM POWERS FOR A *SECOND* AND THEN IT *KILLS* THEM.
KILLS.
SO I'M ASKING YOU FOR A HUGE FAVOR, AND I KNOW I DON'T DESERVE IT...

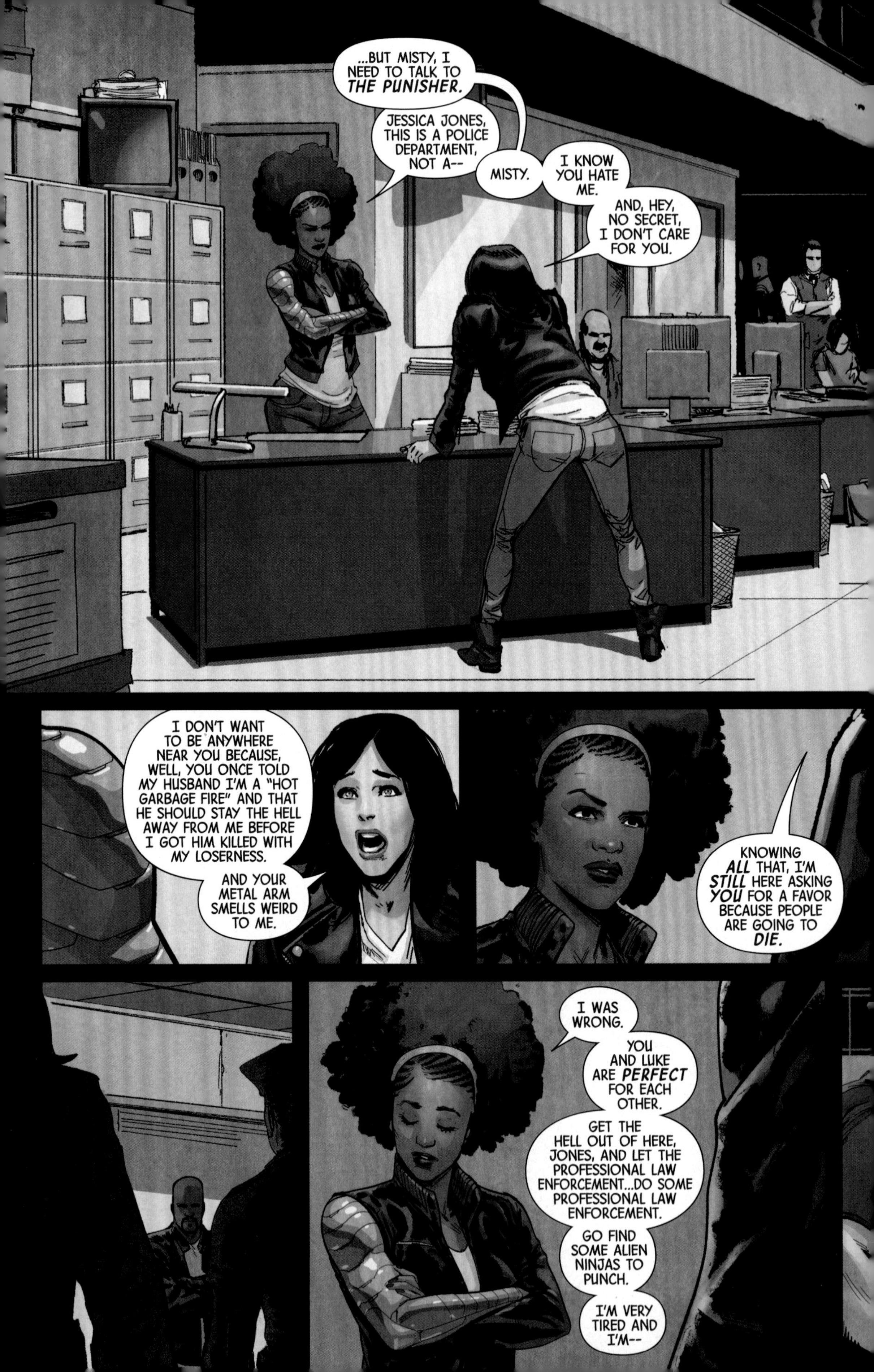
...BUT MISTY, I NEED TO TALK TO *THE PUNISHER.*
JESSICA JONES, THIS IS A POLICE DEPARTMENT, NOT A--
MISTY.
I KNOW YOU HATE ME.
AND, HEY, NO SECRET, I DON'T CARE FOR YOU.
I DON'T WANT TO BE ANYWHERE NEAR YOU BECAUSE, WELL, YOU ONCE TOLD MY HUSBAND I'M A "HOT GARBAGE FIRE" AND THAT HE SHOULD STAY THE HELL AWAY FROM ME BEFORE I GOT HIM KILLED WITH MY LOSERNESS.
AND YOUR METAL ARM SMELLS WEIRD TO ME.
KNOWING *ALL* THAT, I'M *STILL* HERE ASKING *YOU* FOR A FAVOR BECAUSE PEOPLE ARE GOING TO *DIE.*
I WAS WRONG.
YOU AND LUKE ARE *PERFECT* FOR EACH OTHER.
GET THE HELL OUT OF HERE, JONES, AND LET THE PROFESSIONAL LAW ENFORCEMENT...DO SOME PROFESSIONAL LAW ENFORCEMENT.
GO FIND SOME ALIEN NINJAS TO PUNCH.
I'M VERY TIRED AND I'M--

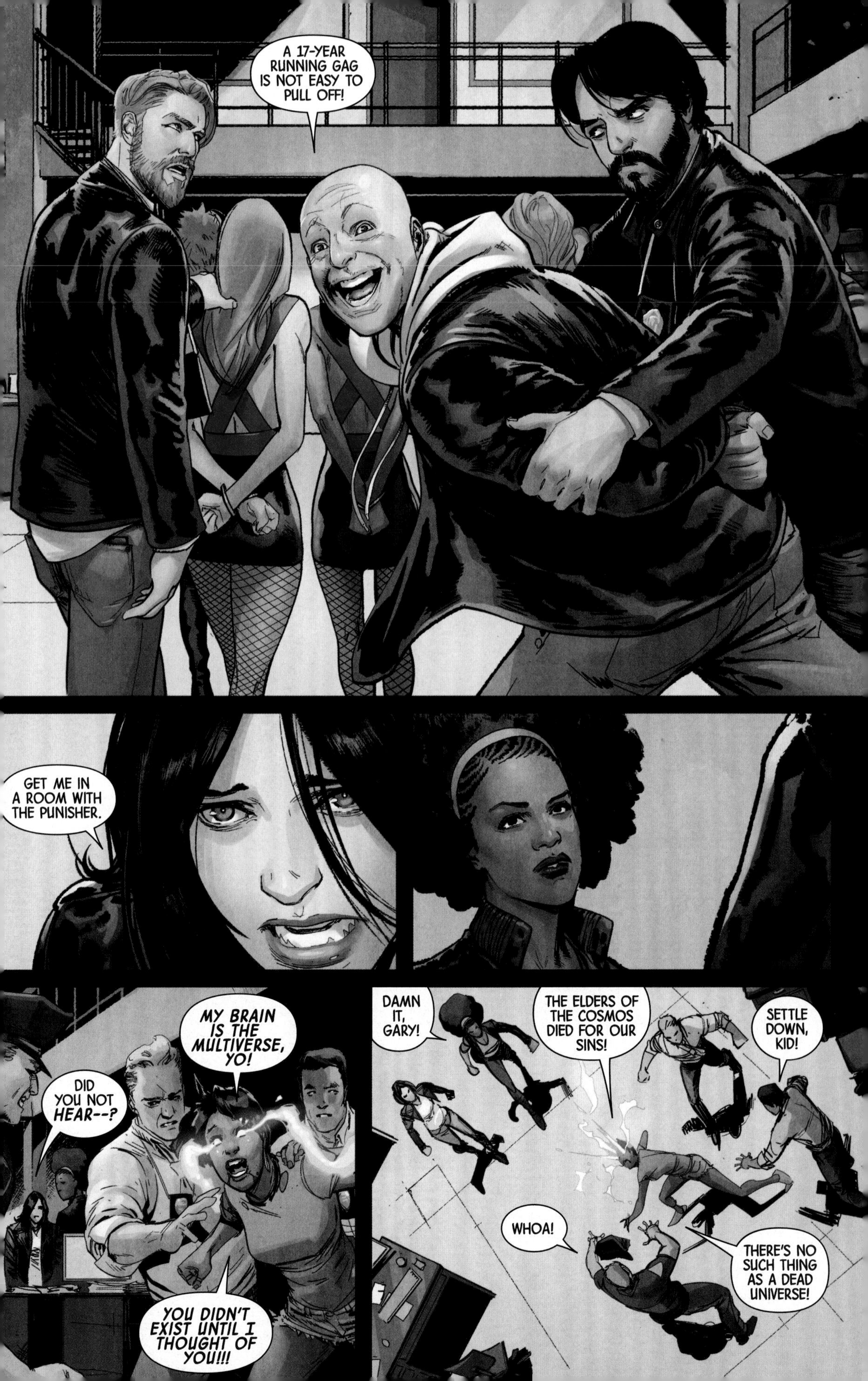
A 17-YEAR RUNNING GAG IS NOT EASY TO PULL OFF!
GET ME IN A ROOM WITH THE PUNISHER.
MY BRAIN IS THE MULTIVERSE, YO!
DID YOU NOT HEAR--?
YOU DIDN'T EXIST UNTIL I THOUGHT OF YOU!!!
DAMN IT, GARY!
THE ELDERS OF THE COSMOS DIED FOR OUR SINS!
SETTLE DOWN, KID!
WHOA!
THERE'S NO SUCH THING AS A DEAD UNIVERSE!

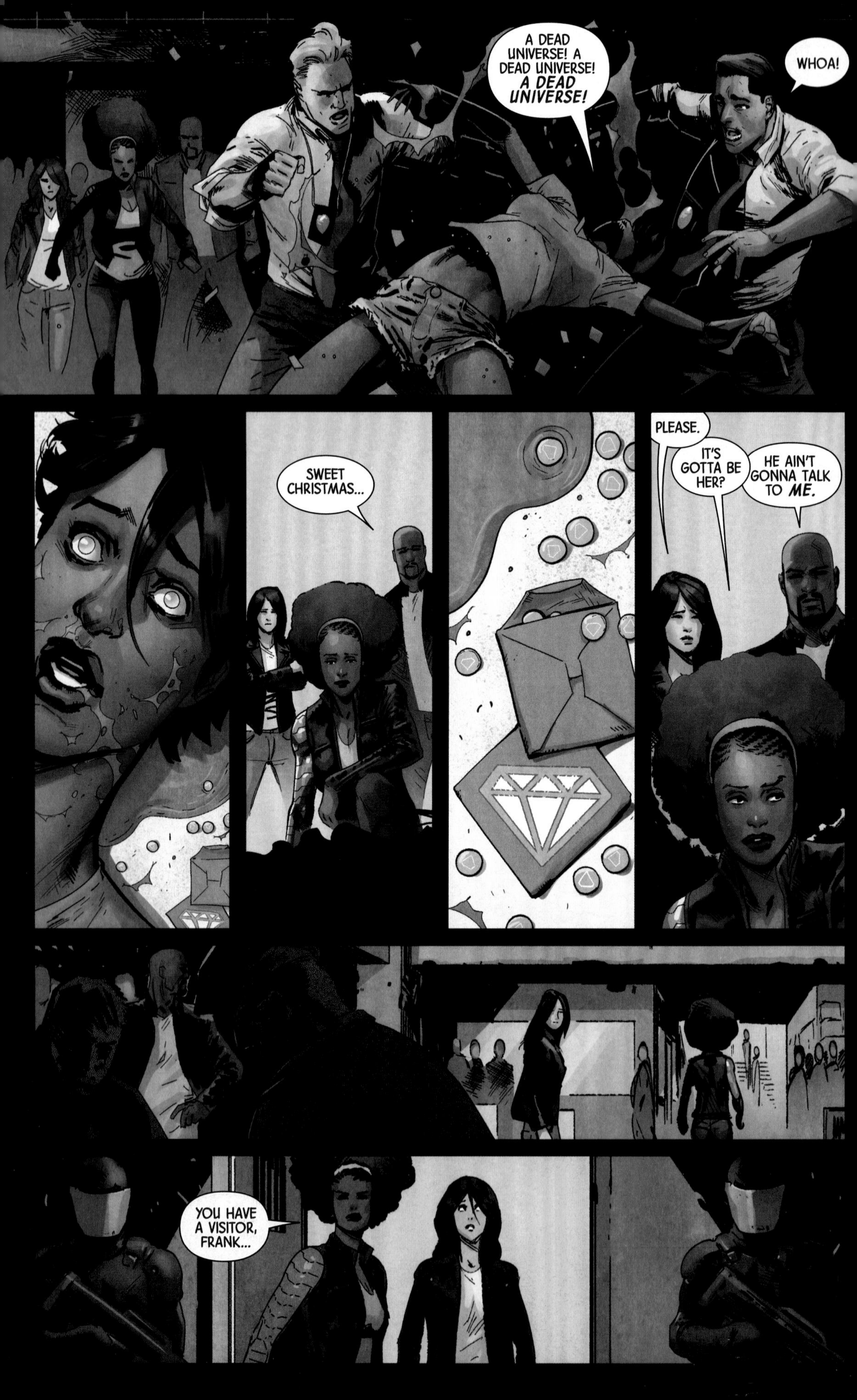
A DEAD UNIVERSE! A DEAD UNIVERSE! A DEAD UNIVERSE!
WHOA!
SWEET CHRISTMAS...
PLEASE.
IT'S GOTTA BE HER?
HE AIN'T GONNA TALK TO ME.
YOU HAVE A VISITOR, FRANK...

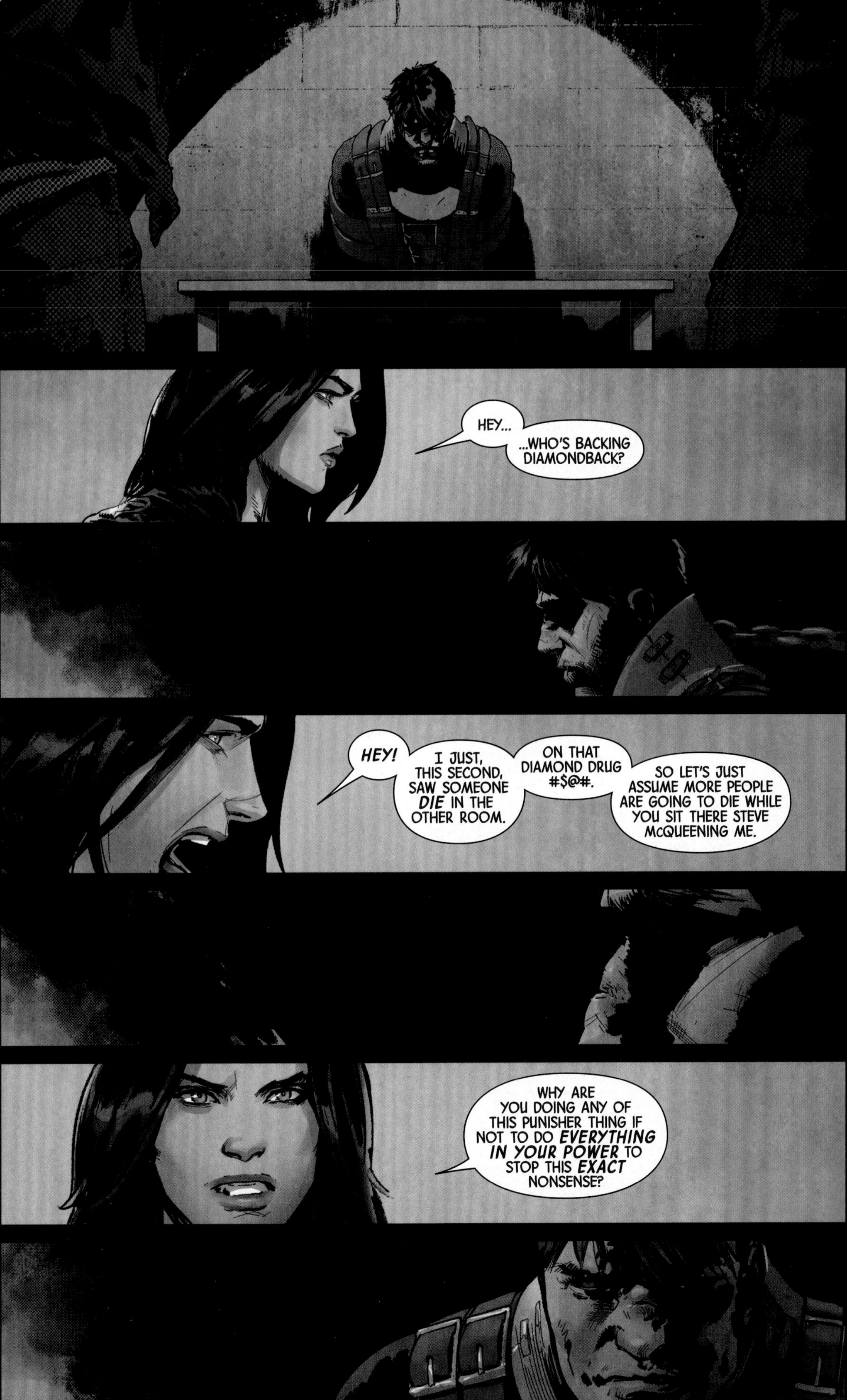
HEY...
...WHO'S BACKING DIAMONDBACK?
HEY!
I JUST, THIS SECOND, SAW SOMEONE DIE IN THE OTHER ROOM.
ON THAT DIAMOND DRUG #$@#.
SO LET'S JUST ASSUME MORE PEOPLE ARE GOING TO DIE WHILE YOU SIT THERE STEVE McQUEENING ME.
WHY ARE YOU DOING ANY OF THIS PUNISHER THING IF NOT TO DO EVERYTHING IN YOUR POWER TO STOP THIS EXACT NONSENSE?

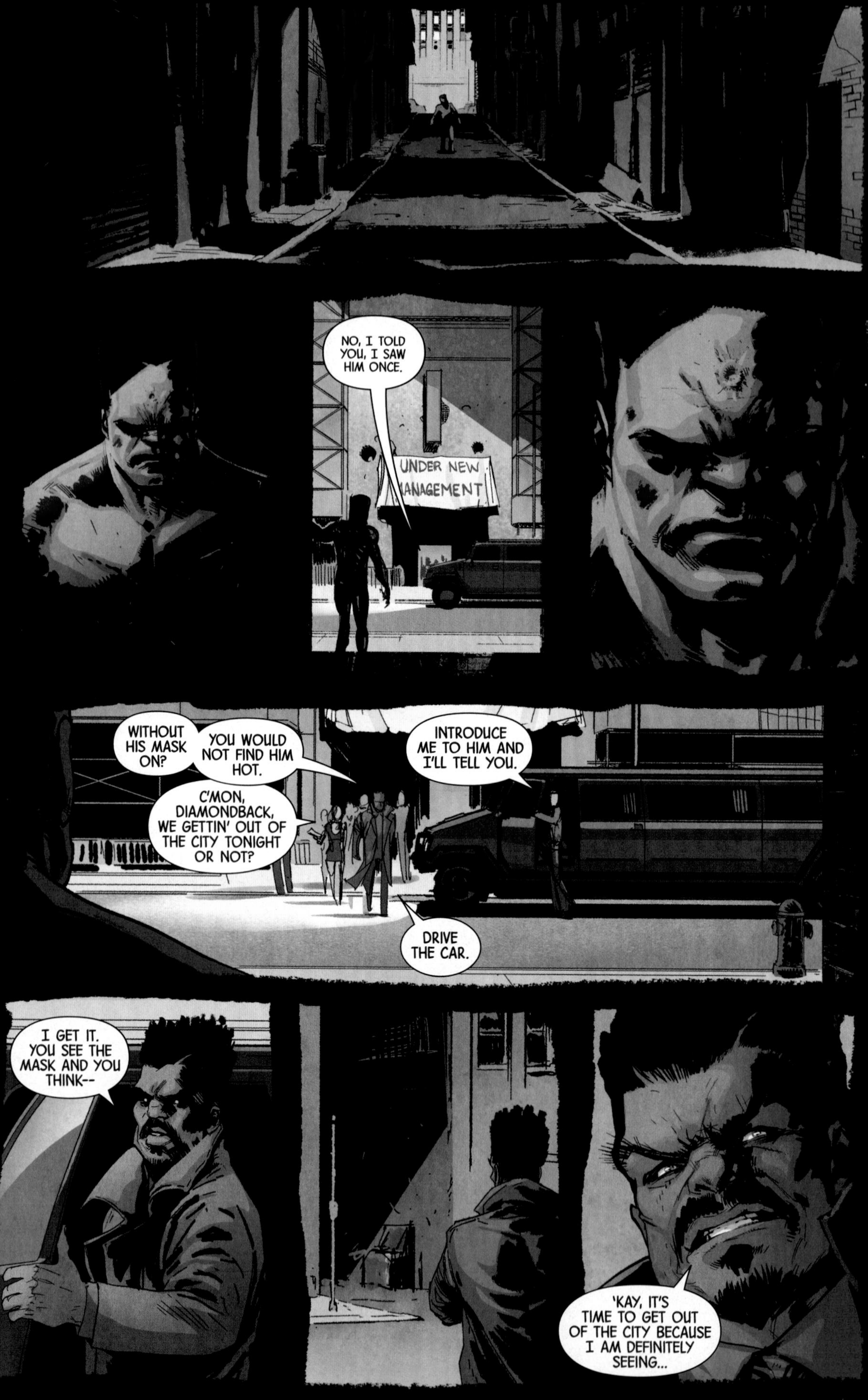

NO, I TOLD YOU, I SAW HIM ONCE.
UNDER NEW MANAGEMENT
WITHOUT HIS MASK ON?
YOU WOULD NOT FIND HIM HOT.
INTRODUCE ME TO HIM AND I'LL TELL YOU.
C'MON, DIAMONDBACK, WE GETTIN' OUT OF THE CITY TONIGHT OR NOT?
DRIVE THE CAR.
I GET IT. YOU SEE THE MASK AND YOU THINK--
'KAY, IT'S TIME TO GET OUT OF THE CITY BECAUSE I AM DEFINITELY SEEING...

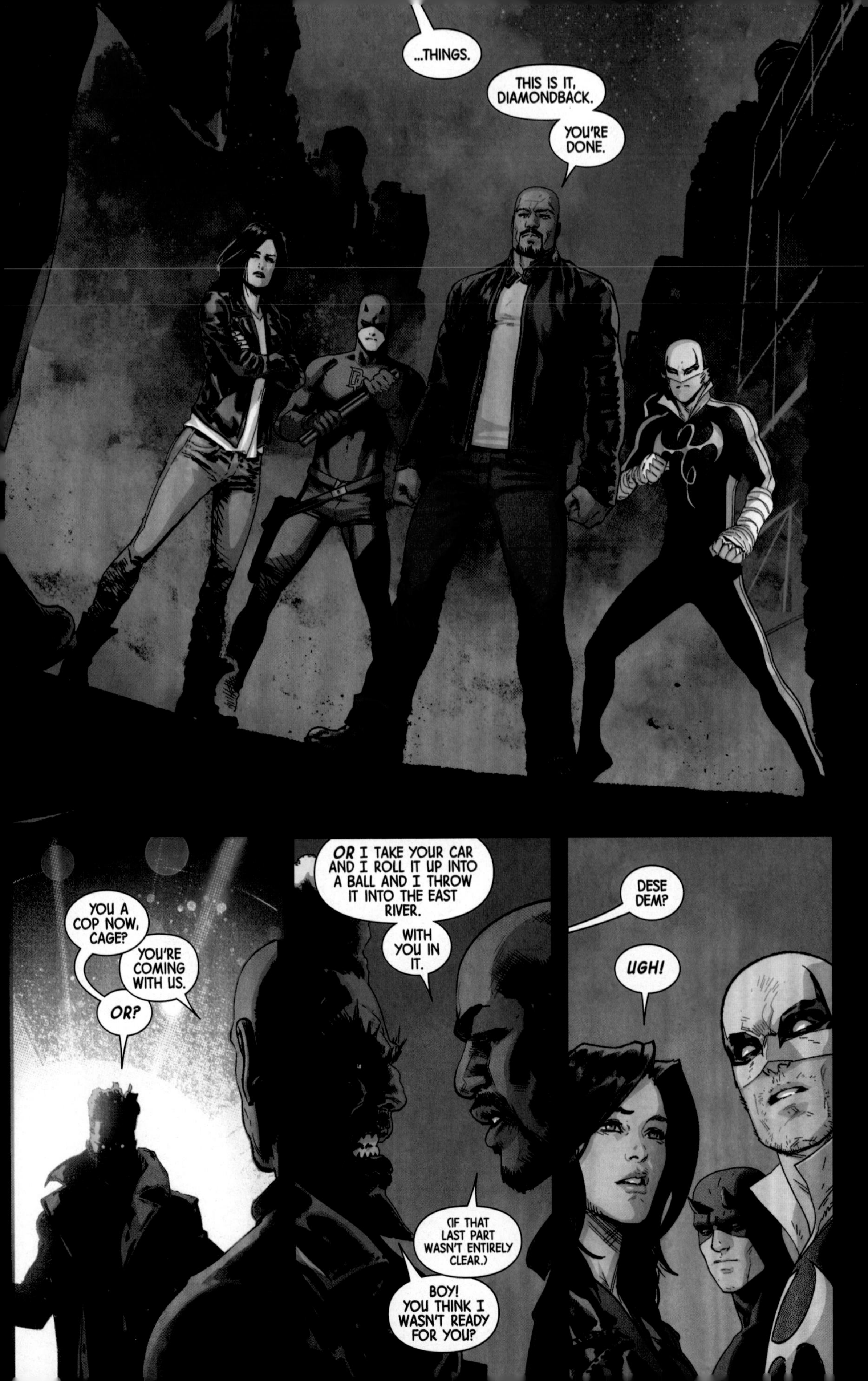
...THINGS.
THIS IS IT, DIAMONDBACK.
YOU'RE DONE.
YOU A COP NOW, CAGE?
YOU'RE COMING WITH US.
OR?
OR I TAKE YOUR CAR AND I ROLL IT UP INTO A BALL AND I THROW IT INTO THE EAST RIVER.
WITH YOU IN IT.
(IF THAT LAST PART WASN'T ENTIRELY CLEAR.)
BOY! YOU THINK I WASN'T READY FOR YOU?
DESE DEM?
UGH!

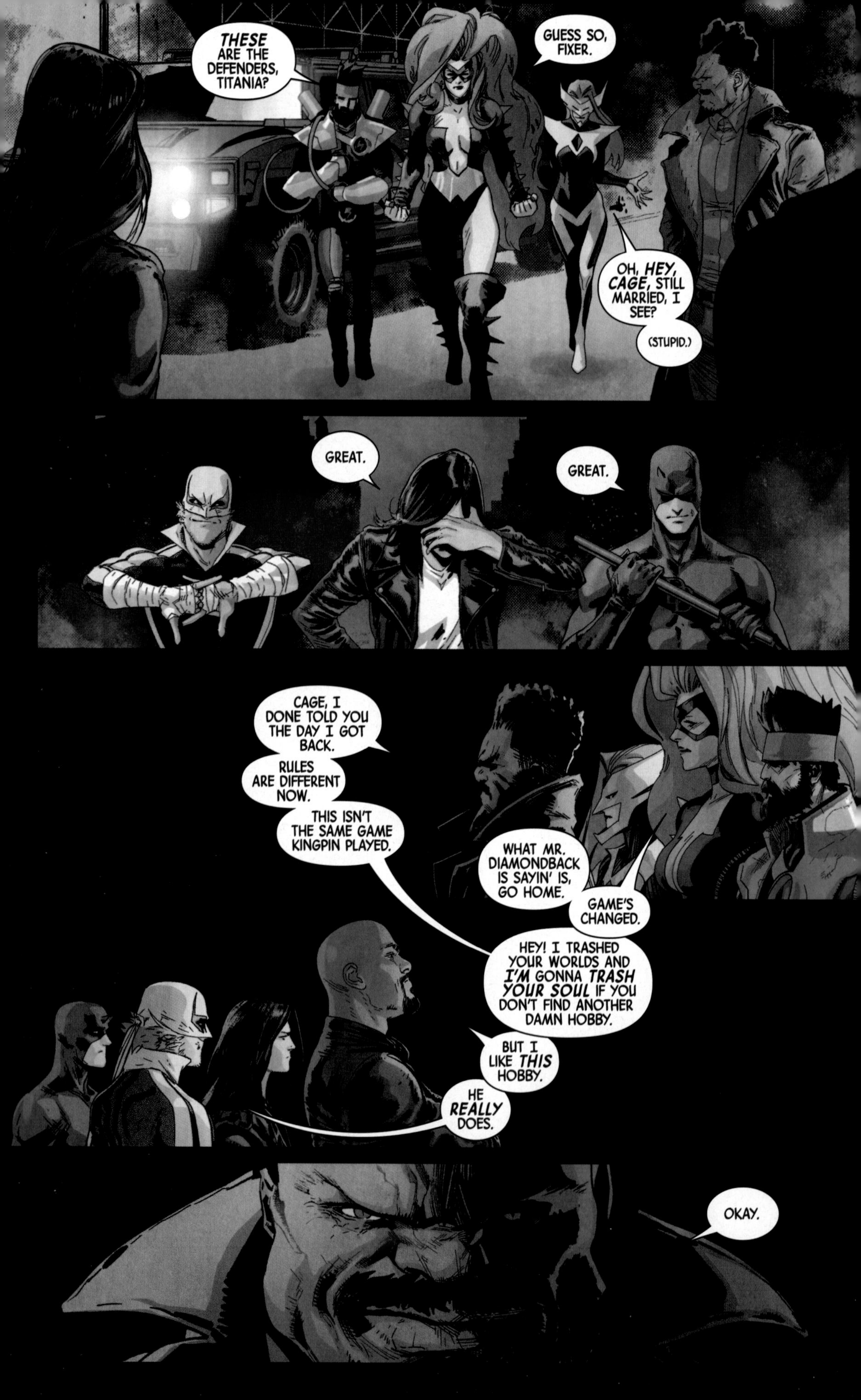
THESE ARE THE DEFENDERS, TITANIA?
GUESS SO, FIXER.
OH, HEY, CAGE, STILL MARRIED, I SEE?
(STUPID.)
GREAT.
GREAT.
CAGE, I DONE TOLD YOU THE DAY I GOT BACK.
RULES ARE DIFFERENT NOW.
THIS ISN'T THE SAME GAME KINGPIN PLAYED.
WHAT MR. DIAMONDBACK IS SAYIN' IS, GO HOME.
GAME'S CHANGED.
HEY! I TRASHED YOUR WORLDS AND I'M GONNA TRASH YOUR SOUL IF YOU DON'T FIND ANOTHER DAMN HOBBY.
BUT I LIKE THIS HOBBY.
HE REALLY DOES.
OKAY.

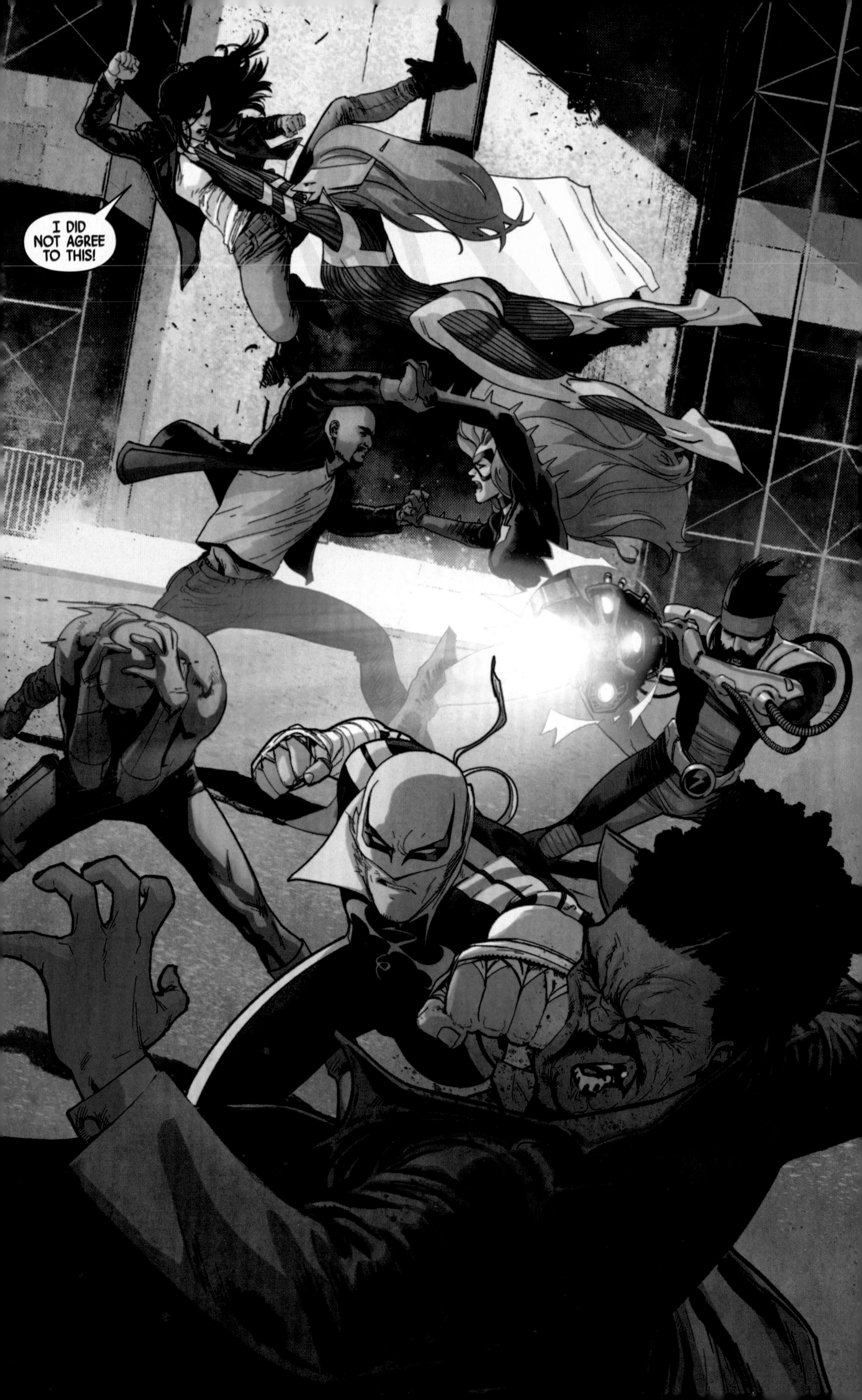
I DID NOT AGREE TO THIS!

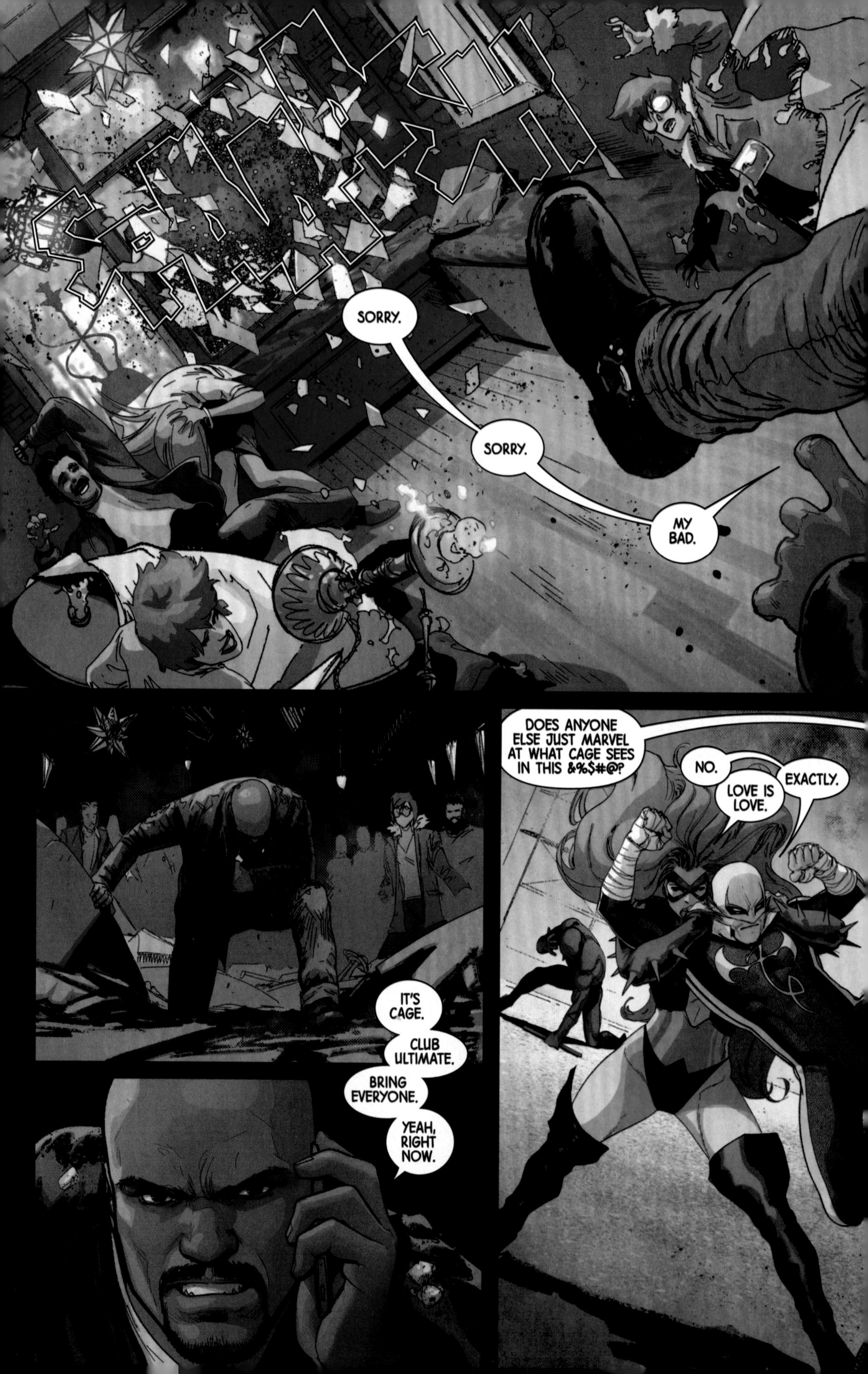
SORRY.
SORRY.
MY BAD.
IT'S CAGE.
CLUB ULTIMATE.
BRING EVERYONE.
YEAH, RIGHT NOW.
DOES ANYONE ELSE JUST MARVEL AT WHAT CAGE SEES IN THIS &%$#@?
NO.
LOVE IS LOVE.
EXACTLY.

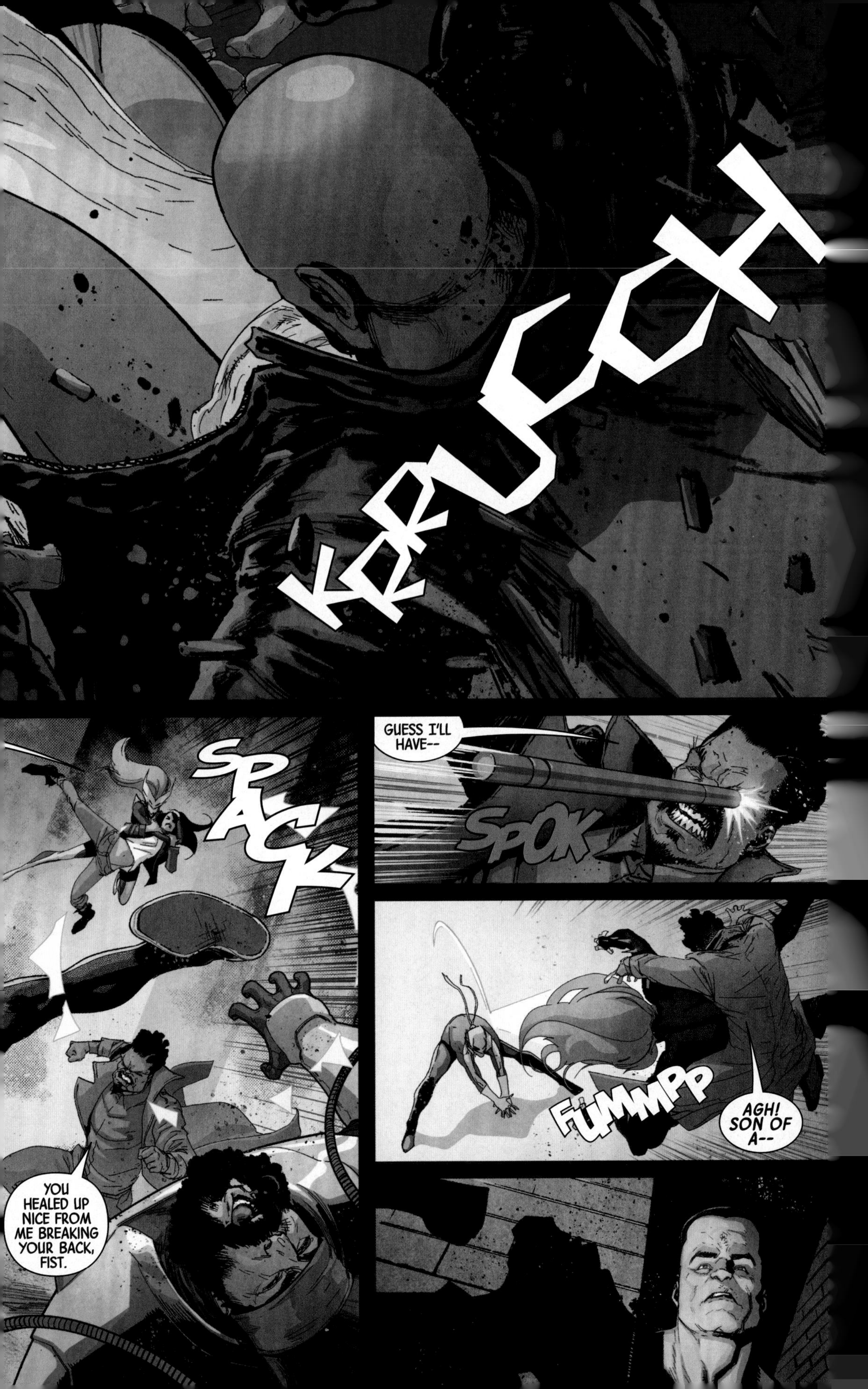
KKRUCCH
SPACK
GUESS I'LL HAVE--
SPOK
FUMMPP
AGH! SON OF A--
YOU HEALED UP NICE FROM ME BREAKING YOUR BACK, FIST.

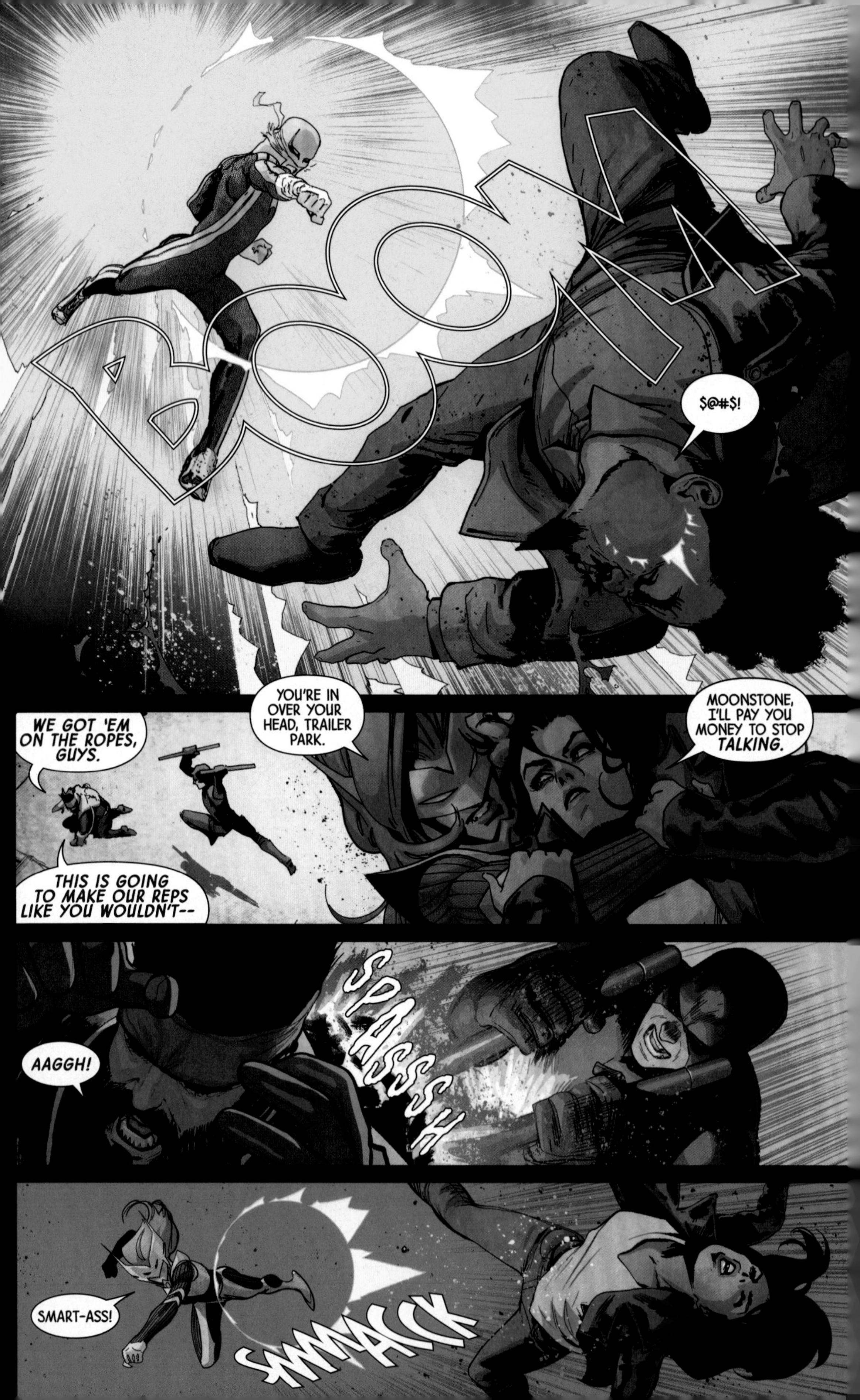
BOOM
$@#$!
WE GOT 'EM ON THE ROPES, GUYS.
THIS IS GOING TO MAKE OUR REPS LIKE YOU WOULDN'T--
YOU'RE IN OVER YOUR HEAD, TRAILER PARK.
MOONSTONE, I'LL PAY YOU MONEY TO STOP TALKING.
SPASSSH
AAGGH!
SMART-ASS!
SMMACK

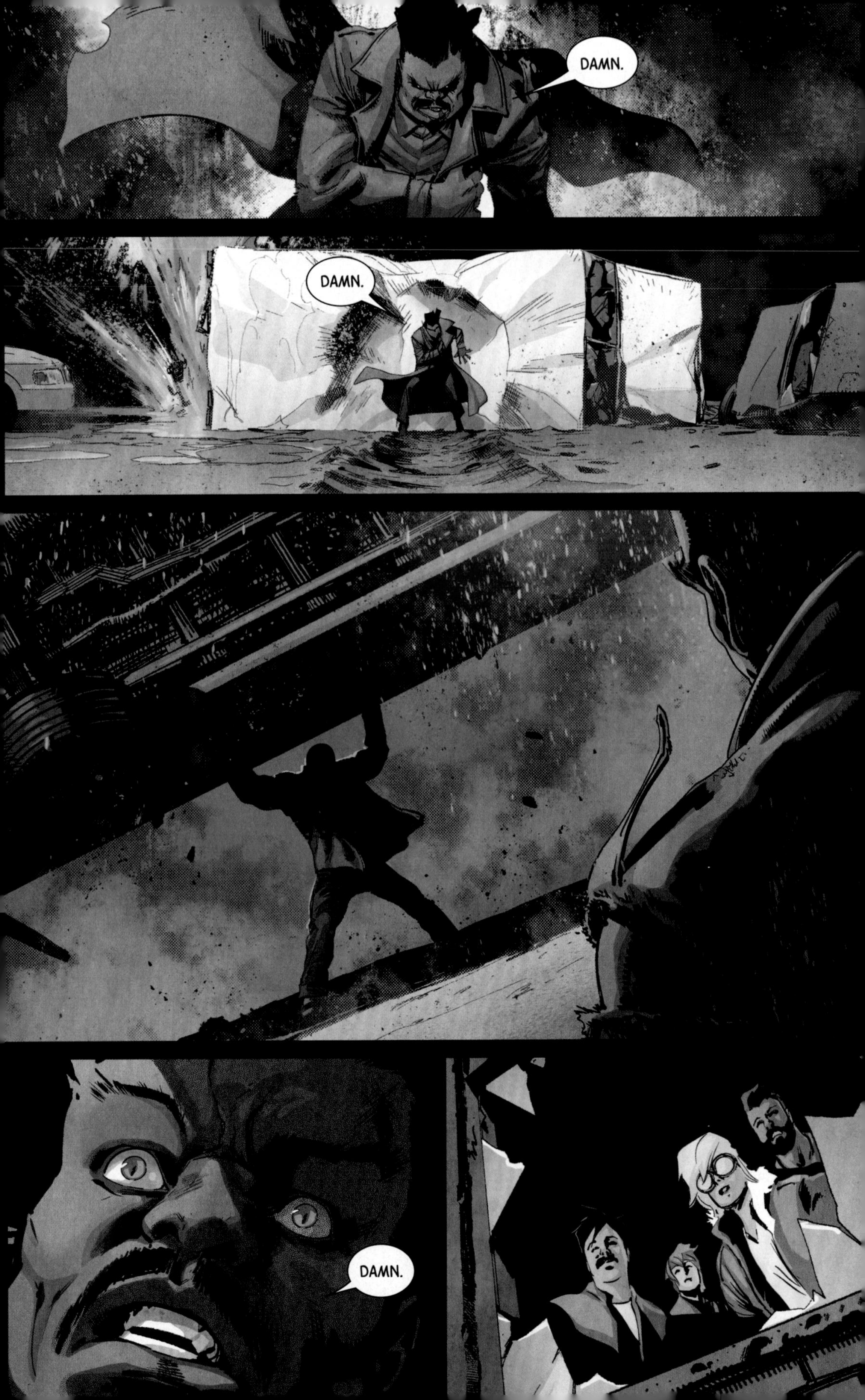
DAMN.
DAMN.
DAMN.

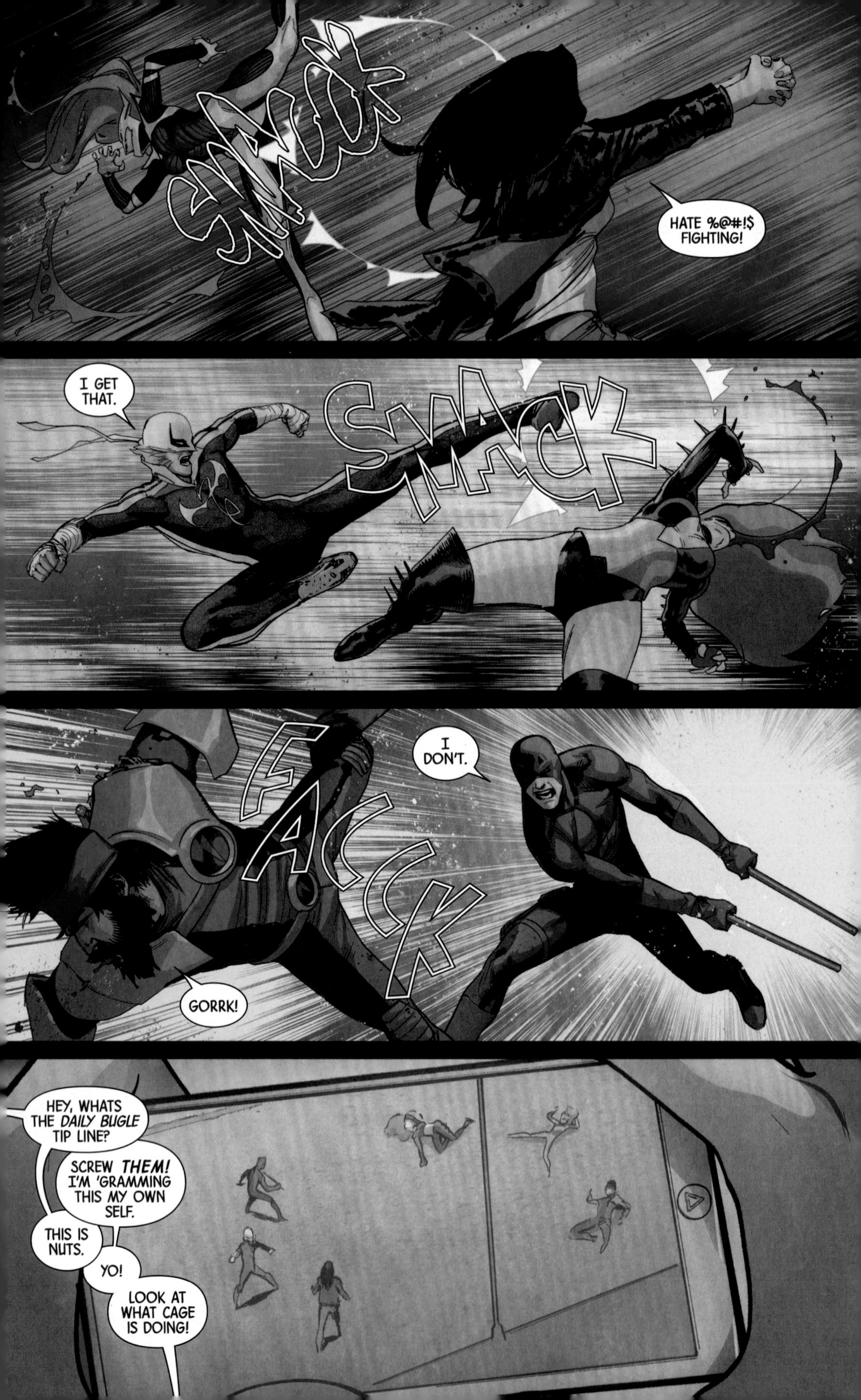
SMACK
HATE %@#!$ FIGHTING!
I GET THAT.
SMACK
FACCK
I DON'T.
GORRK!
HEY, WHATS THE *DAILY BUGLE* TIP LINE?
SCREW *THEM!* I'M 'GRAMMING THIS MY OWN SELF.
THIS IS NUTS.
YO!
LOOK AT WHAT CAGE IS DOING!

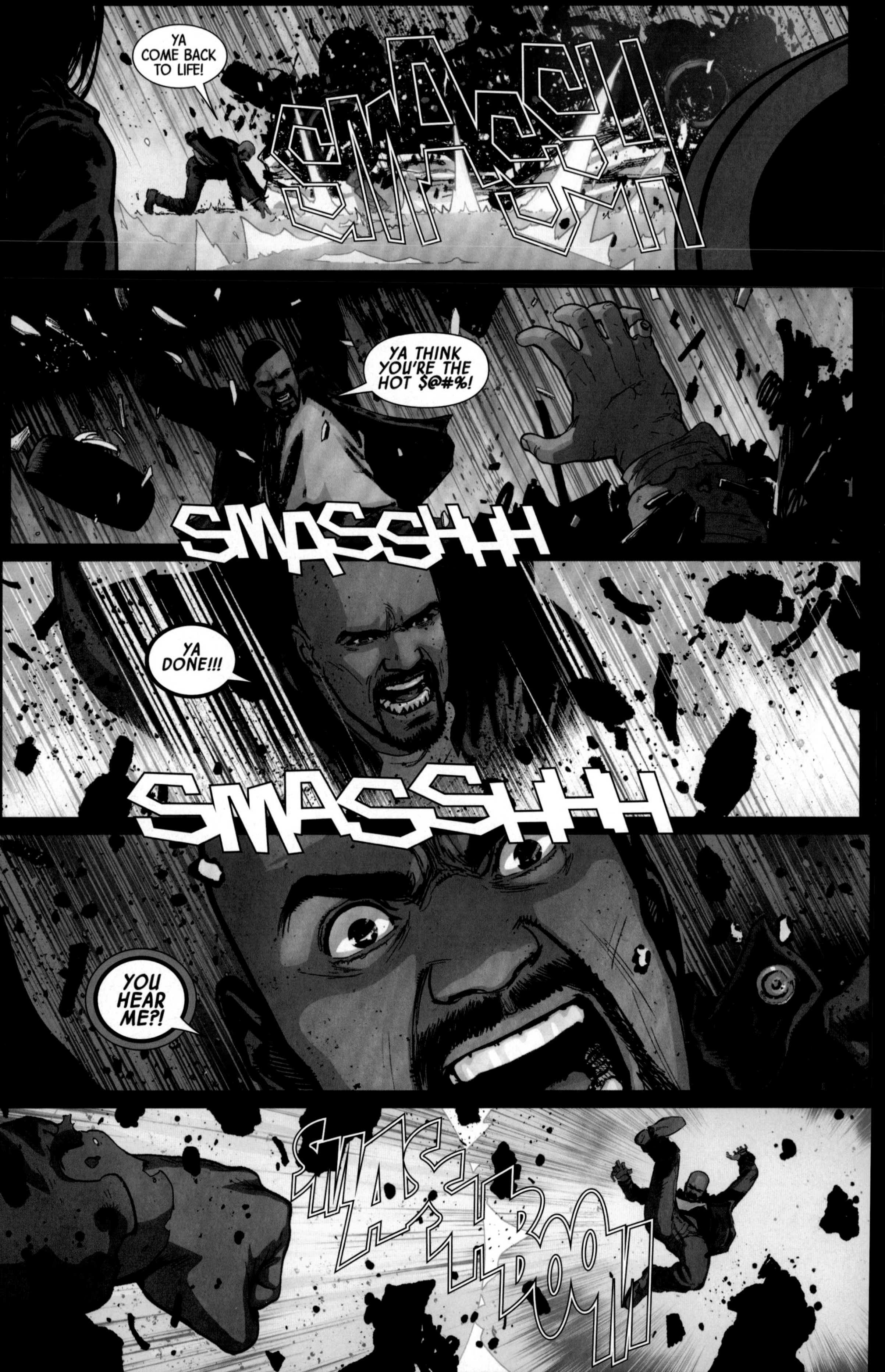
YA COME BACK TO LIFE!
SMASSH
YA THINK YOU'RE THE HOT $@#%!
SMASSHHH
YA DONE!!!
SMASSHHH
YOU HEAR ME?!

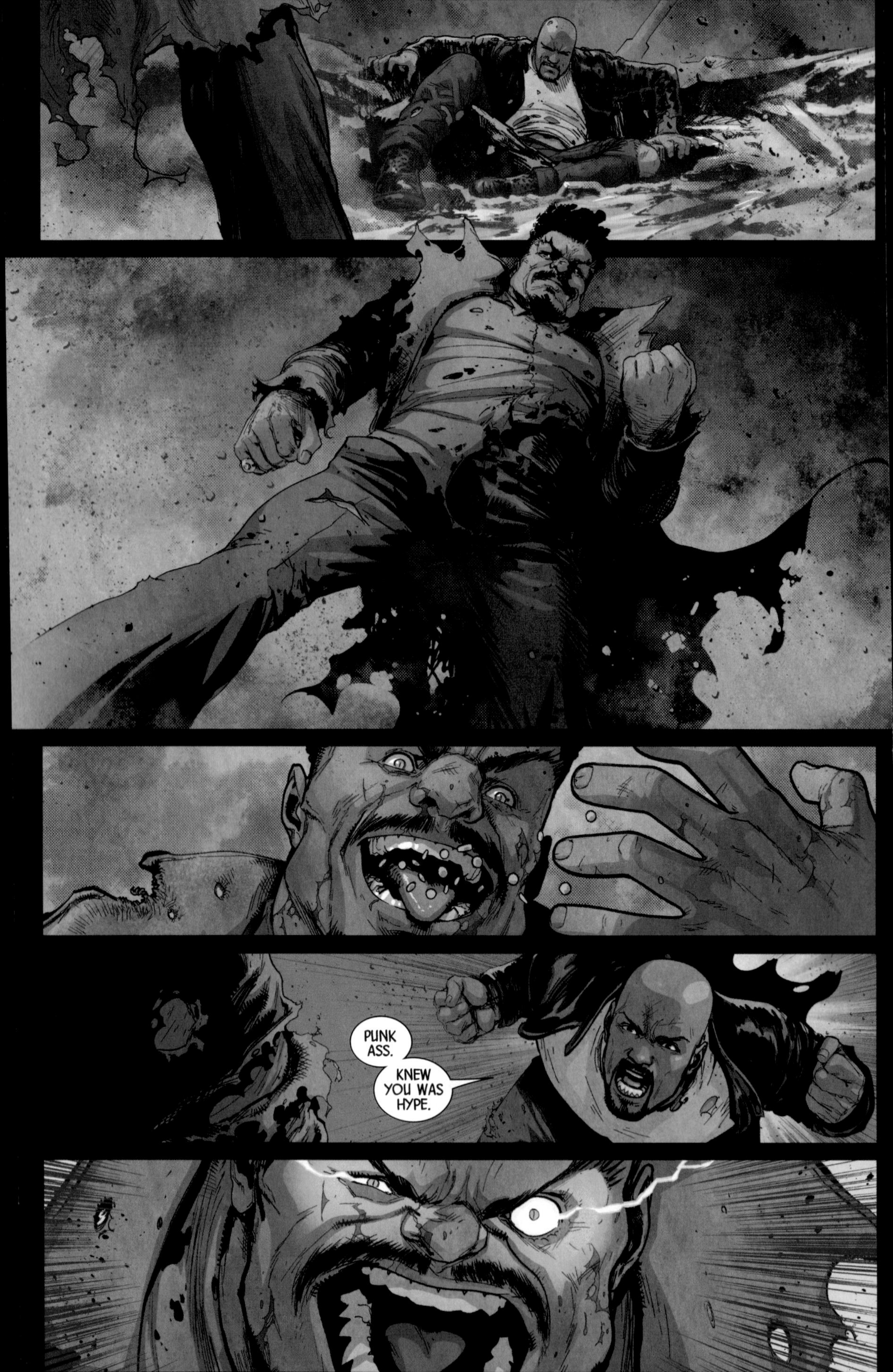
PUNK ASS.
KNEW YOU WAS HYPE.

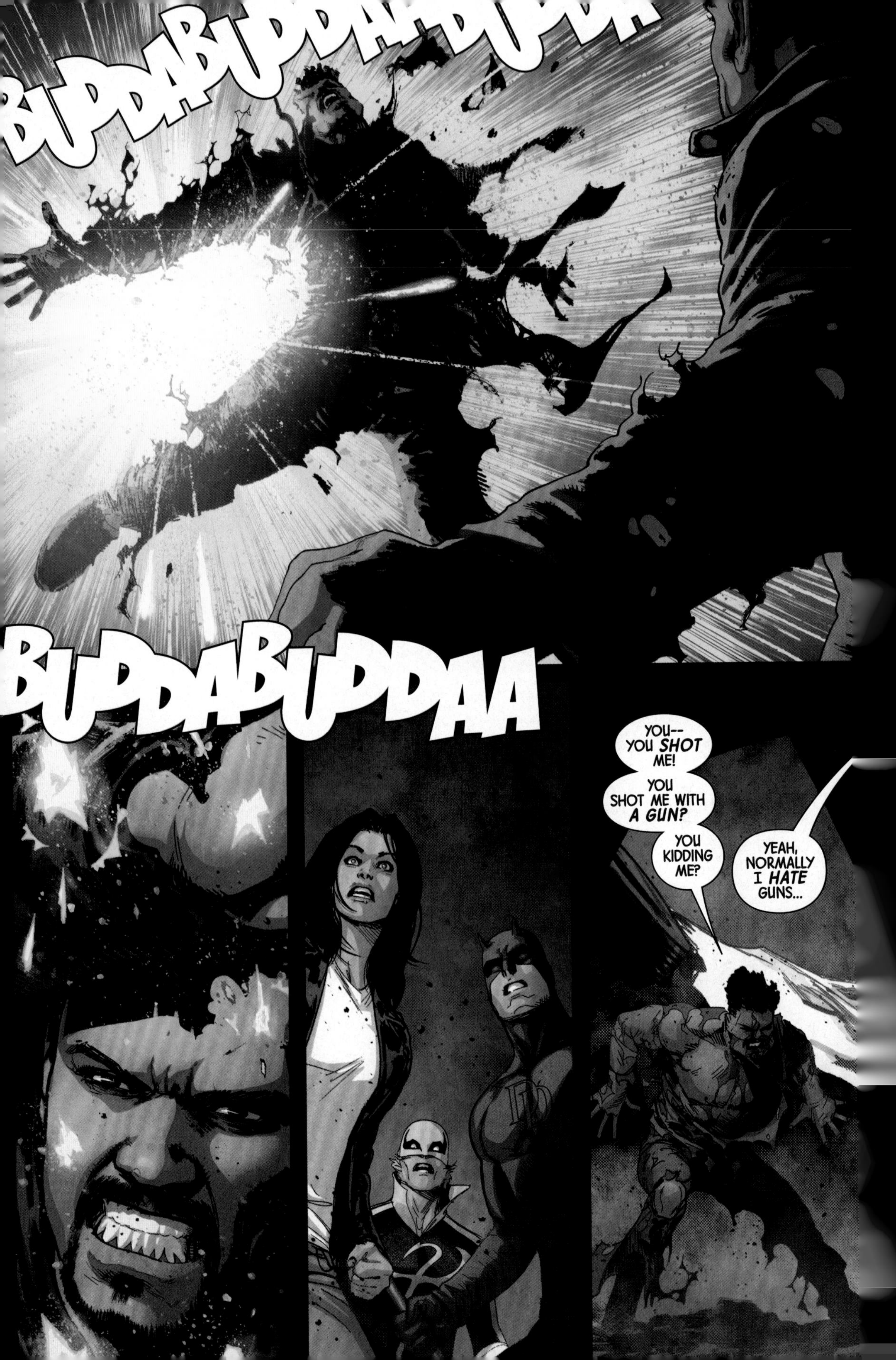
BUDDABUDDABUDDA
BUDDABUDDAA
YOU-- YOU SHOT ME!
YOU SHOT ME WITH A GUN?
YOU KIDDING ME?
YEAH, NORMALLY I HATE GUNS...

I HATE THEM SOMETHING TERRIBLE.

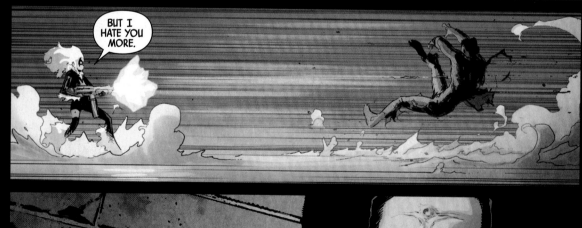

BUT I HATE YOU MORE.

BLACK CAT...

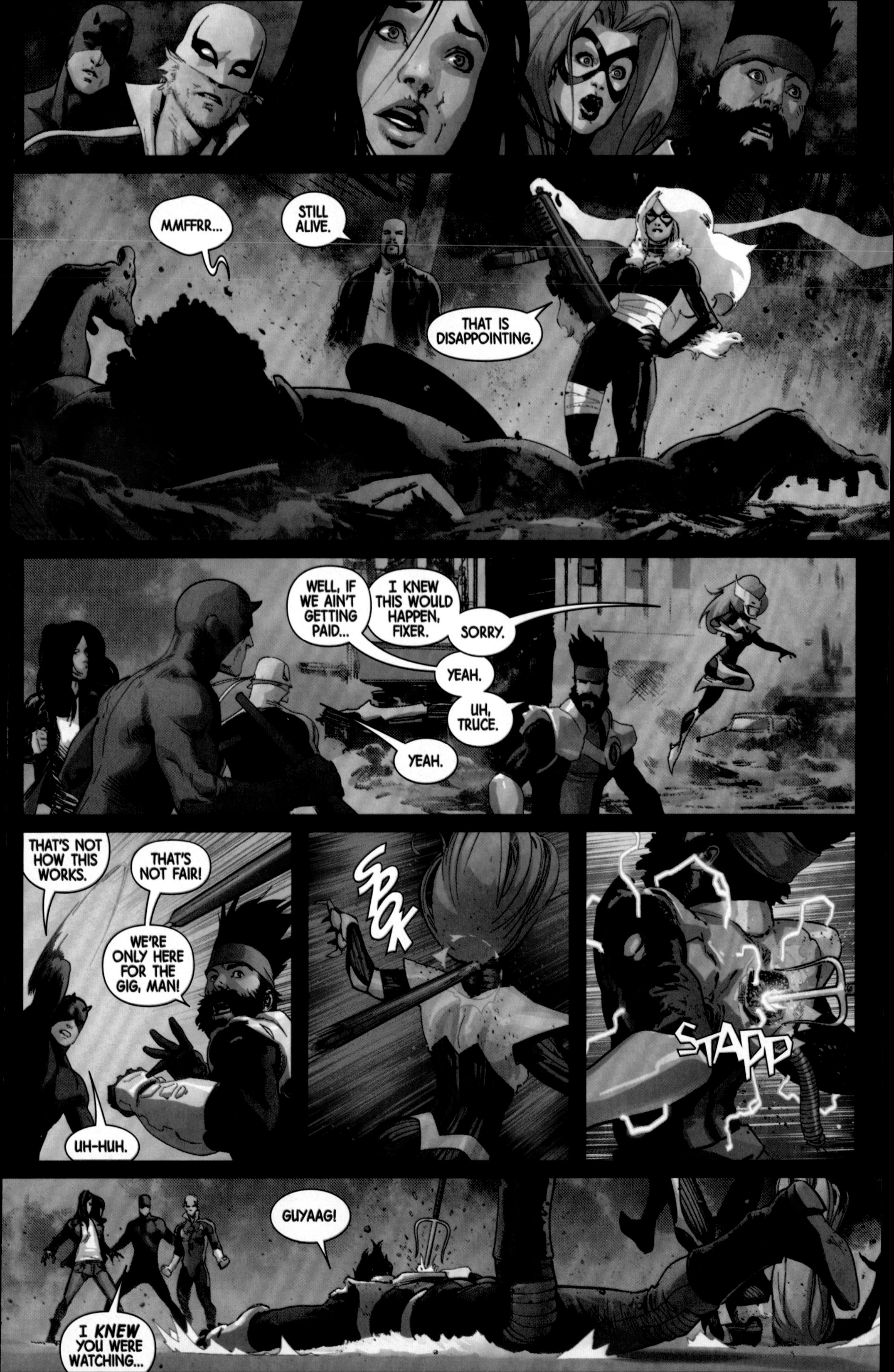
MMFFRR...
STILL ALIVE.
THAT IS DISAPPOINTING.
WELL, IF WE AIN'T GETTING PAID...
I KNEW THIS WOULD HAPPEN, FIXER.
SORRY.
YEAH.
UH, TRUCE.
YEAH.
THAT'S NOT HOW THIS WORKS.
THAT'S NOT FAIR!
WE'RE ONLY HERE FOR THE GIG, MAN!
UH-HUH.
SPOK
STAPP
GUYAAG!
I KNEW YOU WERE WATCHING...

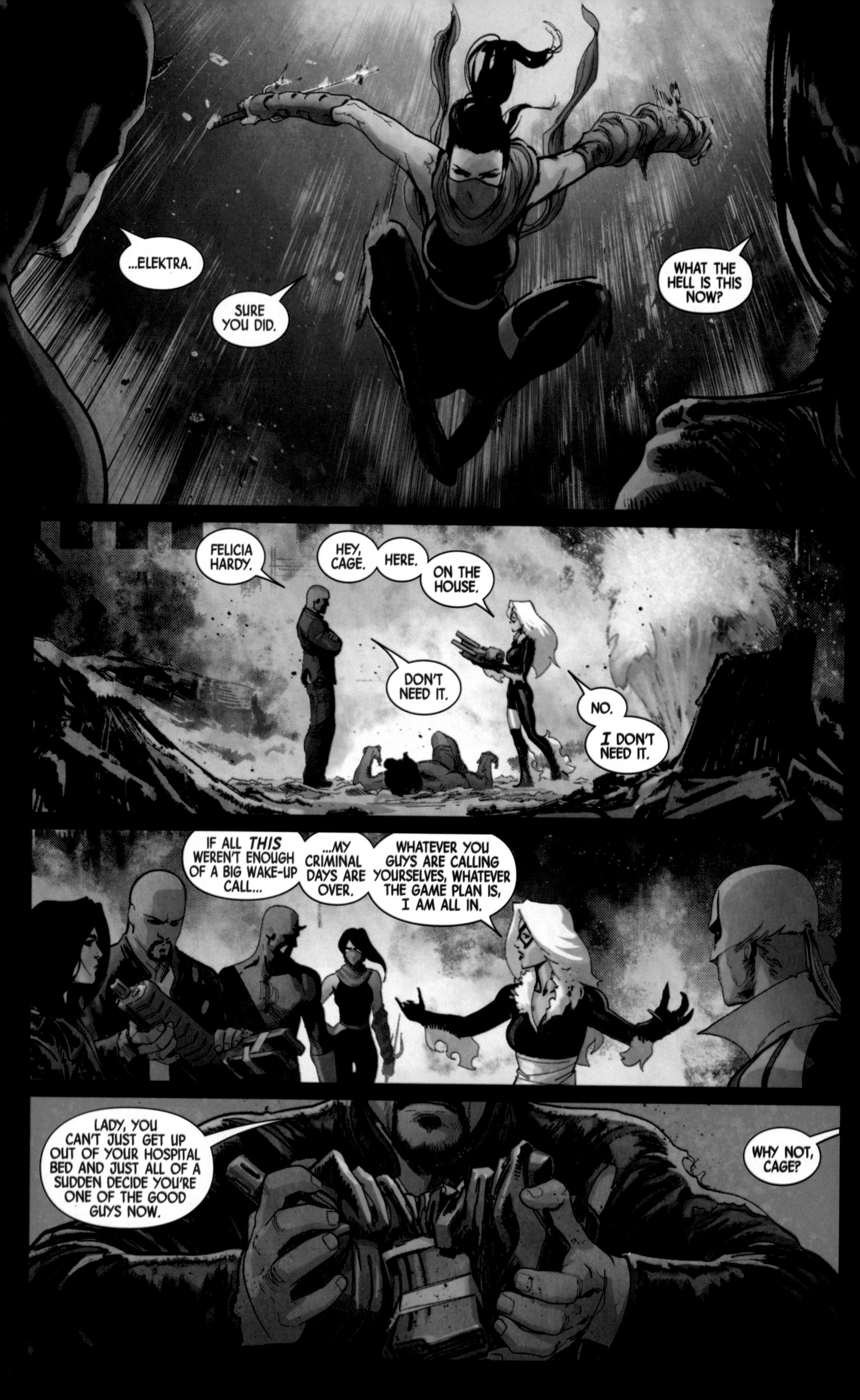

...ELEKTRA.
SURE YOU DID.
WHAT THE HELL IS THIS NOW?
FELICIA HARDY.
HEY, CAGE.
HERE.
ON THE HOUSE.
DON'T NEED IT.
NO.
I DON'T NEED IT.
IF ALL THIS WEREN'T ENOUGH OF A BIG WAKE-UP CALL...
...MY CRIMINAL DAYS ARE OVER.
WHATEVER YOU GUYS ARE CALLING YOURSELVES, WHATEVER THE GAME PLAN IS, I AM ALL IN.
LADY, YOU CAN'T JUST GET UP OUT OF YOUR HOSPITAL BED AND JUST ALL OF A SUDDEN DECIDE YOU'RE ONE OF THE GOOD GUYS NOW.
WHY NOT, CAGE?

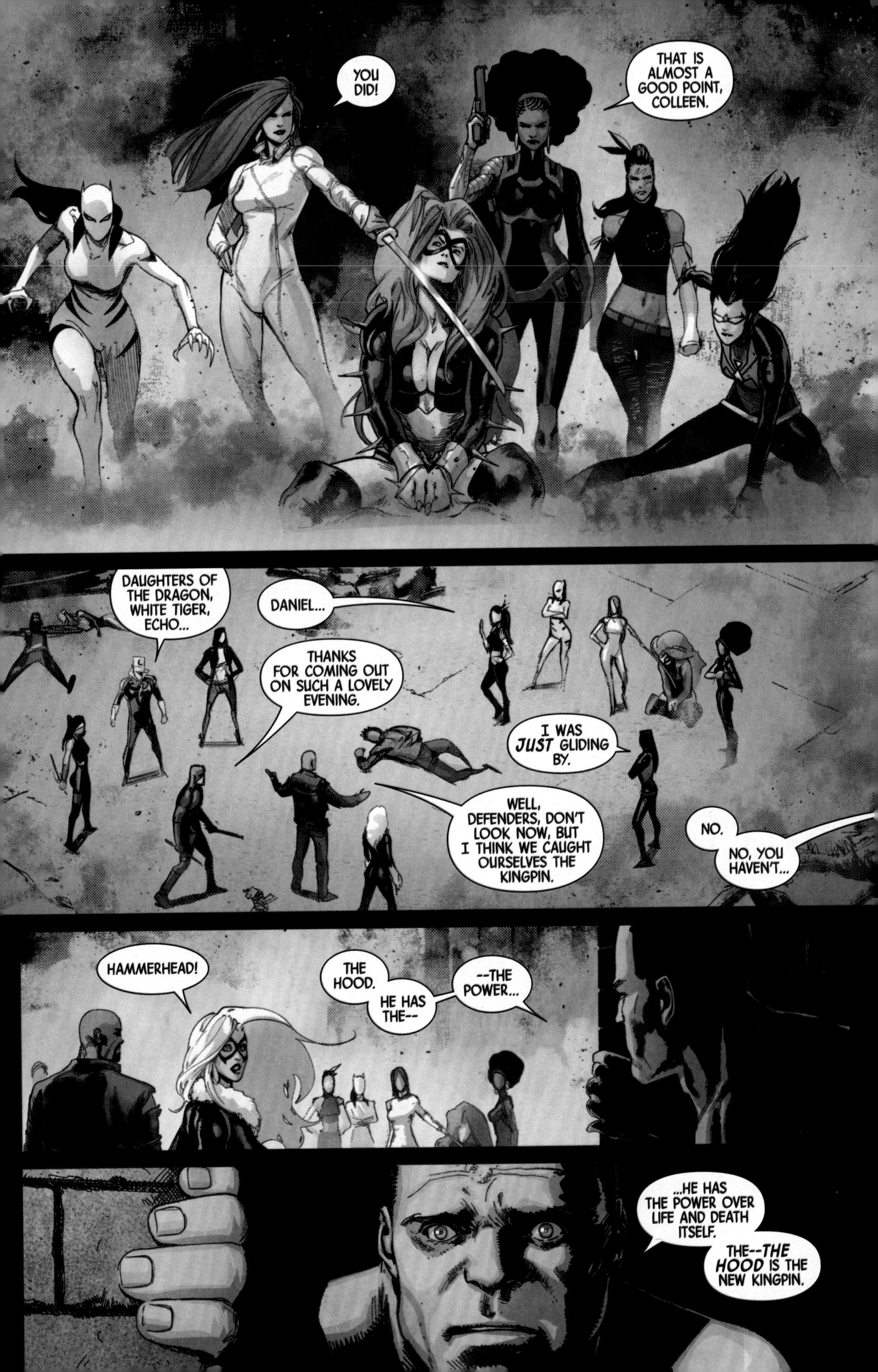
YOU DID!
THAT IS ALMOST A GOOD POINT, COLLEEN.
DAUGHTERS OF THE DRAGON, WHITE TIGER, ECHO...
DANIEL...
THANKS FOR COMING OUT ON SUCH A LOVELY EVENING.
I WAS JUST GLIDING BY.
WELL, DEFENDERS, DON'T LOOK NOW, BUT I THINK WE CAUGHT OURSELVES THE KINGPIN.
NO.
NO, YOU HAVEN'T...
HAMMERHEAD!
THE HOOD.
HE HAS THE--
--THE POWER...
...HE HAS THE POWER OVER LIFE AND DEATH ITSELF.
THE--THE HOOD IS THE NEW KINGPIN.

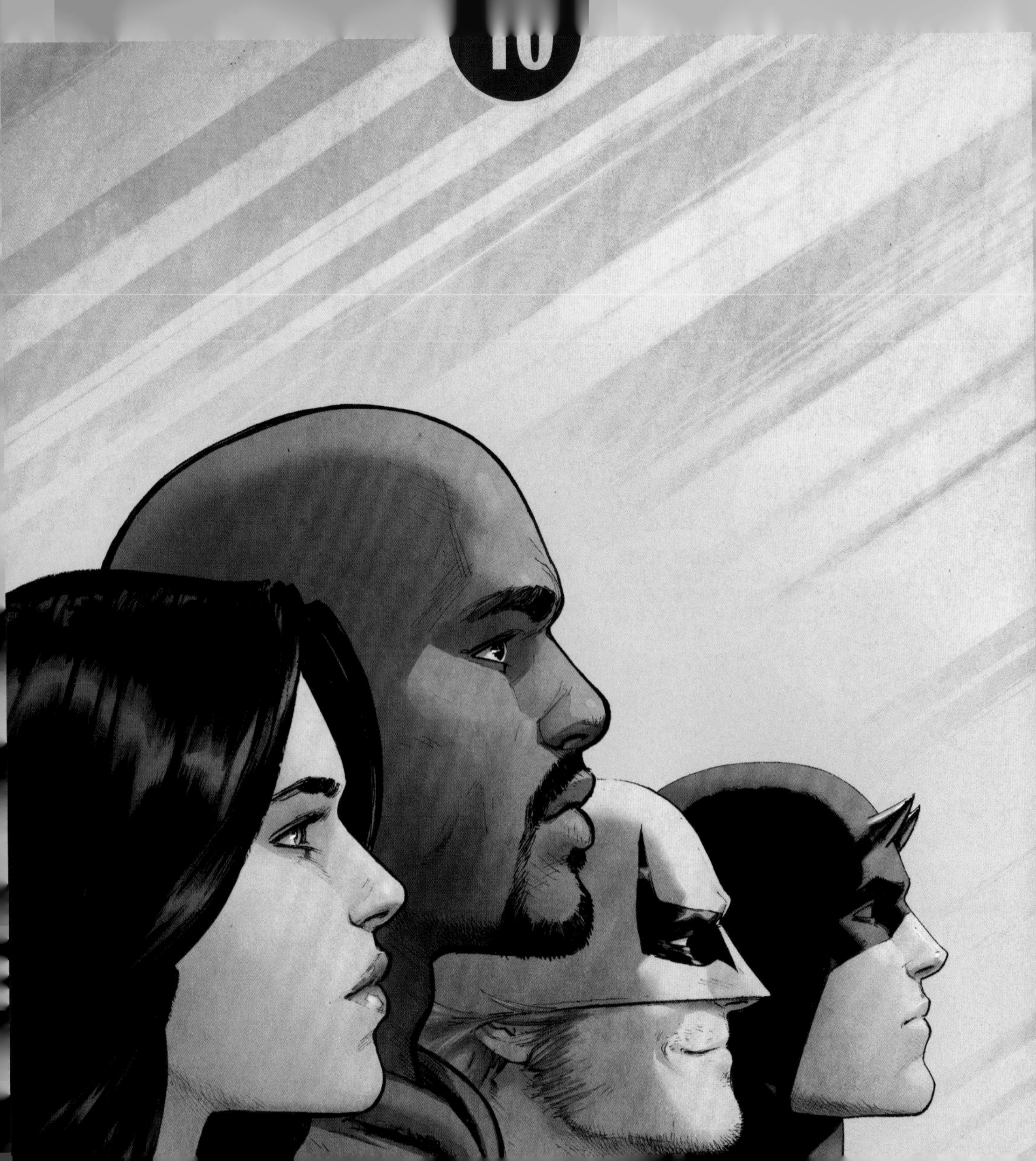

THE DEFENDERS

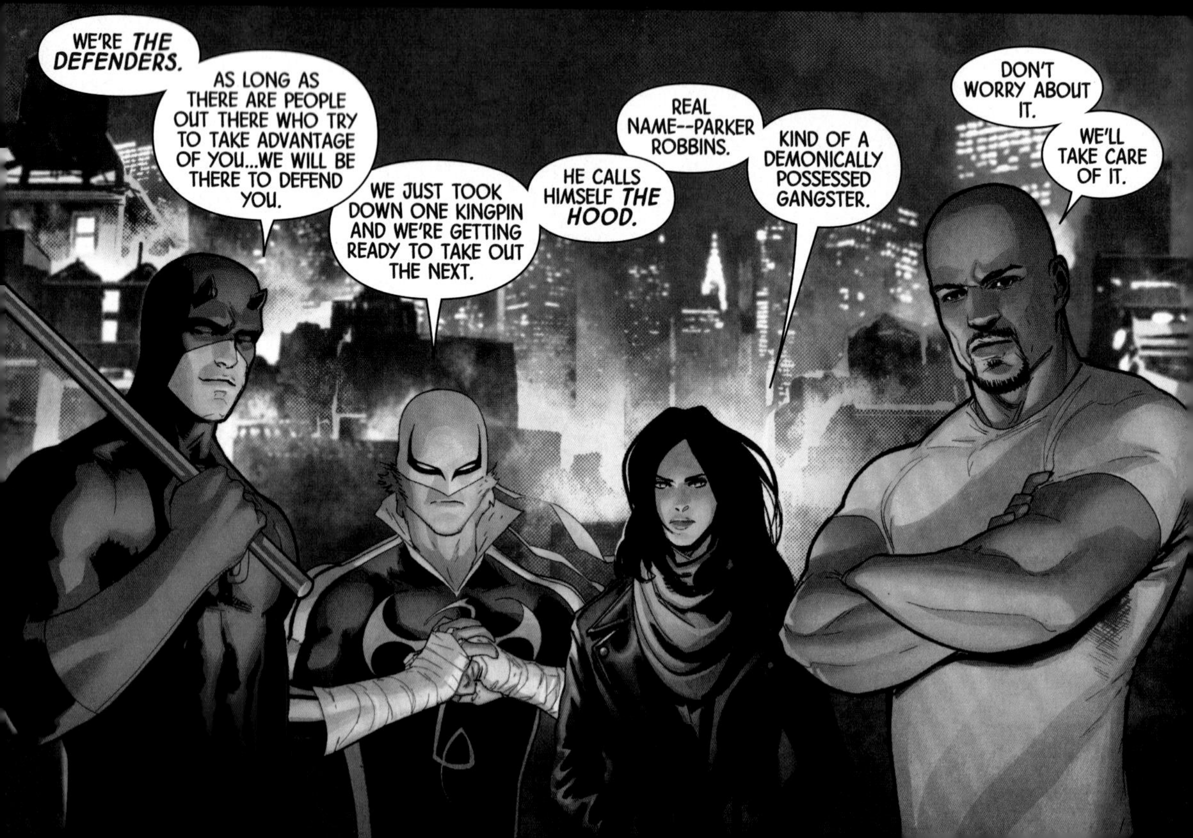
WE'RE *THE DEFENDERS.*
AS LONG AS THERE ARE PEOPLE OUT THERE WHO TRY TO TAKE ADVANTAGE OF YOU...WE WILL BE THERE TO DEFEND YOU.
WE JUST TOOK DOWN ONE KINGPIN AND WE'RE GETTING READY TO TAKE OUT THE NEXT.
HE CALLS HIMSELF *THE HOOD.*
REAL NAME--PARKER ROBBINS.
KIND OF A DEMONICALLY POSSESSED GANGSTER.
DON'T WORRY ABOUT IT.
WE'LL TAKE CARE OF IT.

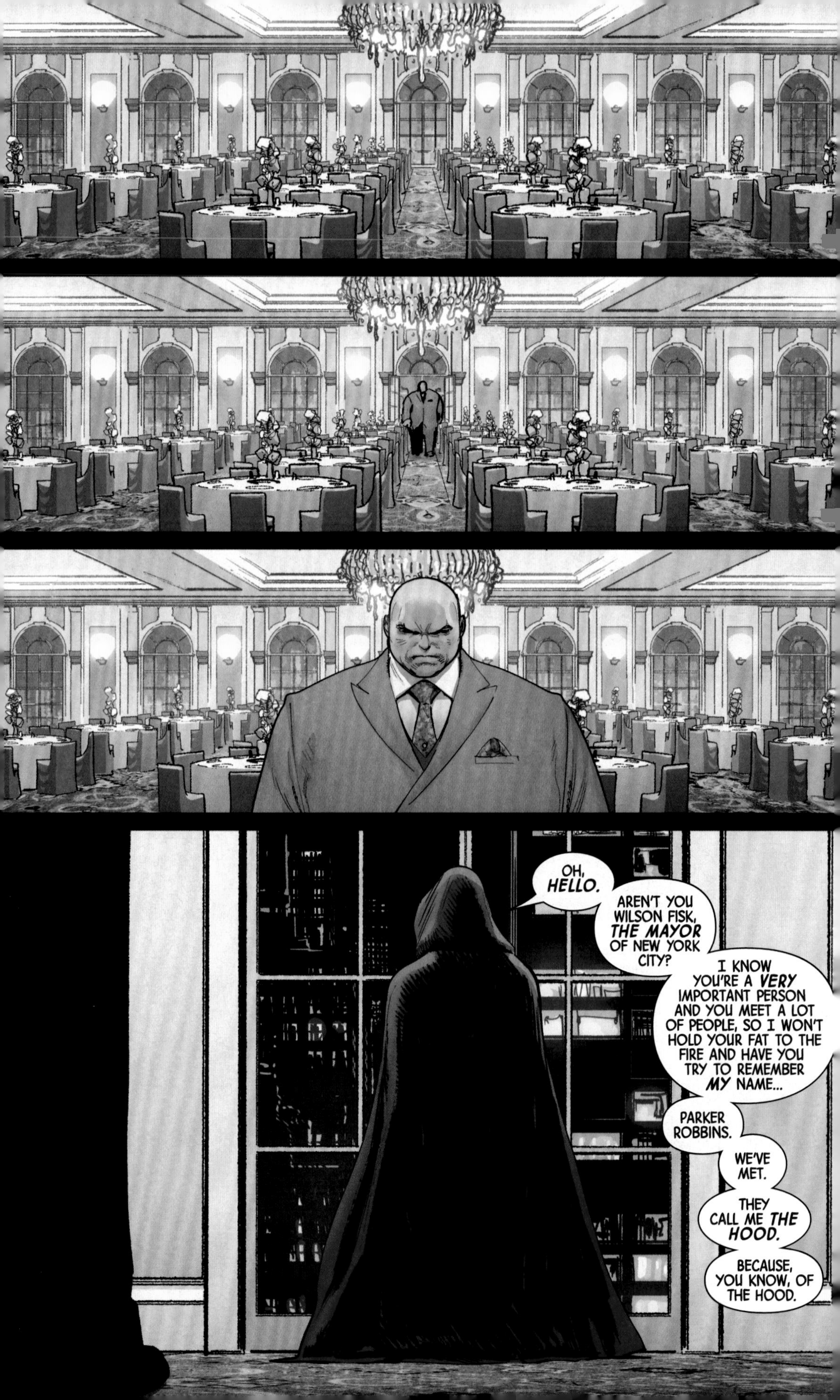
OH, HELLO.
AREN'T YOU WILSON FISK, THE MAYOR OF NEW YORK CITY?
I KNOW YOU'RE A VERY IMPORTANT PERSON AND YOU MEET A LOT OF PEOPLE, SO I WON'T HOLD YOUR FAT TO THE FIRE AND HAVE YOU TRY TO REMEMBER MY NAME...
PARKER ROBBINS.
WE'VE MET.
THEY CALL ME THE HOOD.
BECAUSE, YOU KNOW, OF THE HOOD.

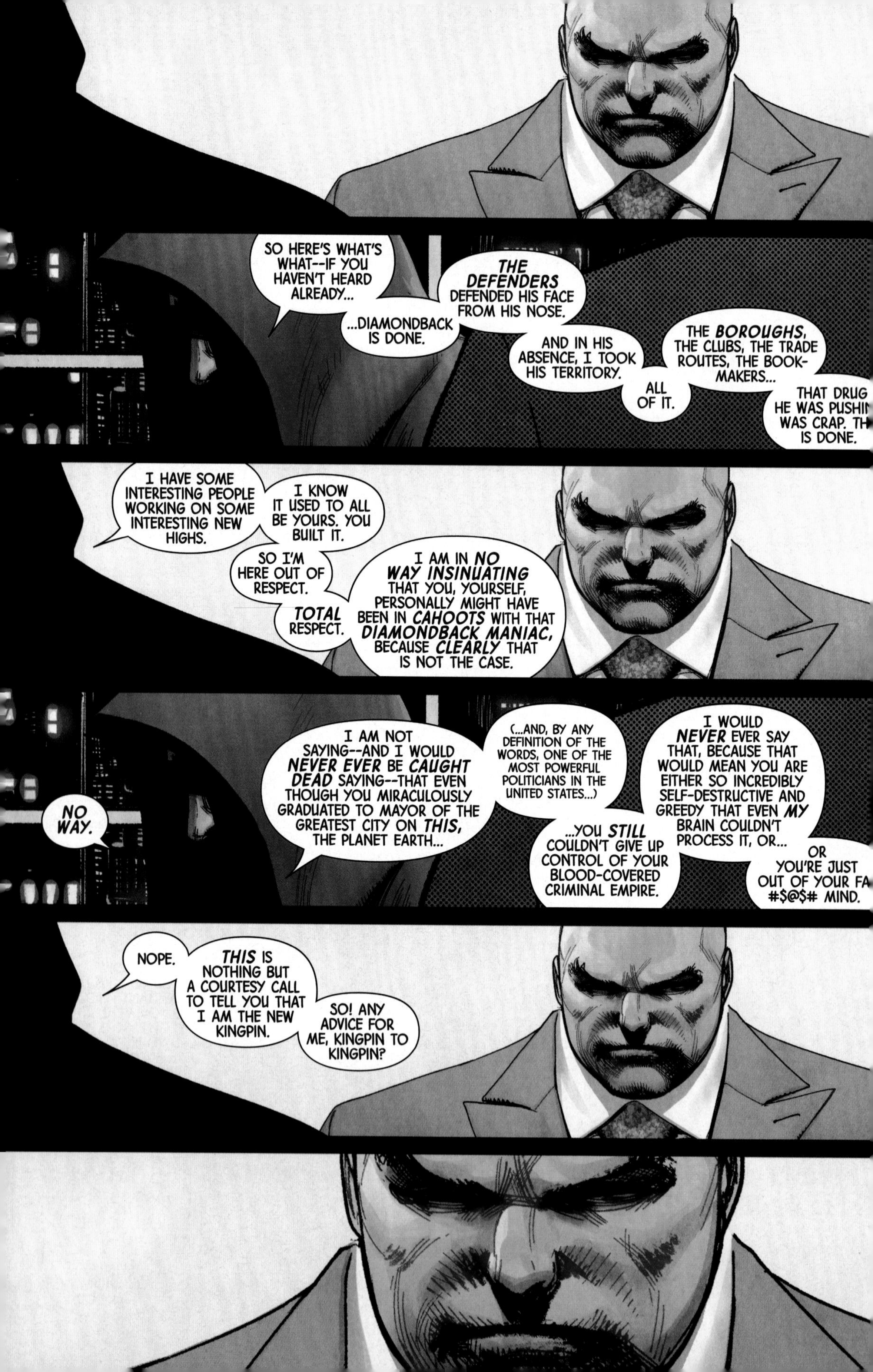
SO HERE'S WHAT'S WHAT--IF YOU HAVEN'T HEARD ALREADY...
...DIAMONDBACK IS DONE.
THE DEFENDERS DEFENDED HIS FACE FROM HIS NOSE.
AND IN HIS ABSENCE, I TOOK HIS TERRITORY.
ALL OF IT.
THE BOROUGHS, THE CLUBS, THE TRADE ROUTES, THE BOOK-MAKERS...
THAT DRUG HE WAS PUSHIN WAS CRAP. TH IS DONE.
I HAVE SOME INTERESTING PEOPLE WORKING ON SOME INTERESTING NEW HIGHS.
I KNOW IT USED TO ALL BE YOURS. YOU BUILT IT.
SO I'M HERE OUT OF RESPECT.
TOTAL RESPECT.
I AM IN NO WAY INSINUATING THAT YOU, YOURSELF, PERSONALLY MIGHT HAVE BEEN IN CAHOOTS WITH THAT DIAMONDBACK MANIAC, BECAUSE CLEARLY THAT IS NOT THE CASE.
NO WAY.
I AM NOT SAYING--AND I WOULD NEVER EVER BE CAUGHT DEAD SAYING--THAT EVEN THOUGH YOU MIRACULOUSLY GRADUATED TO MAYOR OF THE GREATEST CITY ON THIS, THE PLANET EARTH...
(...AND, BY ANY DEFINITION OF THE WORDS, ONE OF THE MOST POWERFUL POLITICIANS IN THE UNITED STATES...)
...YOU STILL COULDN'T GIVE UP CONTROL OF YOUR BLOOD-COVERED CRIMINAL EMPIRE.
I WOULD NEVER EVER SAY THAT, BECAUSE THAT WOULD MEAN YOU ARE EITHER SO INCREDIBLY SELF-DESTRUCTIVE AND GREEDY THAT EVEN MY BRAIN COULDN'T PROCESS IT, OR...
OR YOU'RE JUST OUT OF YOUR FA #$@$# MIND.
NOPE.
THIS IS NOTHING BUT A COURTESY CALL TO TELL YOU THAT I AM THE NEW KINGPIN.
SO! ANY ADVICE FOR ME, KINGPIN TO KINGPIN?

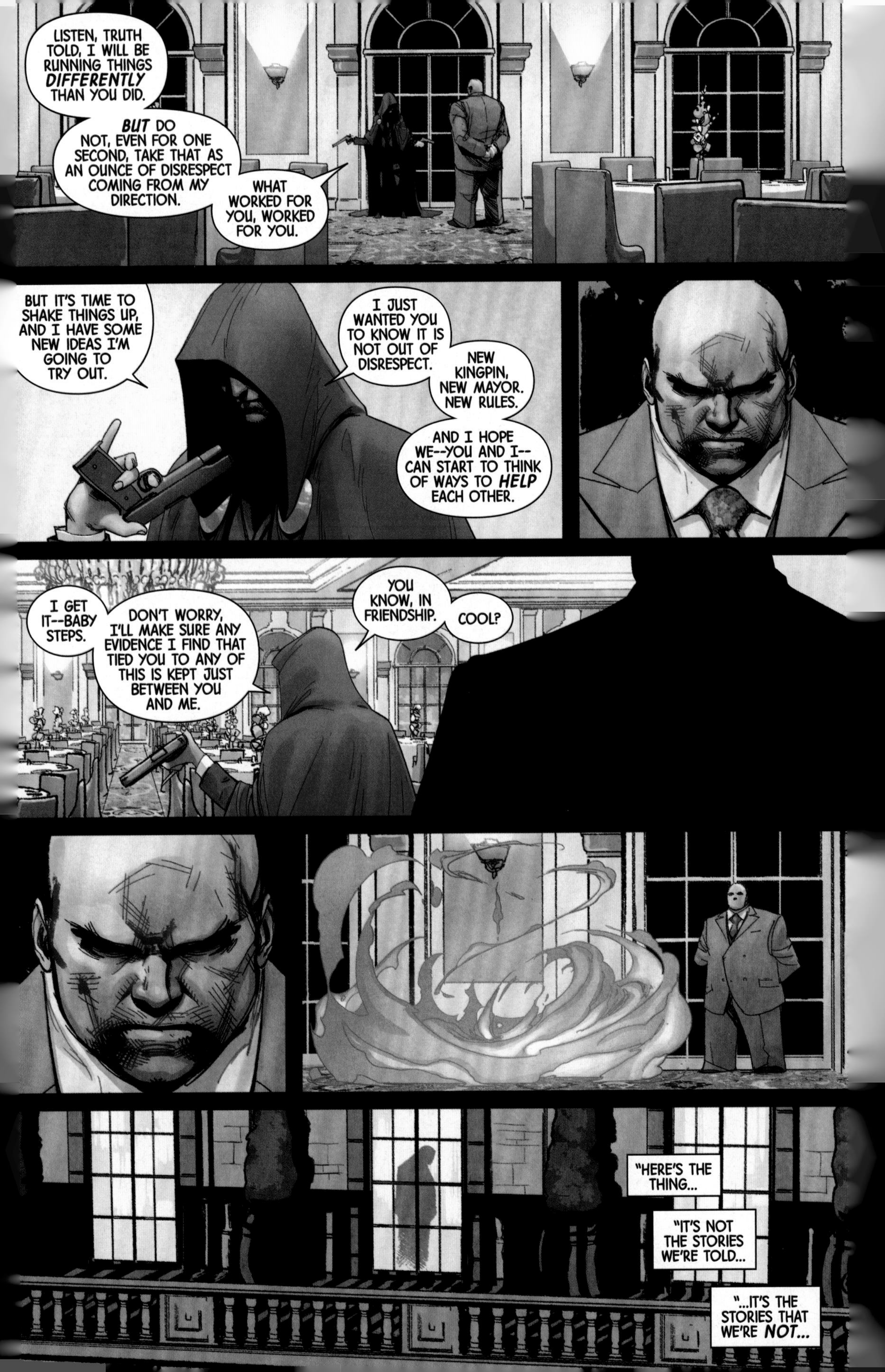

LISTEN, TRUTH TOLD, I WILL BE RUNNING THINGS DIFFERENTLY THAN YOU DID.
BUT DO NOT, EVEN FOR ONE SECOND, TAKE THAT AS AN OUNCE OF DISRESPECT COMING FROM MY DIRECTION.
WHAT WORKED FOR YOU, WORKED FOR YOU.
BUT IT'S TIME TO SHAKE THINGS UP, AND I HAVE SOME NEW IDEAS I'M GOING TO TRY OUT.
I JUST WANTED YOU TO KNOW IT IS NOT OUT OF DISRESPECT.
NEW KINGPIN, NEW MAYOR. NEW RULES.
AND I HOPE WE--YOU AND I--CAN START TO THINK OF WAYS TO HELP EACH OTHER.
I GET IT--BABY STEPS.
DON'T WORRY, I'LL MAKE SURE ANY EVIDENCE I FIND THAT TIED YOU TO ANY OF THIS IS KEPT JUST BETWEEN YOU AND ME.
YOU KNOW, IN FRIENDSHIP.
COOL?
"HERE'S THE THING...
"IT'S NOT THE STORIES WE'RE TOLD...
"...IT'S THE STORIES THAT WE'RE NOT...

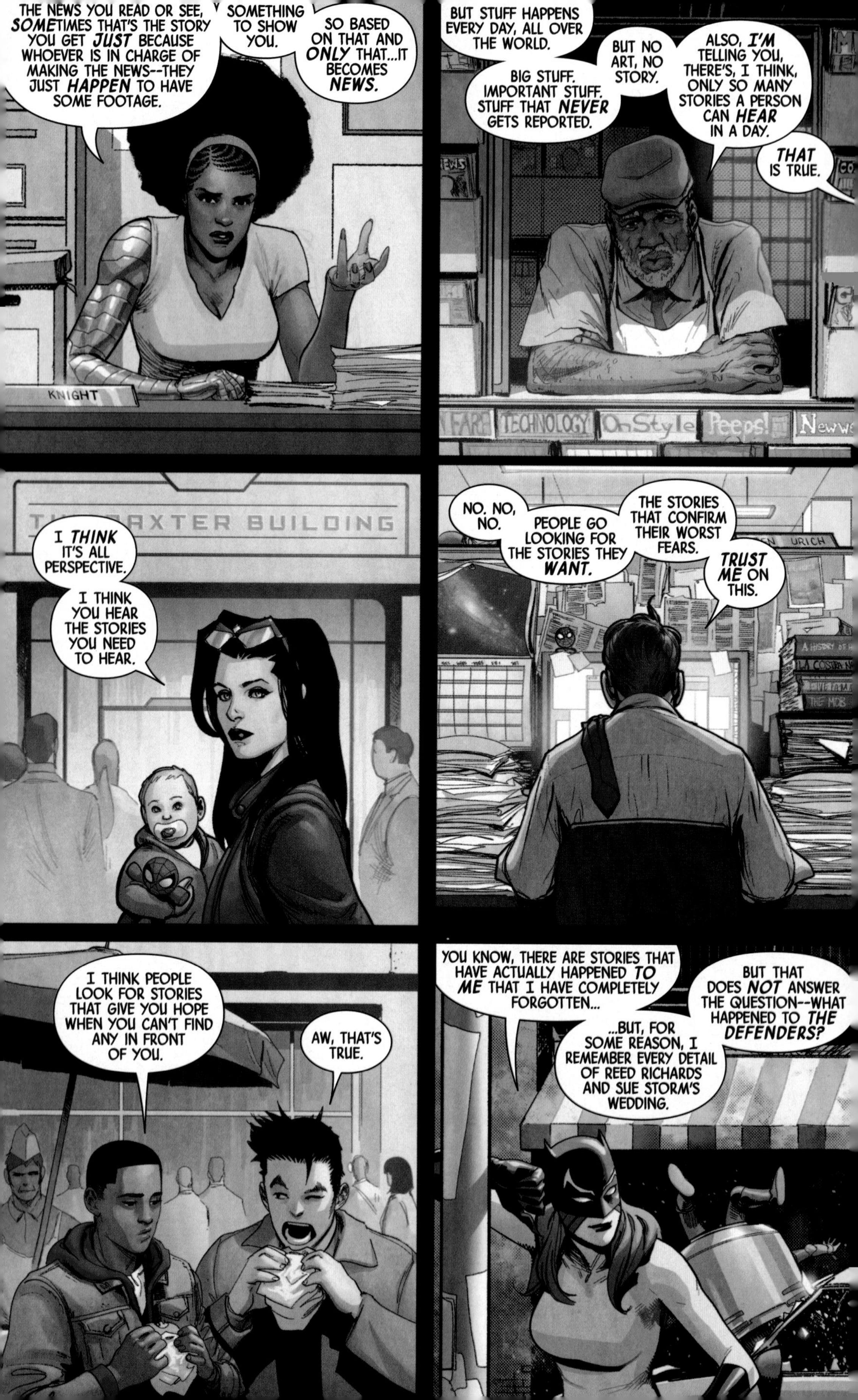
THE NEWS YOU READ OR SEE, SOMETIMES THAT'S THE STORY YOU GET JUST BECAUSE WHOEVER IS IN CHARGE OF MAKING THE NEWS--THEY JUST HAPPEN TO HAVE SOME FOOTAGE.
SOMETHING TO SHOW YOU.
SO BASED ON THAT AND ONLY THAT...IT BECOMES NEWS.
KNIGHT
BUT STUFF HAPPENS EVERY DAY, ALL OVER THE WORLD.
BIG STUFF. IMPORTANT STUFF. STUFF THAT NEVER GETS REPORTED.
BUT NO ART, NO STORY.
ALSO, I'M TELLING YOU, THERE'S, I THINK, ONLY SO MANY STORIES A PERSON CAN HEAR IN A DAY.
THAT IS TRUE.
TECHNOLOGY
OnStyle
Peeps!
I THINK IT'S ALL PERSPECTIVE.
I THINK YOU HEAR THE STORIES YOU NEED TO HEAR.
NO. NO, NO.
PEOPLE GO LOOKING FOR THE STORIES THEY WANT.
THE STORIES THAT CONFIRM THEIR WORST FEARS.
TRUST ME ON THIS.
URICH
THE MOB
I THINK PEOPLE LOOK FOR STORIES THAT GIVE YOU HOPE WHEN YOU CAN'T FIND ANY IN FRONT OF YOU.
AW, THAT'S TRUE.
YOU KNOW, THERE ARE STORIES THAT HAVE ACTUALLY HAPPENED TO ME THAT I HAVE COMPLETELY FORGOTTEN...
...BUT, FOR SOME REASON, I REMEMBER EVERY DETAIL OF REED RICHARDS AND SUE STORM'S WEDDING.
BUT THAT DOES NOT ANSWER THE QUESTION--WHAT HAPPENED TO THE DEFENDERS?

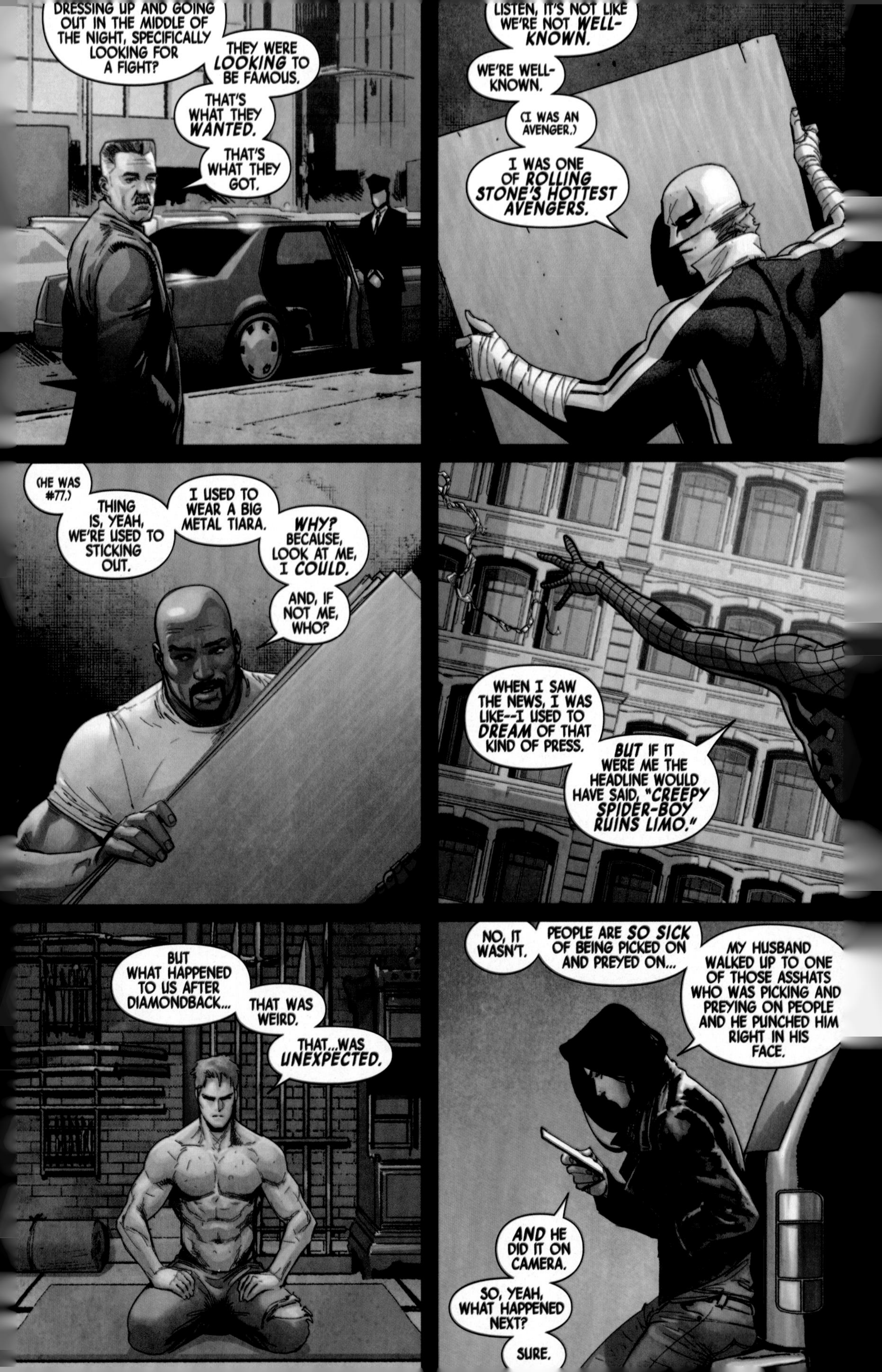
DRESSING UP AND GOING OUT IN THE MIDDLE OF THE NIGHT, SPECIFICALLY LOOKING FOR A FIGHT?
THEY WERE LOOKING TO BE FAMOUS.
THAT'S WHAT THEY WANTED.
THAT'S WHAT THEY GOT.
LISTEN, IT'S NOT LIKE WE'RE NOT WELL-KNOWN.
WE'RE WELL-KNOWN.
(I WAS AN AVENGER.)
I WAS ONE OF ROLLING STONE'S HOTTEST AVENGERS.
(HE WAS #77.)
THING IS, YEAH, WE'RE USED TO STICKING OUT.
I USED TO WEAR A BIG METAL TIARA.
WHY? BECAUSE, LOOK AT ME, I COULD.
AND, IF NOT ME, WHO?
WHEN I SAW THE NEWS, I WAS LIKE--I USED TO DREAM OF THAT KIND OF PRESS.
BUT IF IT WERE ME THE HEADLINE WOULD HAVE SAID, "CREEPY SPIDER-BOY RUINS LIMO."
BUT WHAT HAPPENED TO US AFTER DIAMONDBACK...
THAT WAS WEIRD.
THAT...WAS UNEXPECTED.
NO, IT WASN'T.
PEOPLE ARE SO SICK OF BEING PICKED ON AND PREYED ON...
MY HUSBAND WALKED UP TO ONE OF THOSE ASSHATS WHO WAS PICKING AND PREYING ON PEOPLE AND HE PUNCHED HIM RIGHT IN HIS FACE.
AND HE DID IT ON CAMERA.
SO, YEAH, WHAT HAPPENED NEXT?
SURE.

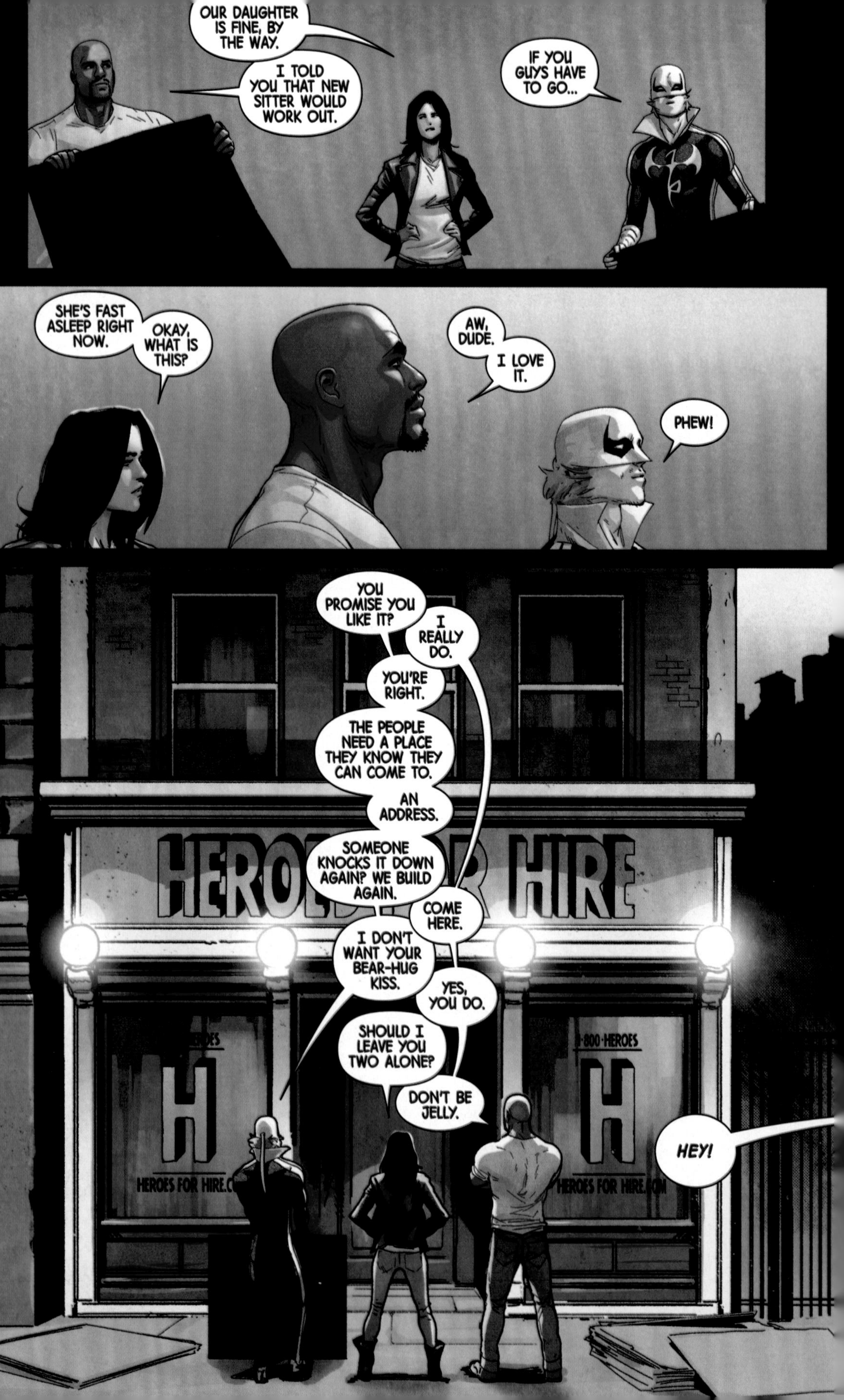
OUR DAUGHTER IS FINE, BY THE WAY.
I TOLD YOU THAT NEW SITTER WOULD WORK OUT.
IF YOU GUYS HAVE TO GO...
SHE'S FAST ASLEEP RIGHT NOW.
OKAY, WHAT IS THIS?
AW, DUDE.
I LOVE IT.
PHEW!
YOU PROMISE YOU LIKE IT?
I REALLY DO.
YOU'RE RIGHT.
THE PEOPLE NEED A PLACE THEY KNOW THEY CAN COME TO.
AN ADDRESS.
SOMEONE KNOCKS IT DOWN AGAIN? WE BUILD AGAIN.
COME HERE.
I DON'T WANT YOUR BEAR-HUG KISS.
YES, YOU DO.
SHOULD I LEAVE YOU TWO ALONE?
DON'T BE JELLY.
HEY!
HEROES FOR HIRE
1-800-HEROES
H
HEROES FOR HIRE.COM

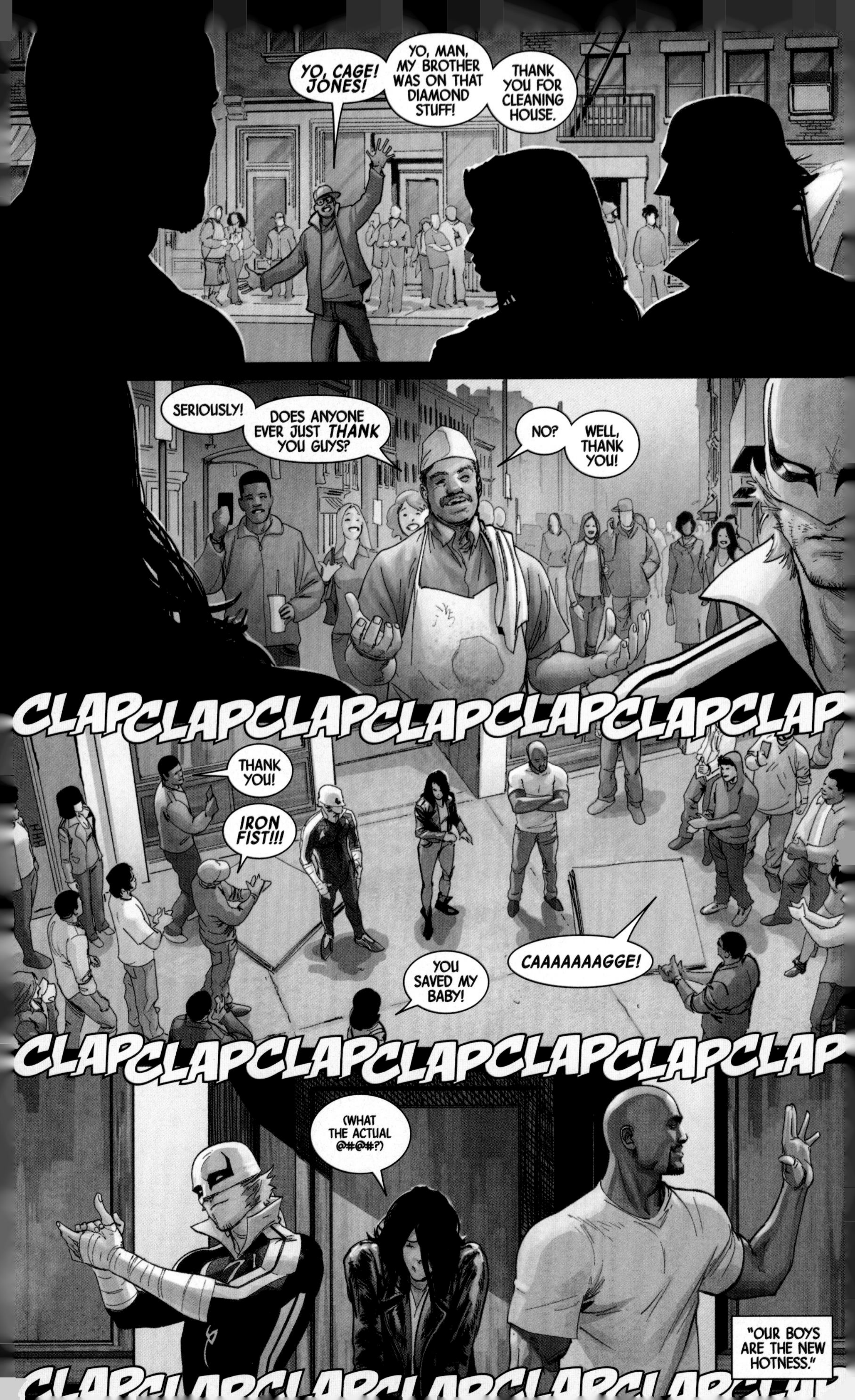
YO, CAGE! JONES!
YO, MAN, MY BROTHER WAS ON THAT DIAMOND STUFF!
THANK YOU FOR CLEANING HOUSE.
SERIOUSLY!
DOES ANYONE EVER JUST THANK YOU GUYS?
NO?
WELL, THANK YOU!
CLAPCLAPCLAPCLAPCLAPCLAPCLAP
THANK YOU!
IRON FIST!!!
YOU SAVED MY BABY!
CAAAAAAAGGE!
CLAPCLAPCLAPCLAPCLAPCLAPCLAP
(WHAT THE ACTUAL @#@#?)
"OUR BOYS ARE THE NEW HOTNESS."

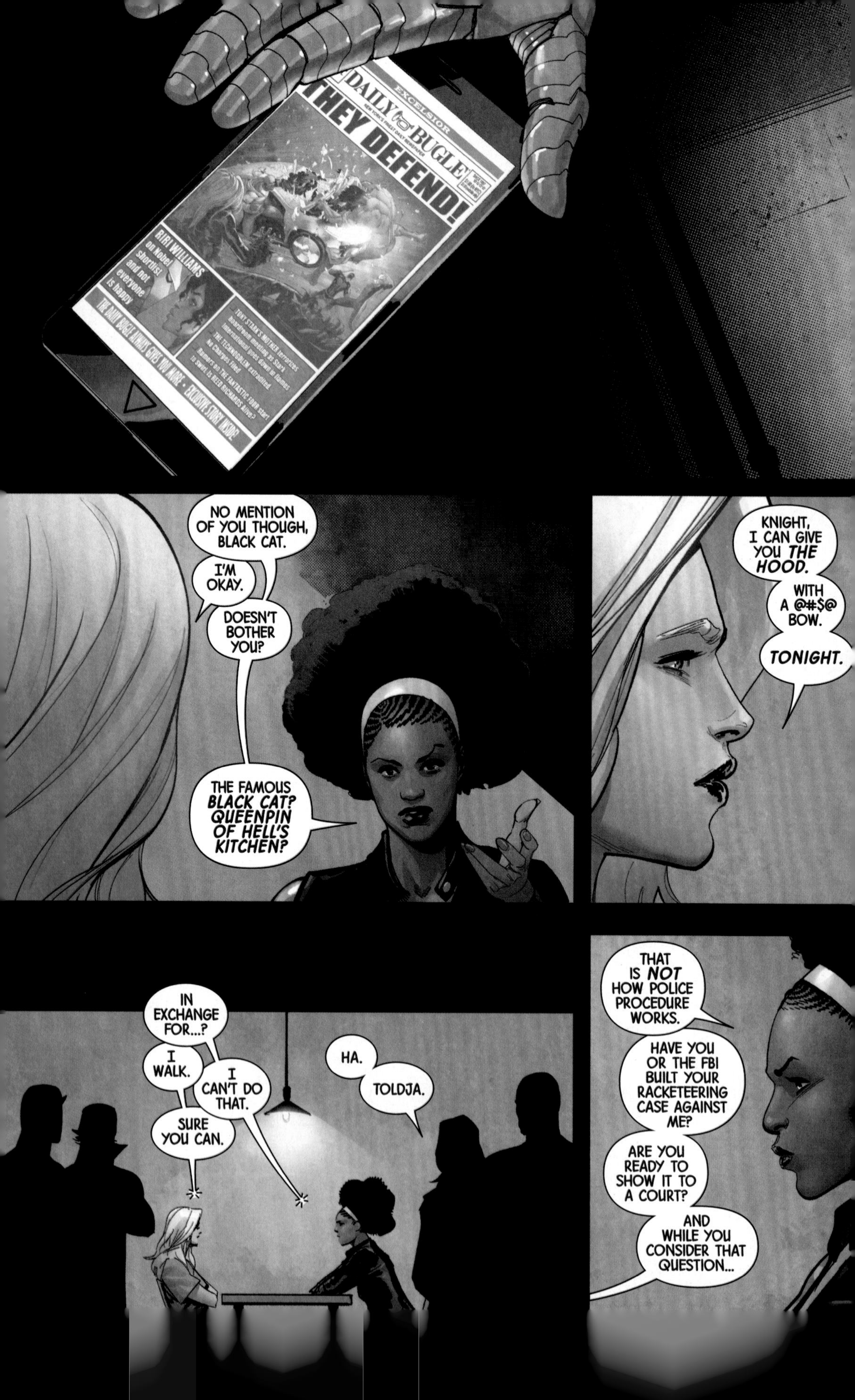
EXCELSIOR
DAILY BUGLE
THEY DEFEND!
RIRI WILLIAMS on Nobel shortlist and not everyone is happy
THE DAILY BUGLE ALWAYS GIVES YOU MORE • EXCLUSIVE STORY INSIDE
NO MENTION OF YOU THOUGH, BLACK CAT.
I'M OKAY.
DOESN'T BOTHER YOU?
THE FAMOUS BLACK CAT? QUEENPIN OF HELL'S KITCHEN?
KNIGHT, I CAN GIVE YOU THE HOOD.
WITH A @#$@ BOW.
TONIGHT.
IN EXCHANGE FOR...?
I WALK.
I CAN'T DO THAT.
SURE YOU CAN.
HA.
TOLDJA.
THAT IS NOT HOW POLICE PROCEDURE WORKS.
HAVE YOU OR THE FBI BUILT YOUR RACKETEERING CASE AGAINST ME?
ARE YOU READY TO SHOW IT TO A COURT?
AND WHILE YOU CONSIDER THAT QUESTION...

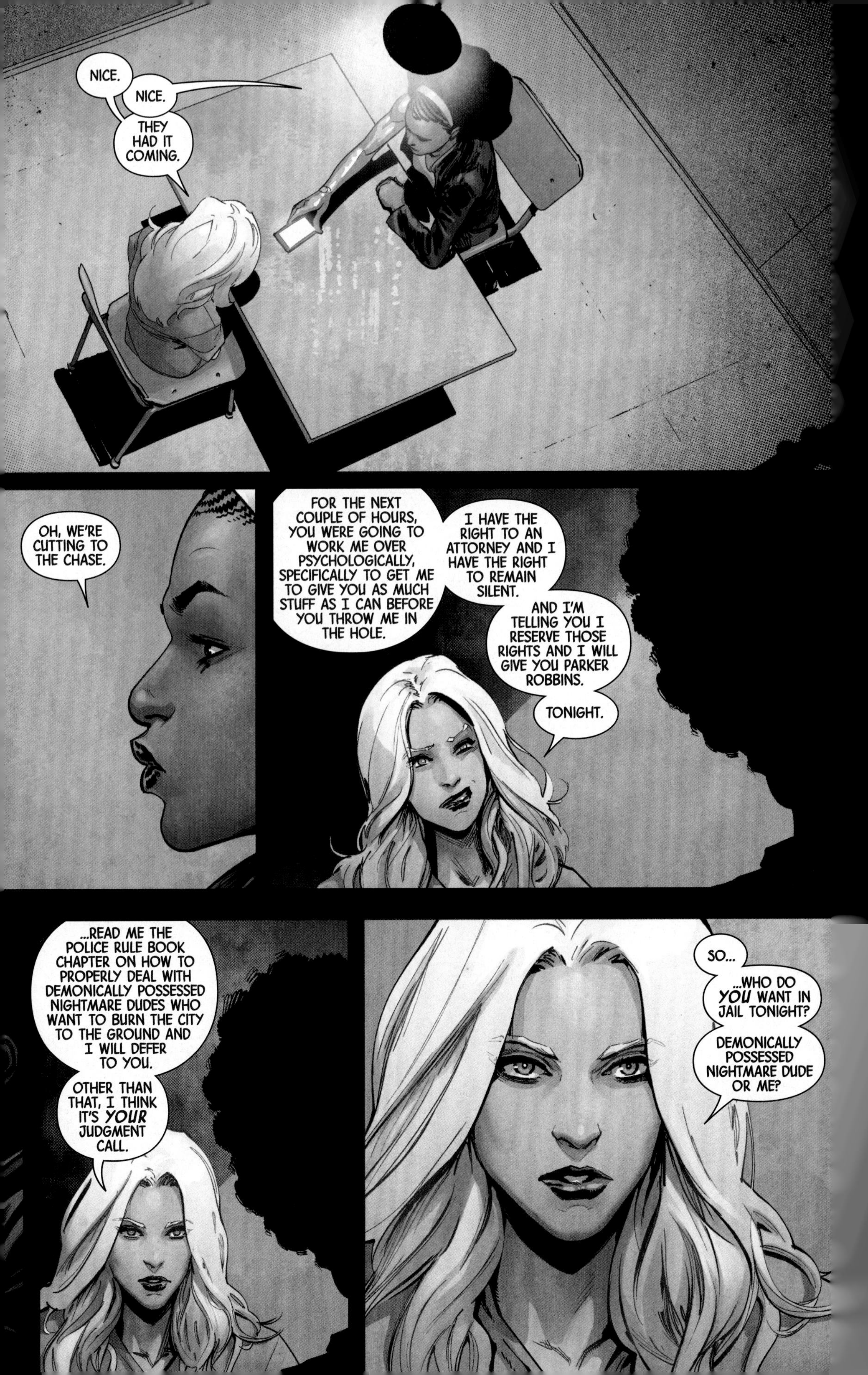
NICE.
NICE.
THEY HAD IT COMING.
OH, WE'RE CUTTING TO THE CHASE.
FOR THE NEXT COUPLE OF HOURS, YOU WERE GOING TO WORK ME OVER PSYCHOLOGICALLY, SPECIFICALLY TO GET ME TO GIVE YOU AS MUCH STUFF AS I CAN BEFORE YOU THROW ME IN THE HOLE.
I HAVE THE RIGHT TO AN ATTORNEY AND I HAVE THE RIGHT TO REMAIN SILENT.
AND I'M TELLING YOU I RESERVE THOSE RIGHTS AND I WILL GIVE YOU PARKER ROBBINS.
TONIGHT.
...READ ME THE POLICE RULE BOOK CHAPTER ON HOW TO PROPERLY DEAL WITH DEMONICALLY POSSESSED NIGHTMARE DUDES WHO WANT TO BURN THE CITY TO THE GROUND AND I WILL DEFER TO YOU.
OTHER THAN THAT, I THINK IT'S *YOUR* JUDGMENT CALL.
SO...
...WHO DO *YOU* WANT IN JAIL TONIGHT?
DEMONICALLY POSSESSED NIGHTMARE DUDE OR ME?

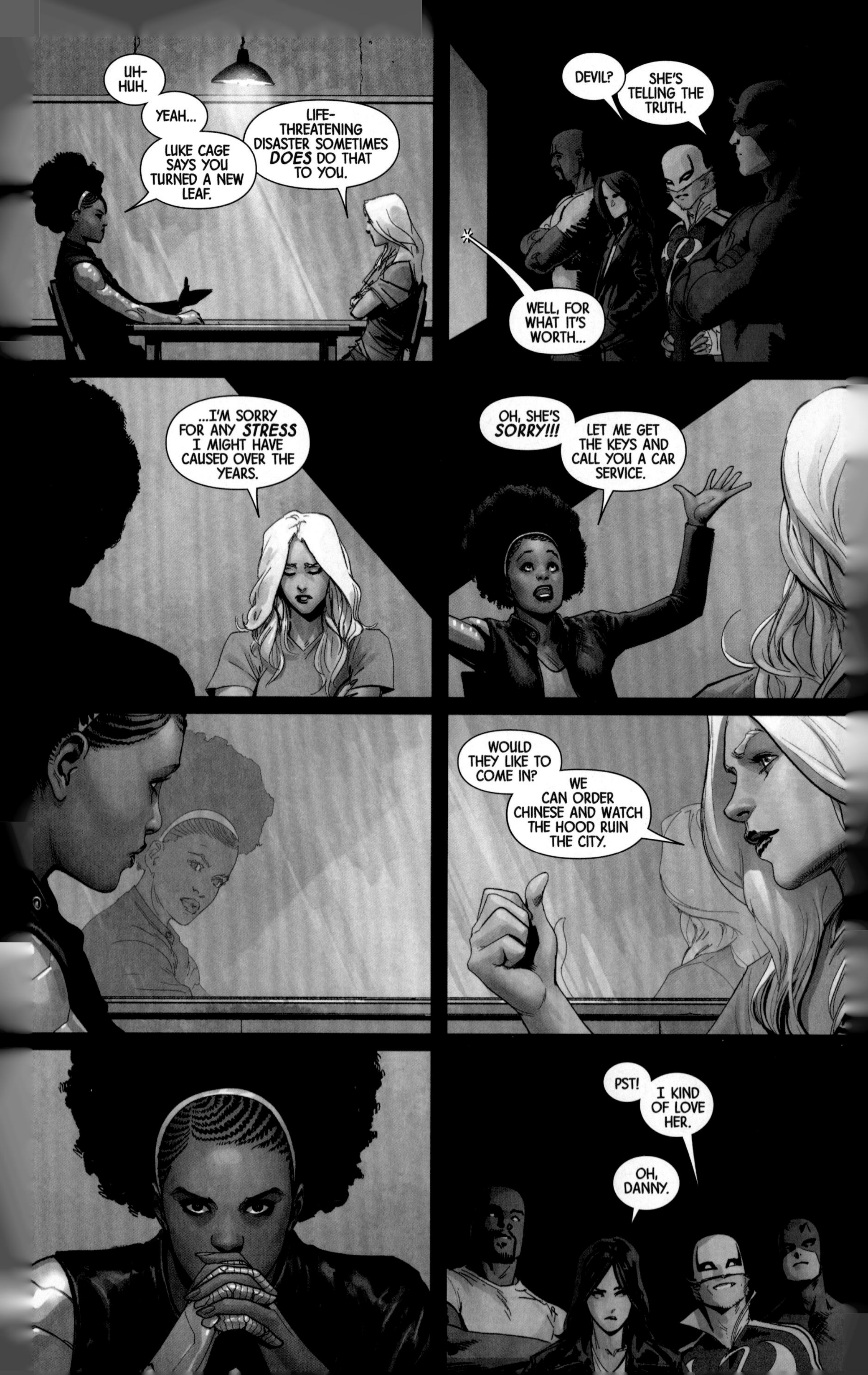
UH-HUH.
YEAH...
LUKE CAGE SAYS YOU TURNED A NEW LEAF.
LIFE-THREATENING DISASTER SOMETIMES DOES DO THAT TO YOU.
DEVIL?
SHE'S TELLING THE TRUTH.
WELL, FOR WHAT IT'S WORTH...
...I'M SORRY FOR ANY STRESS I MIGHT HAVE CAUSED OVER THE YEARS.
OH, SHE'S SORRY!!!
LET ME GET THE KEYS AND CALL YOU A CAR SERVICE.
WOULD THEY LIKE TO COME IN?
WE CAN ORDER CHINESE AND WATCH THE HOOD RUIN THE CITY.
PST!
I KIND OF LOVE HER.
OH, DANNY.

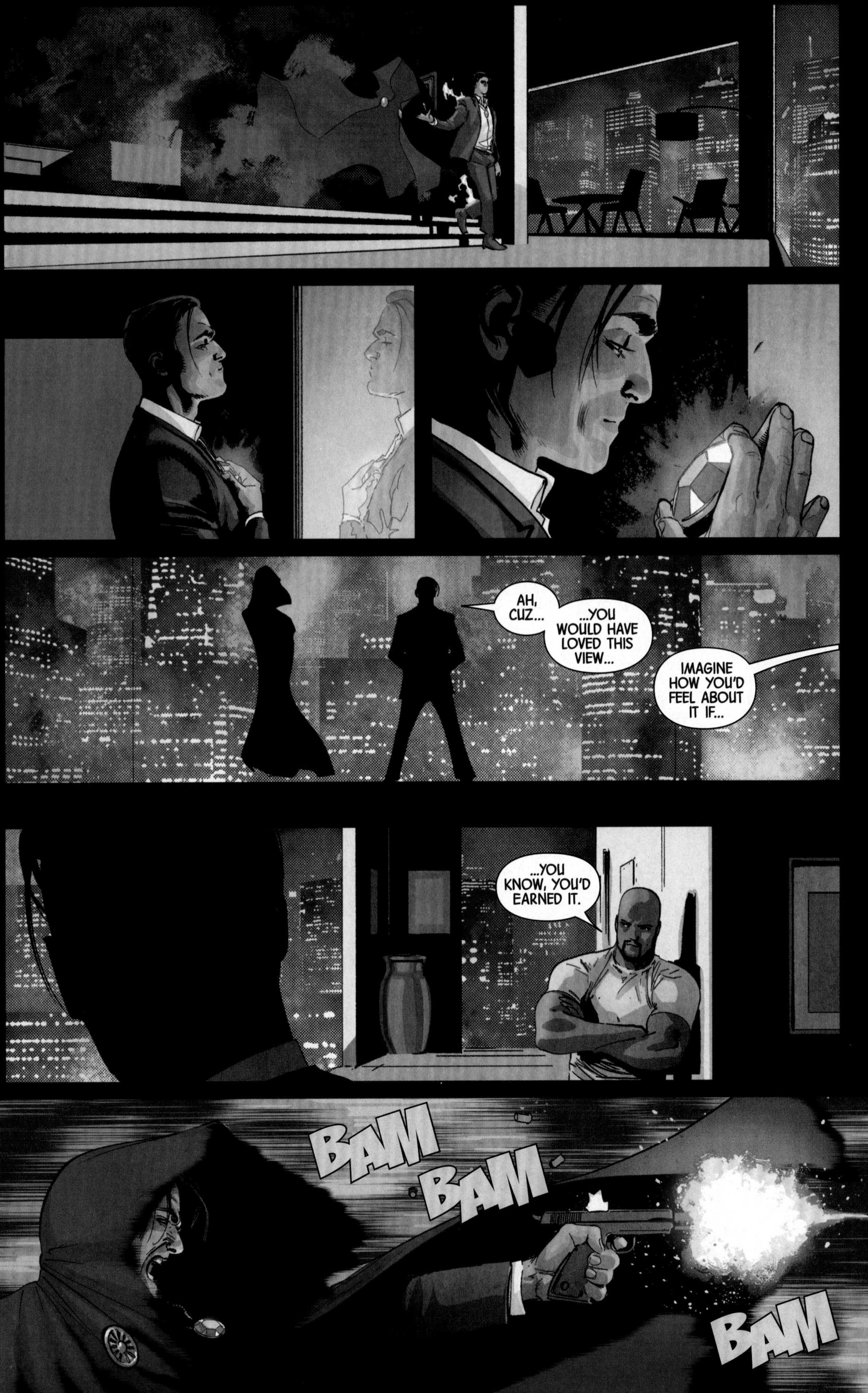
AH, CUZ...
...YOU WOULD HAVE LOVED THIS VIEW...
IMAGINE HOW YOU'D FEEL ABOUT IT IF...
...YOU KNOW, YOU'D EARNED IT.
BAM
BAM
BAM

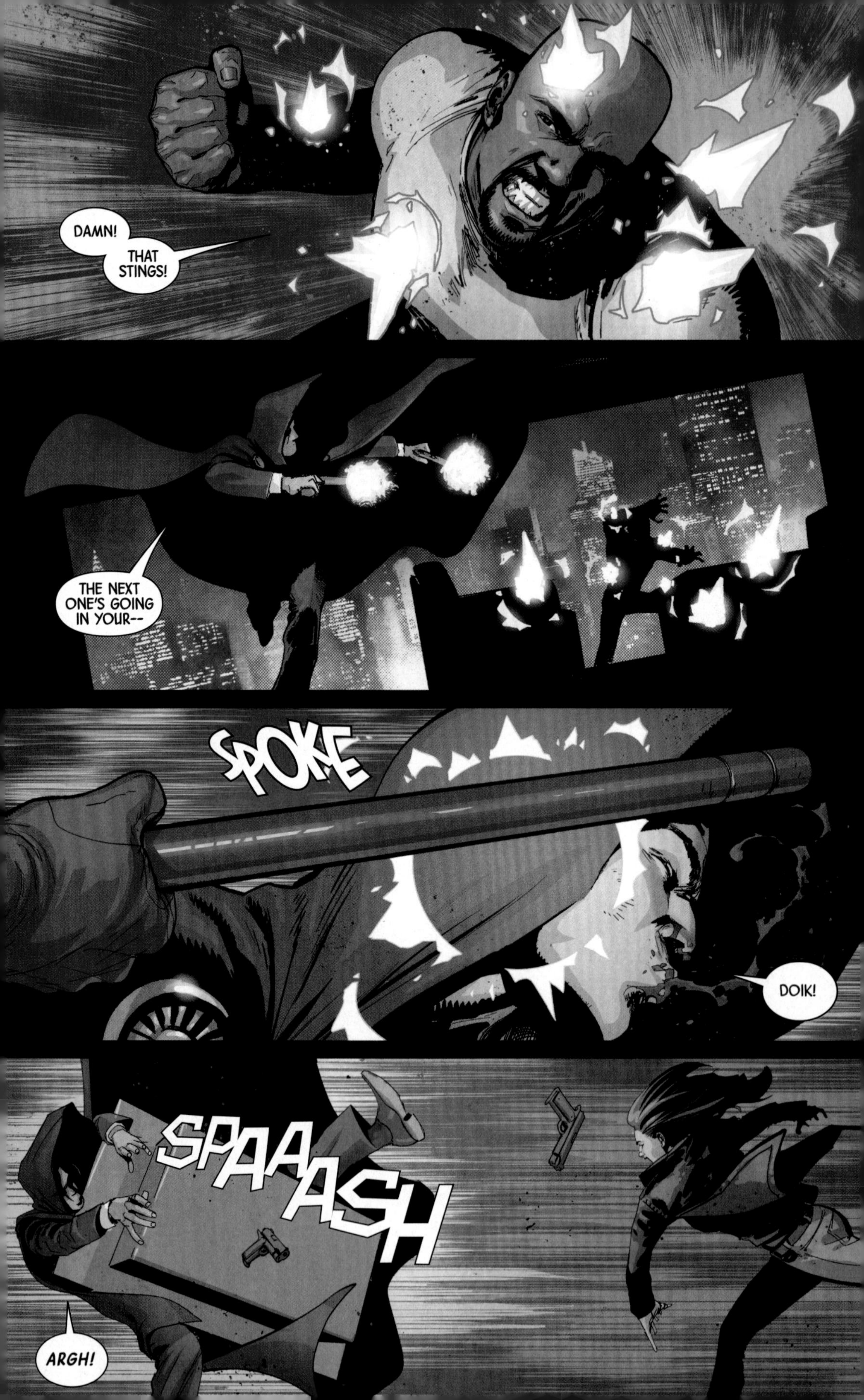
DAMN! THAT STINGS!
THE NEXT ONE'S GOING IN YOUR--
SPOKE
DOIK!
SPAAAASH
ARGH!

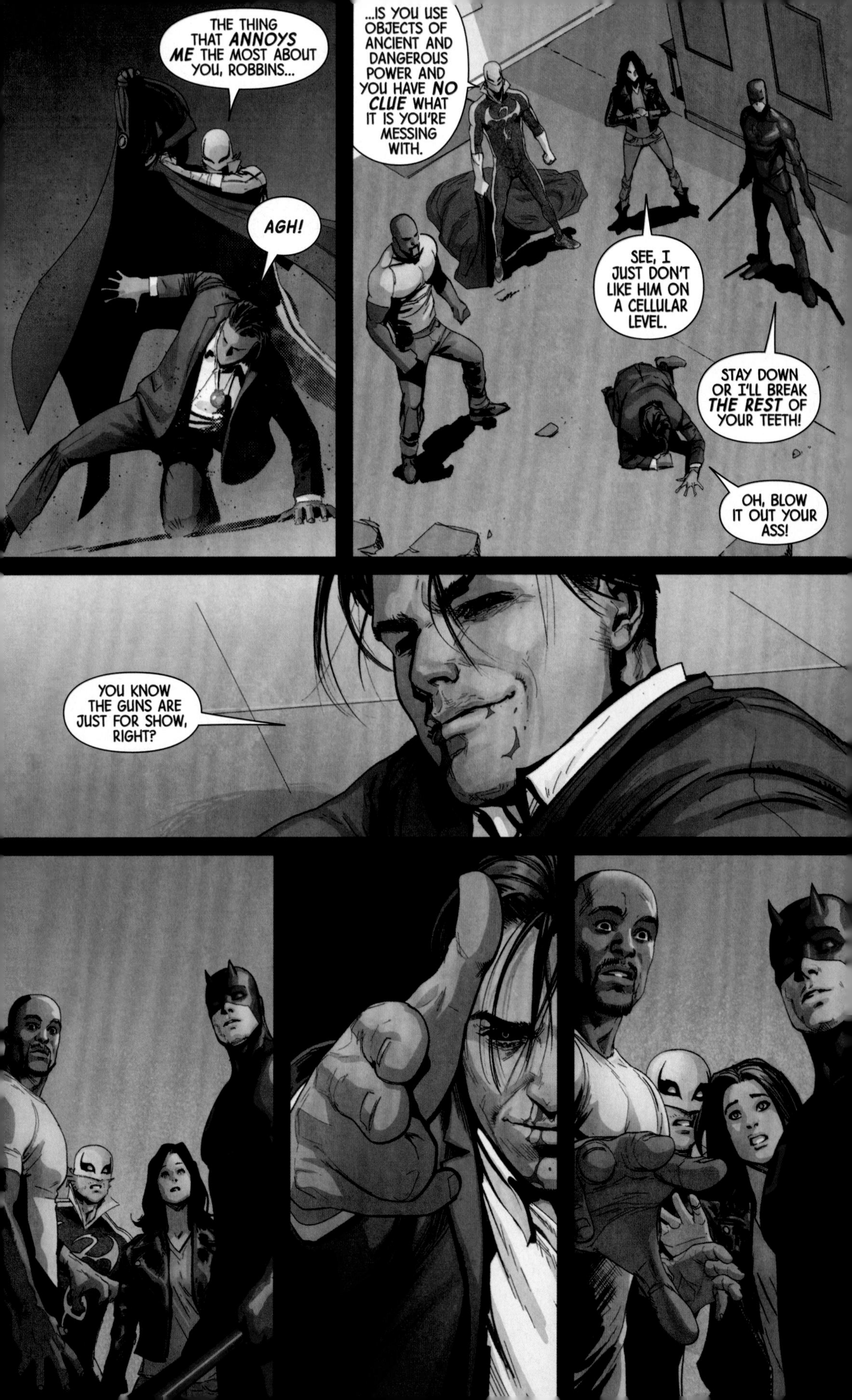
THE THING THAT ANNOYS ME THE MOST ABOUT YOU, ROBBINS...
AGH!
...IS YOU USE OBJECTS OF ANCIENT AND DANGEROUS POWER AND YOU HAVE NO CLUE WHAT IT IS YOU'RE MESSING WITH.
SEE, I JUST DON'T LIKE HIM ON A CELLULAR LEVEL.
STAY DOWN OR I'LL BREAK THE REST OF YOUR TEETH!
OH, BLOW IT OUT YOUR ASS!
YOU KNOW THE GUNS ARE JUST FOR SHOW, RIGHT?

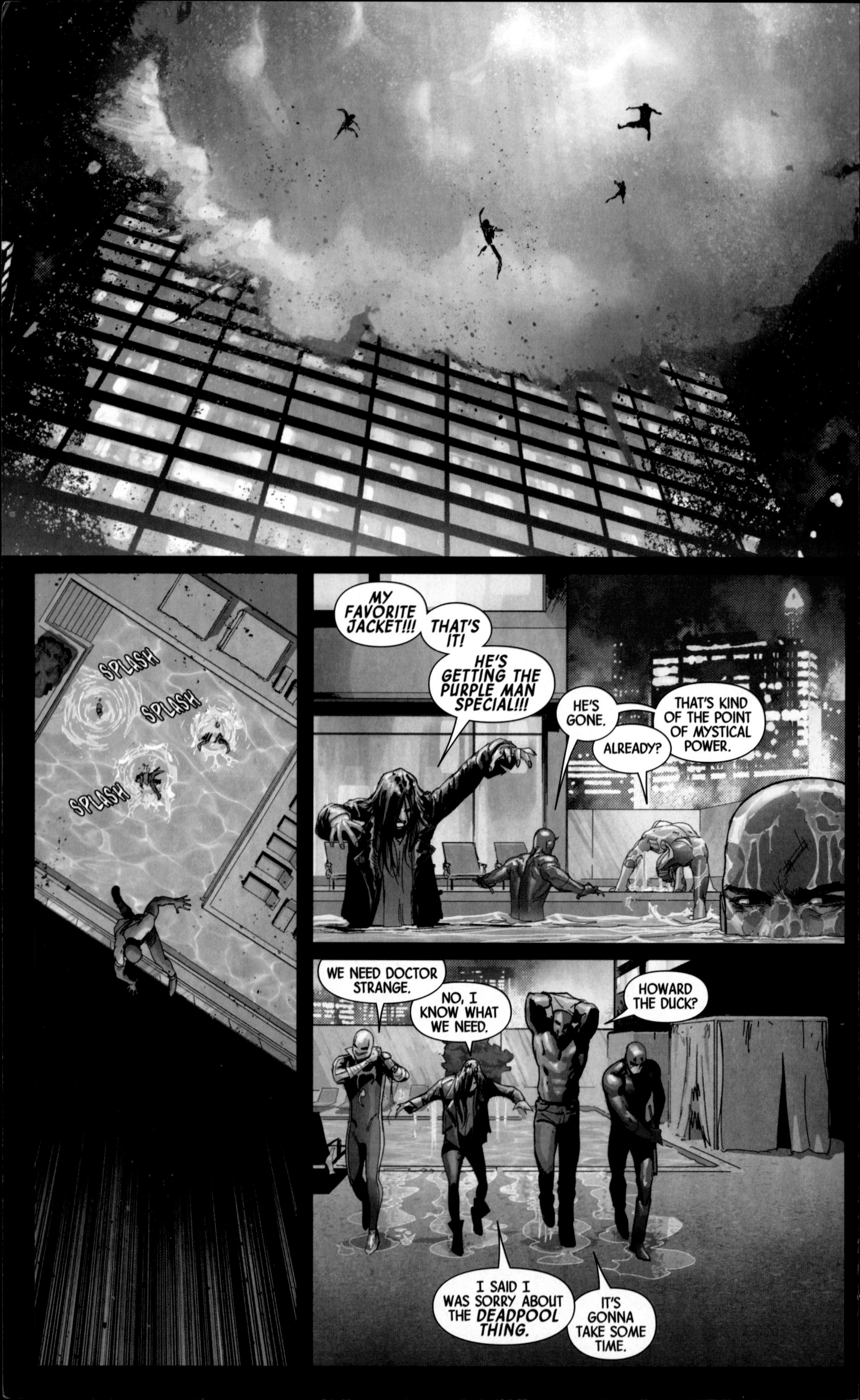
SPLASH
SPLASH
SPLASH
MY FAVORITE JACKET!!!
THAT'S IT!
HE'S GETTING THE PURPLE MAN SPECIAL!!!
HE'S GONE.
ALREADY?
THAT'S KIND OF THE POINT OF MYSTICAL POWER.
WE NEED DOCTOR STRANGE.
NO, I KNOW WHAT WE NEED.
HOWARD THE DUCK?
I SAID I WAS SORRY ABOUT THE DEADPOOL THING.
IT'S GONNA TAKE SOME TIME.

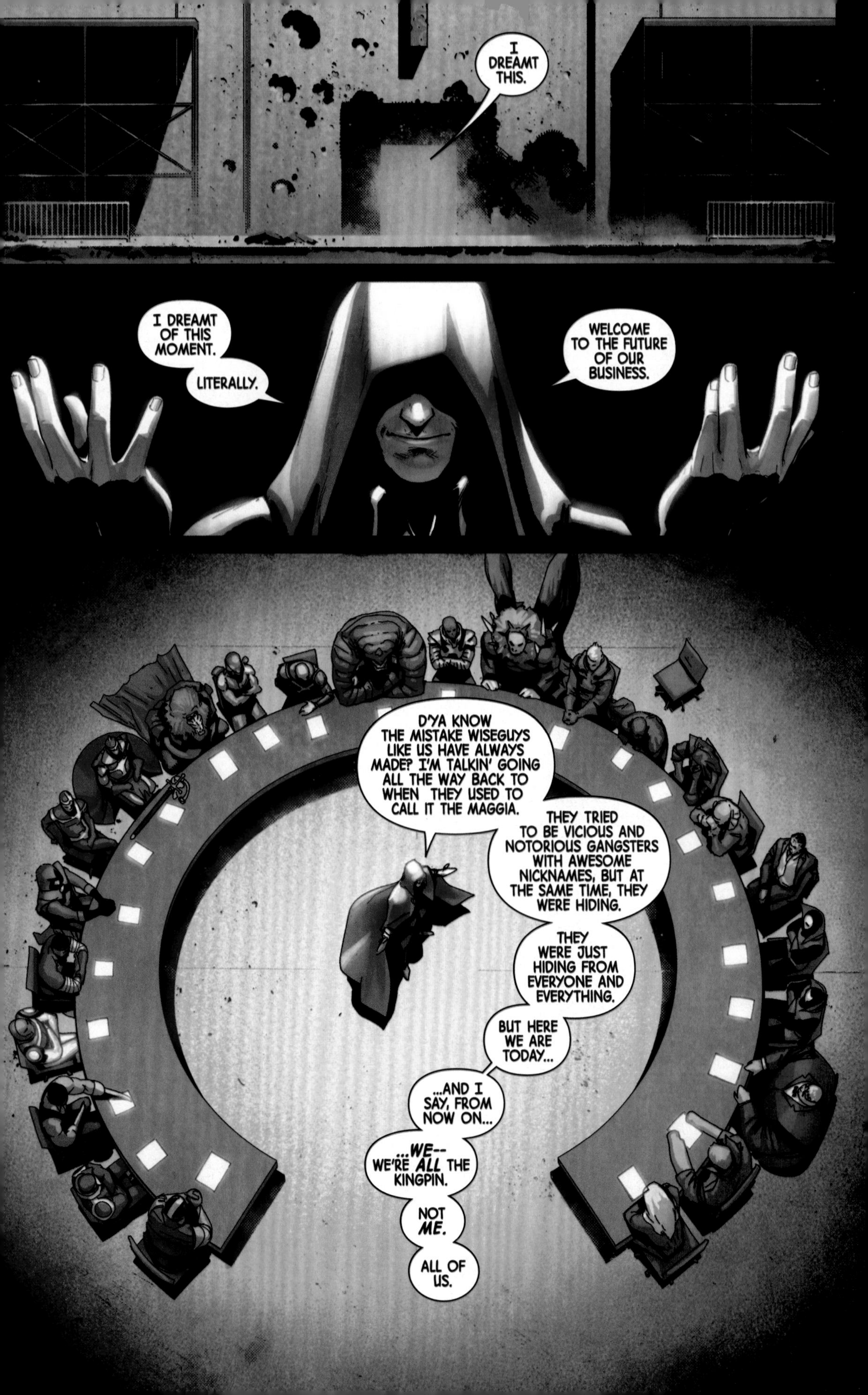
I DREAMT THIS.
I DREAMT OF THIS MOMENT.
LITERALLY.
WELCOME TO THE FUTURE OF OUR BUSINESS.
D'YA KNOW THE MISTAKE WISEGUYS LIKE US HAVE ALWAYS MADE? I'M TALKIN' GOING ALL THE WAY BACK TO WHEN THEY USED TO CALL IT THE MAGGIA.
THEY TRIED TO BE VICIOUS AND NOTORIOUS GANGSTERS WITH AWESOME NICKNAMES, BUT AT THE SAME TIME, THEY WERE HIDING.
THEY WERE JUST HIDING FROM EVERYONE AND EVERYTHING.
BUT HERE WE ARE TODAY...
...AND I SAY, FROM NOW ON...
...WE-- WE'RE ALL THE KINGPIN.
NOT ME.
ALL OF US.

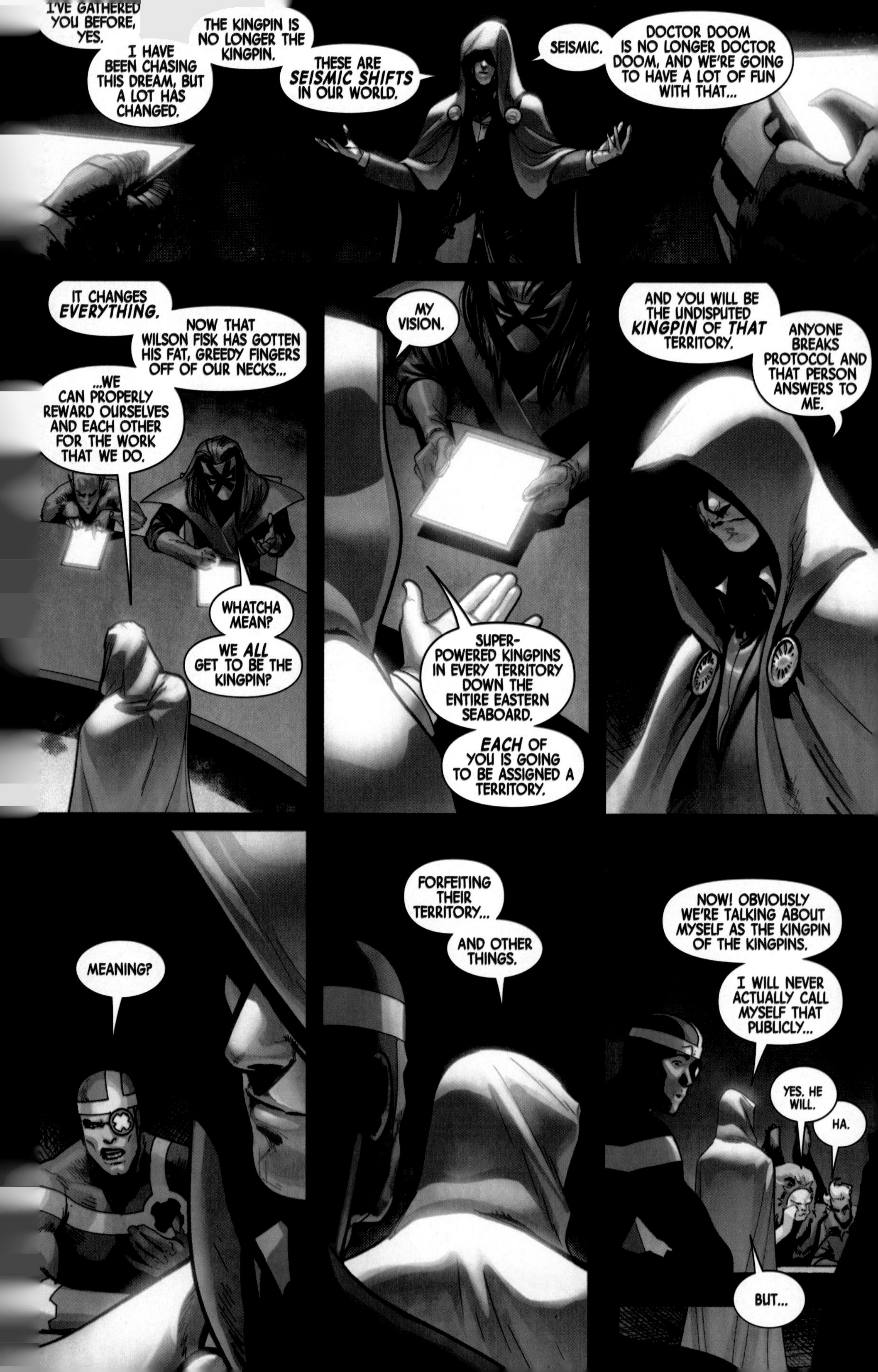
I'VE GATHERED YOU BEFORE, YES.
I HAVE BEEN CHASING THIS DREAM, BUT A LOT HAS CHANGED.
THE KINGPIN IS NO LONGER THE KINGPIN.
THESE ARE SEISMIC SHIFTS IN OUR WORLD.
SEISMIC.
DOCTOR DOOM IS NO LONGER DOCTOR DOOM, AND WE'RE GOING TO HAVE A LOT OF FUN WITH THAT...
IT CHANGES EVERYTHING.
NOW THAT WILSON FISK HAS GOTTEN HIS FAT, GREEDY FINGERS OFF OF OUR NECKS...
...WE CAN PROPERLY REWARD OURSELVES AND EACH OTHER FOR THE WORK THAT WE DO.
WHATCHA MEAN?
WE ALL GET TO BE THE KINGPIN?
MY VISION.
SUPER-POWERED KINGPINS IN EVERY TERRITORY DOWN THE ENTIRE EASTERN SEABOARD.
EACH OF YOU IS GOING TO BE ASSIGNED A TERRITORY.
AND YOU WILL BE THE UNDISPUTED KINGPIN OF THAT TERRITORY.
ANYONE BREAKS PROTOCOL AND THAT PERSON ANSWERS TO ME.
MEANING?
FORFEITING THEIR TERRITORY...
AND OTHER THINGS.
NOW! OBVIOUSLY WE'RE TALKING ABOUT MYSELF AS THE KINGPIN OF THE KINGPINS.
I WILL NEVER ACTUALLY CALL MYSELF THAT PUBLICLY...
YES. HE WILL.
HA.
BUT...

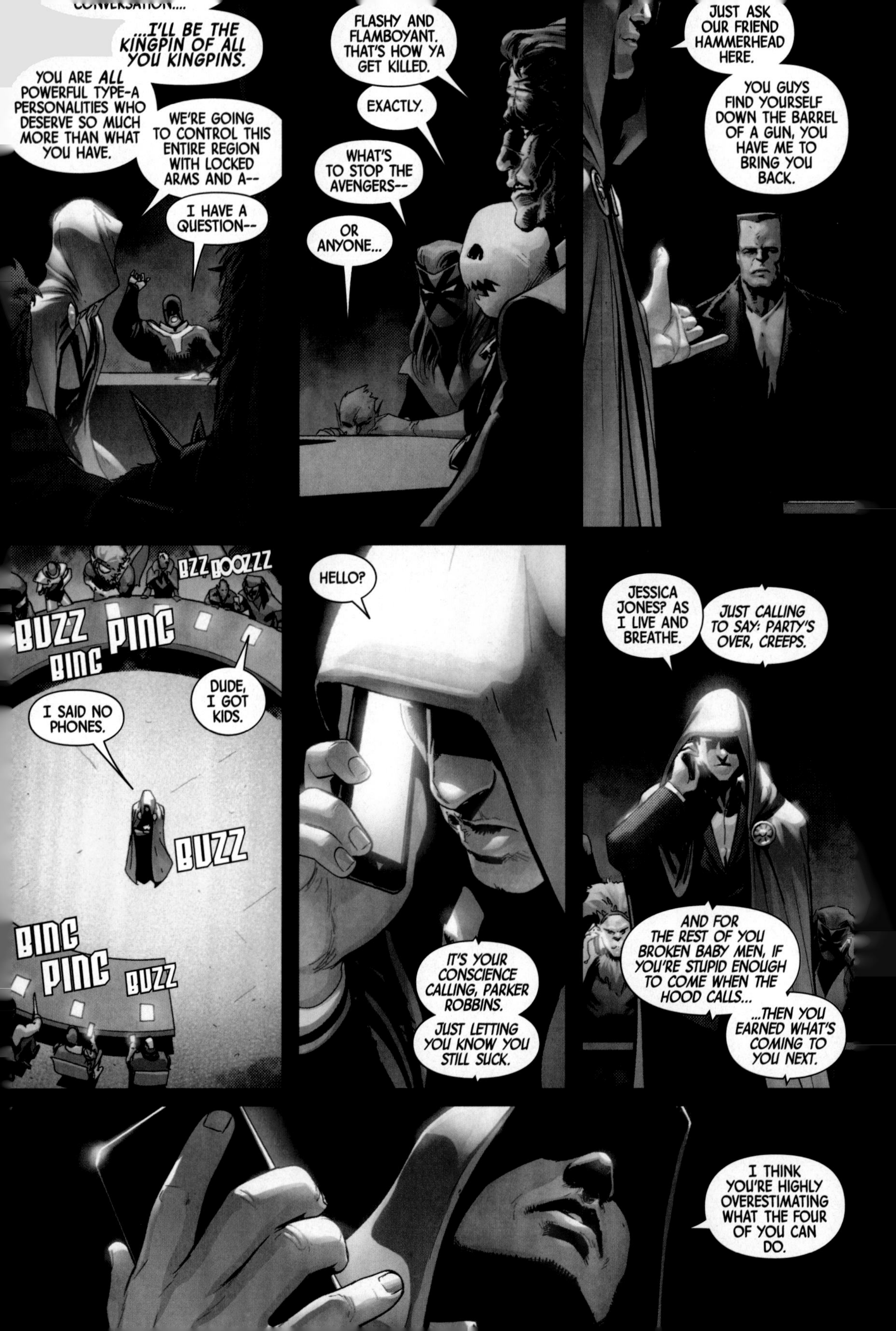
CONVERSATION....
...I'LL BE THE KINGPIN OF ALL YOU KINGPINS.
YOU ARE ALL POWERFUL TYPE-A PERSONALITIES WHO DESERVE SO MUCH MORE THAN WHAT YOU HAVE.
WE'RE GOING TO CONTROL THIS ENTIRE REGION WITH LOCKED ARMS AND A--
I HAVE A QUESTION--
FLASHY AND FLAMBOYANT. THAT'S HOW YA GET KILLED.
EXACTLY.
WHAT'S TO STOP THE AVENGERS--
OR ANYONE...
JUST ASK OUR FRIEND HAMMERHEAD HERE.
YOU GUYS FIND YOURSELF DOWN THE BARREL OF A GUN, YOU HAVE ME TO BRING YOU BACK.
BZZ BOOZZZ
BUZZ PING
BING
DUDE, I GOT KIDS.
I SAID NO PHONES.
BUZZ
BING
PING
BUZZ
HELLO?
IT'S YOUR CONSCIENCE CALLING, PARKER ROBBINS.
JUST LETTING YOU KNOW YOU STILL SUCK.
JESSICA JONES? AS I LIVE AND BREATHE.
JUST CALLING TO SAY: PARTY'S OVER, CREEPS.
AND FOR THE REST OF YOU BROKEN BABY MEN, IF YOU'RE STUPID ENOUGH TO COME WHEN THE HOOD CALLS...
...THEN YOU EARNED WHAT'S COMING TO YOU NEXT.
I THINK YOU'RE HIGHLY OVERESTIMATING WHAT THE FOUR OF YOU CAN DO.

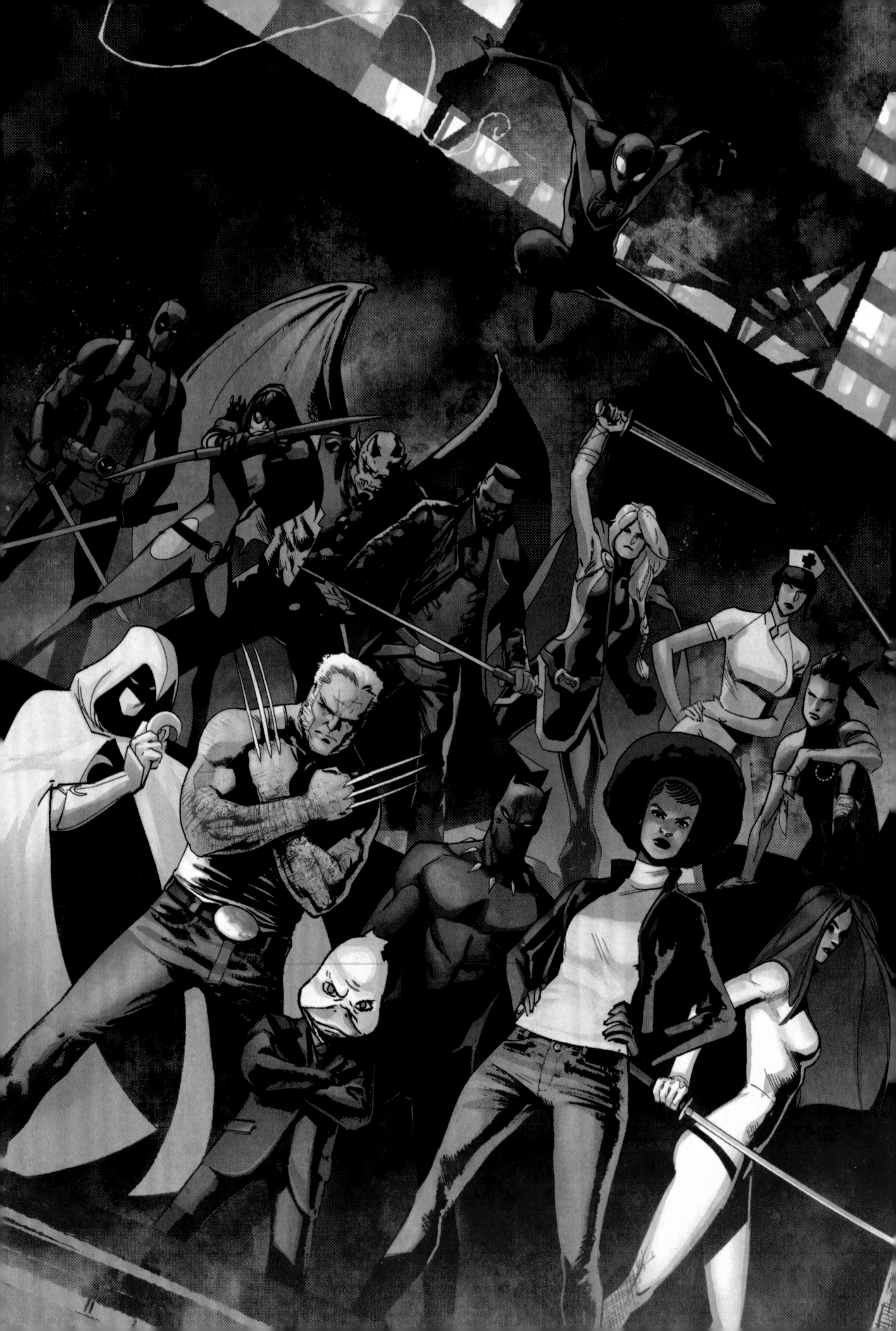

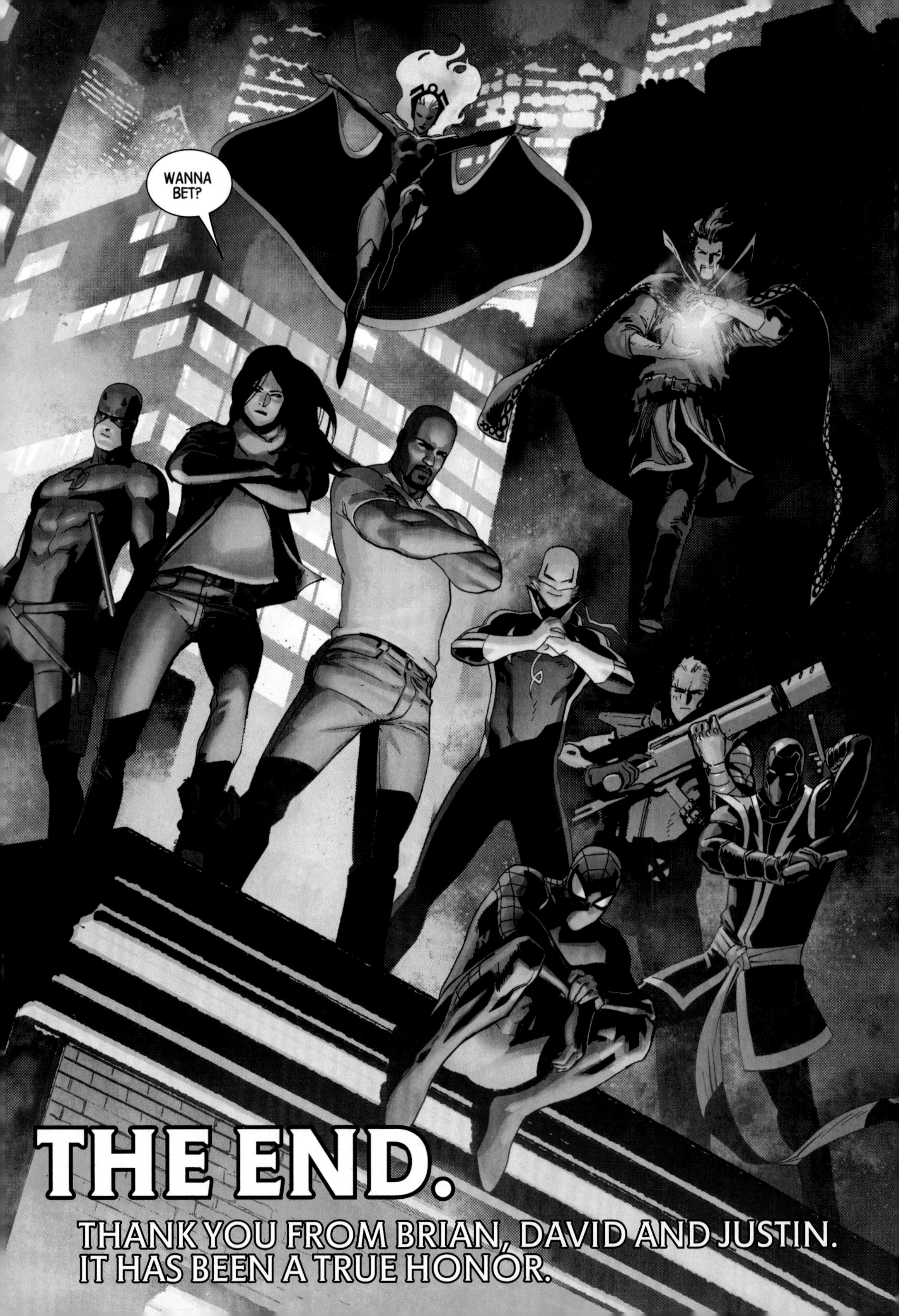
WANNA BET?
THE END.
THANK YOU FROM BRIAN, DAVID AND JUSTIN.
IT HAS BEEN A TRUE HONOR.

HOW TO DRAW LUKE CAGE
IN SIX EASY STEPS!

BY CHIP "'HERO' FOR HIRE" ZDARSKY

Wow! A "sketch variant cover"! A simple, yet elegant, way to get your art on the cover of a Marvel comic! Anyway, here's a fun and informative step-by-step guide to drawing LUKE CAGE!

1

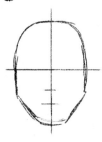

First step is to outline his head. Rounder top half, more squared-off bottom half. Then, lines to indicate center, eyeline, nose and mouth position.

2

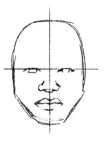

Then start to add features! Eyes roughly one eye apart, mouth slightly wider than nose.

3

Luke sports a goatee, so add that. Then some ears. Eyebrows slightly furrowed, like he's going to take on a bad guy!

4

He's muscular, so go ahead and add a thick neck and trapezius, to give us more context!

5

Now he ... doesn't really have a costume anymore, but he's been known to wear a hoodie, so if you want MORE context for who he is, add one! And some fine detail and shading!

6

The Christmas Suile

TIARA
OUTFITTERS

And finally, to REALLY let people know this is Luke, make a bunch of references to his '70s incarnation!